Personality-Guided Therapy for Posttraumatic Stress Disorder

Personality-Guided Therapy for Posttraumatic Stress Disorder

George S. Everly, Jr.
Jeffrey M. Lating

Series Editor Theodore Millon

AMERICAN PSYCHOLOGICAL ASSOCIATION
WASHINGTON, DC

Published by
American Psychological Association
750 First Street, NE
Washington, DC 20002
www.apa.org

To order
APA Order Department
P.O. Box 92984
Washington, DC 20090-2984
Tel: (800) 374-2721
Direct: (202) 336-5510
Fax: (202) 336-5502
TDD/TTY: (202) 336-6123
Online: www.apa.org/books/
E-mail: order@apa.org

In the U.K., Europe, Africa, and the Middle East, copies may be ordered from
American Psychological Association
3 Henrietta Street
Covent Garden, London
WC2E 8LU England

Typeset in Goudy by World Composition Services, Inc., Sterling, VA

Printer: Sheridan Books, Ann Arbor, MI
Cover Designer: Berg Design, Albany, NY
Project Manager: Debbie Hardin, Carlsbad, CA

The opinions and statements published are the responsibility of the authors, and such opinions and statements do not necessarily represent the policies of the American Psychological Association.

Library of Congress Cataloging-in-Publication Data

Everly, George S., 1950–
    Personality-guided therapy for posttraumatic stress disorder / by George S. Everly, Jr. and Jeffrey M. Lating.—1st ed.
        p. cm.—(Personality-guided psychology)
    Includes bibliographical references and index.
    ISBN 1-59147-044-7 (alk. paper)
        1. Post-traumatic stress disorder—Treatment. 2. Psychotherapy. 3. Personality.
    I. Lating, Jeffrey M. II. Title. III. Series.

RC552.P67E837 2003
616.8′521—dc21   2003050201

British Library Cataloguing-in-Publication Data
A CIP record is available from the British Library.

Printed in the United States of America
First Edition

The study of personality is but a pale academic exercise
until we see it unfold before us in everyday life.
I dedicate this book to three most interesting
and instructive personalities: my children,
Marideth, George, and Andi.
—George S. Everly, Jr.

To my beloved children, Austin and Jenna,
and my wonderful niece Alexandra.
May the joy in your lives far outweigh the adversity.
—Jeffrey M. Lating

CONTENTS

SERIES FOREWORD

The turn of the 20th century saw the emergence of psychological interest in the concept of individual differences, the recognition that the many realms of scientific study then in vogue displayed considerable variability among "laboratory subjects." Sir Francis Galton in Great Britain and many of his disciples, notably Charles Spearman in England, Alfred Binet in France, and James McKeen Cattell in the United States, laid the groundwork for recognizing that intelligence was a major element of import in what came to be called *differential psychology*. Largely through the influence of psychoanalytic thought, and then only indirectly, did this new field expand the topic of individual differences in the direction of character and personality.

And so here we are at the dawn of the 21st century, ready to focus our attentions ever more seriously on the subject of personality trait differences and their impact on a wide variety of psychological subjects—from how they impinge on behavioral medicine outcomes, alter gerontological and adolescent treatment, regulate residential care programs, affect the management of depressive and PTSD patients, transform the style of cognitive–behavioral and interpersonal therapies, guide sophisticated forensic and correctional assessments—a whole bevy of important themes that typify where psychologists center their scientific and applied efforts today.

It is toward the end of alerting psychologists who work in diverse areas of study and practice that the present series, entitled *Personality-Guided Psychology*, has been developed for publication by the American Psychological Association. The originating concept underlying the series may be traced to Henry Murray's seminal proposal in his 1938 volume, *Explorations in Personality*, in which he advanced a new field of study termed *personology*.

It took its contemporary form in a work of mine, published in 1999 under the title *Personality-Guided Therapy*.

The utility and relevance of personality as a variable is spreading in all directions, and the series sets out to illustrate where things stand today. As will be evident as the series' publication progresses, the most prominent work at present is found with creative thinkers whose efforts are directed toward enhancing a more efficacious treatment of patients. We hope to demonstrate, further, some of the newer realms of application and research that lie just at the edge of scientific advances in our field. Thus, we trust that the volumes included in this series will help us look beyond the threshold of the present and toward the vast horizon that represents all of psychology. Fortunately, there is a growing awareness that personality variables can be a guiding factor in all spheres of study. We trust the series will provide a map of an open country that encourages innovative ventures and provides a foundation for investigators who wish to locate directions in which they themselves can assume leading roles.

Theodore Millon, PhD, DSc
Series Editor

PREFACE

This volume is a unique integration of several paths of study, and as such represents an amalgam of several "careers." Integrated within, the reader will find an intertwining of selected aspects of the sciences of personology, human stress and psychophysiology, trauma, communications, and psychotherapy. Only through such an integration, we believe, can the personality-guided therapy of posttraumatic stress be presented. The space available does not allow for in-depth examinations of each of these fields of study, nor is such necessary. Rather, we have chosen to extract what we believe are the most relevant aspects of those fields to the clinical challenge at hand. In the final analysis, this is a textbook written for clinicians, from a unique personologic perspective, which provides insight and clinical guidance for what we believe is the single most severe and therapeutically challenging psychological disorder to affect otherwise healthy women and men in the prime of their lives. Posttraumatic stress syndromes, especially posttraumatic stress disorder (PTSD), have the ability to snatch away careers, marriages, and the satisfaction and vitality of life itself. In childhood presentations, the effects are even more devastating.

This treatise on the personality-guided therapy of PTSD is designed for mental health practitioners and students who are challenged with assisting their patients in making sense out of a world that has become psychologically toxic as a result of psychological trauma and victimization. Although many of the clinical techniques and intervention approaches reviewed and suggested in this book have been subjected to controlled empirical scrutiny as isolated elements, the amalgamated personality-guided approach to the treatment of posttraumatic distress and PTSD has not been subjected to controlled research in its composite entirety. Therefore, the recommendations that follow should be viewed as heuristic and taxonomic rather than rigidly prescriptive. They are designed to provide the clinician with greater insight into the person who suffers from posttraumatic distress. It is hoped that through a better understanding of the person and posttraumatic disorders, the clinician will prove to be a more effective agent in the patient's overall healing process.

ACKNOWLEDGMENTS

We are deeply grateful to Theodore Millon for the opportunity to make this volume a reality. He has provided an illuminating beacon by which practitioners may better understand the true "art of healing."

We are also indebted to Linda McCarter, Susan Reynolds, Debbie Hardin, Doris Manner, and Traci Peragine for their editorial and production assistance in the development of this project.

Finally, I, George S. Everly, Jr., express my deepest appreciation to Theodore Millon for his personal and professional mentorship, now spanning more than 20 years. I also thank my family, from whom this project did take valuable time. I, like many, have learned much about human personality from my children. A true blessing, they have taught me much about priorities as well.

I

ON THE NATURE OF PERSONALITY AND POSTTRAUMATIC STRESS DISORDER

INTRODUCTION: ON THE NATURE OF PERSONALITY AND POSTTRAUMATIC STRESS DISORDER

In the wake of the terrorist attacks on September 11, 2001, there has been a renewed interest from both the professional and public sectors in the phenomenon of posttraumatic stress. Indeed, with the realities of airplane hijackings, biological terrorism, urban snipers, and natural disasters, posttraumatic stress may be viewed within the context of a public health challenge. Even before the terrorism of September 11, however, more than 50% of adult Americans would be expected to be exposed to a traumatic event. Behavioral and psychological reactions following a traumatic event are an inherent part of the human condition (Jones & Barlow, 1990), and the effects of traumatic stressors have been clinically observed for centuries (Holmes, 1985; Shay, 1994). Not until 1980, however, did posttraumatic stress disorder (PTSD) become nosologically defined as a disorder within the taxonomic formulations of the *Diagnostic and Statistical Manual of Mental Disorders*, Third Edition (*DSM–III*; American Psychiatric Association, 1980). PTSD research received additional credibility when *DSM–III–R* and now *DSM–IV* (American Psychiatric Association, 1987, 1994) provided additional diagnostic and phenomenological clarity. More than 20 years after the origin of the modern formulation of PTSD, we offer additional clarification into the phenomenology and treatment of PTSD using a personality-guided perspective.

The treatment of syndromes of posttraumatic distress, especially PTSD, may be viewed as an endeavor within the realm of clinical science. Perhaps the most influential personologist of the past 50 years, Theodore Millon, has proposed that there are four elements to a clinical science (Millon, 1990):

1. *Theory*: A theoretical formulation of the observed clinical manifestation or disorder. In this case, a neuropersonologic theory of posttraumatic stress and PTSD, to be addressed in Part I of this volume;

2. *Taxonomy*: A descriptive classification of PTSD. In this case, PTSD is described as an anxiety disorder (American Psychiatric Association, 1994), a "disorder of arousal" (Everly, 1990, 1993), and as an injury to the foundational schematic fabric of personality, to be addressed in Part I of this volume.

3. *Assessment*: Methods for the identification of the clinical manifestation. In this case, methods for the assessment of PTSD and related syndromes of posttraumatic distress. Psychological, psychophysiological, neurological, and neuropsychological methods will be reviewed in chapters 5 and 6, this volume.

4. *Clinical intervention*: A strategic framework for amelioration or resolution of the observed clinical disorder. In Part III, we explore the synergistic, personality-guided approach (Millon, Grossman, Meagher, Millon, & Everly, 1999) to the treatment of PTSD using a two-factor neuropersonologic approach.

An amalgam of various philosophical and clinical orientations, this personality-guided approach to the treatment of posttraumatic distress and PTSD embraces the synergistic multicomponent approach to therapy advocated by Millon et al. (1999). The key mechanisms described in this book are outlined next and will be explained in detail throughout the remainder of this volume. The key mechanisms involved in the personality-guided approach to the treatment of PTSD are as follows:

1. The use of a personality-guided approach to establishing the therapeutic alliance and creating the foundation for the reconstruction of a "safe" world (preferential process and thematic belief mechanisms);

2. Achievement of a condition of neurologic desensitization, wherein techniques are used to diminish the intensity of the pathognomonic ergotropic state of neurological hypersensitivity and increase perceptions of self-efficacy; and

3. Restoration of functional personality-based assumptive worldviews and integration of the traumatic event.

In Part I, we introduce the reader first to the foundations of the construct of human personality and second to posttraumatic stress in general and PTSD specifically, using relevant theoretical and taxonomic perspectives, as suggested by Millon, Bandura, Maslow, Janoff-Bulman, Lerner, McCann and Pearlman, Herman, and Everly.

1

ONE'S FATE RESIDES IN ONE'S CHARACTER

More than three generations ago, the esteemed Johns Hopkins's physician Sir William Osler (1849–1919) observed, "It is more important to know what kind of patient has the disease than what kind of disease the patient has" (Frank, 2001, p. 212).

More than 70 years later, Stewart Wolf, one of the founders of the field of psychosomatic medicine, commented that to understand the impact of an event, the focus of inquiry must be the individual.

Finally, the Greek philosopher Heraclitus reportedly once observed, "A man's fate is his character." Although it is far too rigid to believe that one's life is completely preordained by virtue of one's character (the term *character* is used in this context as a synonym for the term *personality*), we do believe that the comments of Osler, Wolf, and Heraclitus do serve as useful admonitions for practicing mental health clinicians. More specifically, we agree with Hall and Lindzey (1957)—that the construct of personality offers "order and congruence to all the different kinds of behavior in which the individual engages" (p. 9) and in doing so represents an extremely valuable, and often neglected, corpus of information regarding any given individual.

PERSONALITY AND PSYCHIATRIC SYNDROMES

We agree with Theodore Millon (1969, 1996), who has repeatedly argued that many clinical psychiatric syndromes (many psychiatric disorders codified on Axis I of the *Diagnostic and Statistical Manual of Mental Disorders* [DSM; American Psychiatric Association, 1980, 1994]), are best understood as pathological extensions, or epicenters, of latent personality processes, personality styles, and aggregate personologic constellations. Millon (Millon et al., 1999), however, is careful to make the distinction between *simple clinical reactions* (SCRs) and *complex clinical syndromes* (CCSs), both of which are manifest on Axis I of the *DSM*.

SCRs represent Axis I psychiatric presentations that derive from

> specific neurochemical dysfunctions or are prompted by rather distinctive stimulus experiences. Simple reactions operate somewhat independently of the patient's overall personality pattern; their form and content are determined largely by the character of a biologic vulnerability or the specifics of an external precipitant. (Millon et al., 1999, p. 112)

CCSs represent Axis I psychiatric syndromes that are

> rooted in part to pervasive personality vulnerabilities and coping styles. ... Complex syndromes usually arise when the patient's established personality equilibrium has been upset or threatened. ... Complex syndromes usually signify the activation of several traits that make up the varied facets of a personality style.(Millon et al., 1999, p. 112)

We believe that posttraumatic stress disorder (PTSD) represents a CCS.

The concept of CCSs may be thought of as a form of *individual syndromal continuity*, and seems a radical departure, indeed, from formulations wherein personality and its disorders are taught as wholly separate phenomenological entities with little practical clinical relevance, other than as ends unto themselves. Nevertheless, there exists historical and extant evidence that personality styles, or patterns, are indeed associated with

1. The vulnerability to, and phenomenological course of, disordered as well as subclinical psychological presentations (Bornstein, 1998; Costello, 1995; Gittelman-Klein & Klein, 1969; Weissman, Prusoff, & Klerman, 1978);
2. Meaningful psychodiagnostic refinement (Emery & Lesher, 1982; Widiger & Frances, 1985);
3. Psychotherapeutic responsiveness (Emery & Lesher, 1982; Frances & Hale, 1984; Strupp, 1980); and

4. Psychopharmacologic responsiveness (Bielski & Friedel, 1976; Kayser, Robinson, Nies, & Howard, 1985).

Everly (1987) has referred to the synthesis of these notions as *personologic primacy*.

PERSONOLOGIC PSYCHOTHERAPY

As a practical corollary to the aforementioned notions, Everly (1987) further posited that the treatment of many Axis I psychiatric disorders should take into consideration the foundational and potentially more salient personality processes, personality-based schemas and constituent personologic diatheses that undergird many of the Axis I disorders (in addition to more florid psychological symptomatology), to avoid a condition wherein one treats only the symptoms and neglects the more causal, self-perpetuating psychological "lesion." Everly (1987) has referred to this notion as *personologic psychotherapy*. Millon has referred to a similar construction as *personality-guided therapy* (Millon et al., 1999).

The embodiment of Millon's personality-guided therapy is *synergistic psychotherapy*—in other words, using a multitude of psychotherapeutic interventions in their most effective combinations at their most appropriate times. "The process of therapy must be coordinated to the substance of that which is treated" (Millon & Davis, 2000, p. 91).

"The palette of methods and techniques available to the therapist must be commensurate with the idiographic heterogeneity of the patient for whom the methods and techniques are intended" (Millon et al., 1999, p. 145). Thus, synergistic psychotherapy is the application of multiple intervention techniques, either simultaneously (potentiated pairings) or serially (catalytic sequences) in such a tailored manner as to specifically address the essential phenomenological elements of the extant disorder and the unique personologic elements of the individual patient in a combinatorial manner.

In this volume, we focus on one specific Axis I psychiatric disorder from a *personality-guided* perspective. We focus on PTSD. We believe that a synthesizing personologic perspective on PTSD has been largely overlooked to this point. More specifically, although not abandoning more traditional perspectives altogether, we are especially interested in the role that personality factors play in the genesis of PTSD, as well as its psychotherapeutic mitigation and elimination. *In the final analysis, we believe that PTSD represents a phenomenological insult, or injury, to the structure and function of the personality construction.* PTSD represents a contradictory condition wherein the traumatic stressor causes chaotic upheaval within the personality, setting into motion a series of pathognomonic compensatory reactions.

PERSONALITY DEFINED

The term *personality* has historically been defined in numerous, and often divergent, ways. According to Robinson (1999), personality may be thought of as "a relatively stable and enduring set of characteristic behavioral and emotional traits" (p. 3).

In his classic textbook, *Modern Psychopathology*, Millon commented,

> In the first years of life, children engage in a wide variety of spontaneous behaviors. . . . Throughout [the] years, then, a shaping process [takes] place in which the range of initially diverse behaviors becomes narrowed, selective and, finally, crystallized into particular modes of seeking and achieving. . . . Thus, . . . the child develops a distinctive pattern of characteristics that are deeply etched . . . and pervade every aspect of his [or her] functioning. In short, these characteristics *are* the essence and sum of his personality, his automatic way of perceiving, feeling, thinking and behaving. (Millon 1969, p. 221)

Perhaps more narrow in their perspective, Beck and Freeman (1990) noted there exist relatively stable psychological structures that serve to integrate and attach meanings to events that surround or directly affect an individual. These structures further serve to create a rather stable predisposition for behavioral responses to various environmental events. These structures are referred to as *schemas*. These schemas are thought to collectively serve as (a) a fabric of information-processing mechanisms, which (b) then bias the individual toward a preferential and characteristic course of instrumental behavior spanning diverse situations. Schemas serve as the most fundamental units of personality, and as such may serve to shape all aspects of psychological functioning. But we are most interested in the information-processing aspect of personologic schemas. More specifically, we are interested in how personologic schemas shape the perception of reality as they contribute to the meanings and interpretations one assigns to people, places, and things in the environment. Rahe (1974, 1976), for example, has argued that environmental stressors accrue their pathogenic properties by violating, or otherwise breaching, the person's psychological defense mechanisms. Primary among such defense mechanisms may be selective perceptual filters that are personality-based. As sunglasses filter out selected wave bands on the visual spectrum, selective psychological filters usually serve to filter out certain aspects of the environment, serving to mitigate various forms of potential stressors. Environmental stressors become stressors by virtue of their ability to penetrate the usual perceptual filters. From a similar perspective, social psychologists Kiritz and Moos (1974) observed that environmental stimuli do not act directly on the individual but rather are mediated through personality variables. This is consistent with our understanding of the personality construct, from an interpretational information-processing perspective.

With this in mind, we have chosen to use the term *personality* within this volume to mean *a* characteristic and predictable pattern of deeply embedded and broadly exhibited cognitive, affective, and overt behavioral traits that, once developed, tend to persist over the course of a lifetime. We believe that one's personality structure may be thought of as an undergirding framework that gives coherence, provides a structure, and creates an intrinsic order to what may otherwise be misinterpreted as a multitude of discrete, environmentally dictated, psychological and behavioral operations that persist temporally and reach functionally across situations, thus revealing themselves to be more intrinsic and individually characteristic rather than a force, or motivation, situationally determined.

We believe personality traits emerge from a complex matrix of

1. Genetically engendered biological factors;
2. Environmentally engendered biological factors; and
3. Experiential learning.

We also believe that it is important to differentiate the term *personality* from the term *temperament*. We believe that temperament is a biologically determined subset of personality. Neonatal nurses are acutely aware of the differential patterns of temperament exhibited by newborns. Most parents appear capable of recognizing distinctive sensitivities and differential patterns of hunger and sleep between successive offspring. We believe temperament to be a crude physiological foundation for the development of that which we refer to as personality. Robinson (1999) has gone so far as to define personality as the sum of temperament (the biological foundation of personality) and character (the learned aspects of one's personality).

PERSONALITY AS A PSYCHOLOGICAL IMMUNE SYSTEM

Let us continue to extend our examination of personality by developing a biological parallel. The definition of personality offered previously denotes a certain fixity to the constellation we refer to as personality. That suggested psychological fixity is not without a biological parallel.

By the latter half of the 19th century, the great French physiologist Claude Bernard had postulated the proclivity of human physiology to sustain a state of equilibrium, despite external challenges and internal perturbations. Bernard postulated the existence of an elaborate compensatory physiological mechanism (Bernard, 1865/1945). Subsequently, the Nobel laureate Walter Cannon referred to this propensity to maintain constancy as "homeostasis" (Cannon, 1932). It may be that as the human body's physiology struggles to maintain balance, order, and constancy through the establishment of homeostatic mechanisms, so the mind struggles to maintain balance, order, and constancy through the establishment of enduring personality structures that serve to provide consistency and predictability. But our pursuit of physiology as a parallel to personologic psychology must go further still.

More than a century ago, Bernard's contemporary, Louis Pasteur, conducted pioneering research with microbial pathogens that led to a revolutionary approach to medicine. This new approach to the practice of medicine contained individual as well as public health implications. It included a focus on external pathogens as the primary threat to health, an attendant loss of interest in nonmicrobial pathogenic processes, and a structuring of medical education that focused largely on the resultant "one germ–one disease–one treatment" phenomenological model. To Pasteur, manifest disease was a virtual *fait accompli* subsequent to exposure to the microbial pathogen. However, Bernard and other contemporaries of Pasteur sharply criticized his univariate focus. They argued that he was wrongly fixated on the microbe to the exclusion of other factors, especially the physiological environment within which the microbial pathogen is allowed to attach and develop to full pathogenic maturity. On his deathbed, Pasteur reportedly declared that Bernard had been correct all along, acknowledging that the environment within which the pathogen grows is essential to the understanding of the disease process: *"Le germe n'est rien, c'est le terrain qui est tout."* According to Hans Selye (1956), "In most instances disease is due neither to the germ as such, nor to our adaptive reactions as such, but to the inadequacy of our reactions against the germ" (p. 300). Thus, the greatest endocrinologist of the 20th century implicated the immune system—in other words, the body's defense system as a crucial factor in microbial pathogenicity.

Returning to the discussion of psychological disorders, specifically PTSD, it is clear that the one germ–one disease–one treatment model is not applicable. If the traumatic event was the "necessary and sufficient" variable in the equation, then clearly the prevalence of PTSD subsequent to exposure to a traumatic event would have to be 100%. It is not. The U.S. Surgeon General's Report on Mental Health (U.S. DHHS, 1999) stated that the prevalence of PTSD subsequent to exposure to a traumatic event is, on average, 9%. Thus, exposure to the traumatic event may be a necessary aspect of the phenomenological chain of events, but it is not singularly sufficient to cause PTSD. This leads us to query, "Is there a psychological immune system?"

Consistent with the work of Millon (1969; Millon et al., 1996), we believe that the individual's personality serves as the equivalent of a psychological immune system—in other words, a psychological interpreting and filtering mechanism, as noted previously. As the physical immune system protects the person against the majority of ubiquitous environmental pathogens by filtering potentially toxic microbes, so the personality structure protects the person against ubiquitous psychological stressors by filtering the potentially toxic aspects of those stressors (see Rahe, 1974, 1976). The physical pathogen that results in physical illness has, by definition, functionally overwhelmed the biological immune system. The psychological stressor (traumatic event) that leads to PTSD, or its variants, has by definition violated, breached, or otherwise overwhelmed the psychological immune system, in this case the personologic interpreting and filtering system.

PERSONALITY CHARACTERISTICS AND PTSD

The focus of this volume is on "normal," functional, and generally adaptive nonpathological personality styles and their relationship to posttraumatic distress, especially PTSD. Within this volume and relevant to the study of PTSD, we are especially interested in the information interpreting and filtering functions of the personality schemas, because they represent one aspect of the overall personality fabric. Although Beck and Freeman (1990) have recognized the importance of such personality schemas in psychopathology, we shall take a more narrow focus of PTSD. We believe that PTSD develops as a direct result of an injury to one's personality-based schemas. We also believe that the "functional lesion" in PTSD resides within the interpretational schemas that assign meanings to the world as it unfolds before us. We believe that these interpretational schemas are critical functional constituents of the personality fabric.

There is evidence that there exist two forms of personality-based schemas consequential to the study of posttraumatic stress:

1. Personality-specific thematic beliefs; and
2. Broader, overarching assumptive explanatory *worldviews*.

Personality-specific thematic beliefs are fundamental beliefs that appear to be unique to, and serve to distinguish, each of the core differentiated personality styles, or patterns. Later we will present eight primary thematic beliefs, one for each of the differentiated normal personality styles. Their primary relevance to PTSD resides in the treatment of PTSD—more specifically, in the initial formulation of the therapeutic alliance.

Overarching and assumptive explanatory worldviews, or *Weltanschauung*, as they are sometimes considered (Everly, 1994), appear to be present within all normal, functional personality styles. They may simply vary in importance or priority from one personality style to another. Assumptive explanatory worldviews appear to be the core assumptive psychological beliefs rendering safety within the human experience. We believe there are five foundational assumptive explanatory worldviews. The importance of these worldviews to PTSD resides in the genesis of the posttraumatic stress reaction. More specifically, an assault on these beliefs reside at the phenomenological center of the traumatic experience. This *is* the psychological core of the traumatic event, and attendance to these psychological injuries reside at the center of trauma resolution.

We examine both of these personality-based schemas in greater detail in subsequent chapters. For now suffice it to say that, collectively, these beliefs

1. Provide a platform from which inferential understanding may be derived;
2. Assist the individual in functioning within ambiguous situations by establishing taxonomic assumptions on which predictive inferences may be drawn regarding people and situations previously unencountered;
3. Serve to conserve energy by preventing the necessity of analyzing every new person, place, or thing for potential opportunities or threats; and
4. Serve as a means of engendering a sense of self-efficacy and the perception of control over oneself and one's environment.

Thus, both of these personologic elements would appear to have survival value, and thus would appear to be perpetuated except under the most violating, or contradictory, of situations—for example, a traumatic event.

Despite their value, both the personality-specific thematic beliefs and the assumptive explanatory worldviews appear to represent potential diatheses, or vulnerabilities, when considering potentially distressing or traumatic circumstances. More succinctly stated, the essence of psychological trauma is the trauma-induced disruption, contradiction, or violation of one's personality-based schemas. More positively, both the personality-specific thematic beliefs and the assumptive explanatory worldviews play critical roles in the successful psychotherapeutic mitigation and resolution of posttraumatic symptomatology.

Thus, we believe that only through an understanding of these personality-anchored schemas—for example, (a) the personality-specific thematic beliefs and (b) the overarching assumptive worldviews—can the therapist best understand the nature of the posttraumatic reaction and the means by which the posttraumatic distress may be best psychotherapeutically mitigated or resolved. This book is dedicated to that end.

KEY POINT SUMMARY

1. "A man's fate is his character," observed Heraclitus more than 2,000 years ago. This statement clearly implies that the

totality of one's behavior is a function of more than situation-specific cues; that there exists a superordinate and predictable pattern of transituational behavior that we refer to as one's personality style or pattern.

2. The utility of studying personality is that the personality paradigm adds order and congruence to the totality of human behavior, yielding not only descriptive insight but predictive insight as well.

3. *Personality* may be defined as a characteristic and predictable pattern of deeply embedded and broadly exhibited cognitive, affective, and behavioral traits that, once developed, tends to persist over the course of a lifetime. The most fundamental aspect of personality is the schema.

4. According to Millon (1969; Millon et al., 1996), complex clinical psychiatric syndromes (CCSs) typically codified on Axis I of the *DSM* are best understood as pathological extensions, or epicenters, of more fundamental personality styles (individual syndromal continuity). Thus, great value is to be derived from the study of the personality structures that undergird the more florid psychological disorders.

5. Everly (1987) extended this concept by noting that personality styles may not only be important factors in the nature and phenomenological course of Axis I disorders but in psychodiagnostic refinement, in psychotherapeutic responsiveness, and in psychopharmacologic responsiveness. He referred to this notion as *personologic primacy*.

6. Everly (1987) observed that the natural corollary of personologic primacy is *personologic psychotherapy*. Personologic psychotherapy posits that the psychotherapy of Axis I psychological disorders is most effective when more salient foundational personality components, especially the constituent personality-based beliefs (in addition to the more florid symptom presentations) are taken into consideration, to avoid a situation wherein one treats only the symptoms and neglects the causal, self-perpetuating psychological lesion. Millon has referred to such an approach as *personality-guided therapy*.

7. Millon's notion of *synergistic psychotherapy* seems ideally suited to the treatment of PTSD, wherein multiple interventions are tailored in combinatorial fashion to address the key phenomenological constituents of PTSD, as well as the personality of the patient.

8. As the human body has an immune system to protect it against the ubiquitous pathogens in the environment, the

human mind uses personality-based schemas to protect it against the potentially toxic stressors that reside in the environment.

9. The development, and phenomenological course, of PTSD is believed to be associated with one's personality—more specifically, an injury to essential schematic beliefs that make up part of the fabric of personality. It is generally agreed that these schemas do much to shape the perception of environmental events through the assignment of meanings to those events, as it is thought to do in psychological traumatization. Thus, psychological traumatization represents a disruption, contradiction, or violation of one's personality-based schemas and as such this contradiction represents the functional lesion within PTSD.

10. We believe there exist two forms of personality-based schemas relevant to the study of PTSD: *personality-specific thematic beliefs* and broader, overarching *assumptive explanatory worldviews*.

11. Personality-specific thematic beliefs are important in the initial formulation of the therapeutic alliance.

12. Explanatory, assumptive worldviews hold the keys to trauma resolution.

13. In this volume, we explore a personality-guided therapy of PTSD through an examination of these most relevant personologic schemas. We examine the role of these schemas in the development of PTSD, as well as the therapeutic mitigation and resolution of PTSD.

14. In the final analysis, failure to understand the person with PTSD is a failure to understand PTSD.

2

AN INTRODUCTION TO
POSTTRAUMATIC STRESS DISORDER

Chapter 1 introduced the perspective that there is value in considering a personologic perspective when formulating a plan for the treatment of complex Axis I clinical psychiatric syndromes. The focus of this volume is on the personality-guided therapy of one specific psychiatric syndrome, posttraumatic stress disorder (PTSD). PTSD seems to be not only a candidate for a personality-guided psychotherapeutic approach but may be the most egregious candidate for a personality-guided psychotherapy. As noted previously, we believe that PTSD arises because of a direct assault on the functional and structural integrity of the individual's personality. Before delving into this assertion with greater acuity, we provide a brief introduction to the nature and prevalence of PTSD. Before doing so, however, it should be mentioned that PTSD is only one of the syndromes of posttraumatic distress. It seems clear that major depressive episodes, personality dysfunction, phobic formation, panic disorder, dissociative disorders, substance abuse, and even psychotic manifestations may result from exposure to traumatic events.

A BRIEF HISTORY OF PTSD

As already discussed, PTSD was first recognized as an official psychiatric diagnosis in 1980 with the advent of the multiaxial third edition of the

Diagnostic and Statistical Manual of Mental Disorders (American Psychiatric Association, 1980), but its roots far predate the 20th century.

Pre–20th-Century Accounts

It may be that the first written account of the posttraumatic stress syndrome was that provided by Homer. In *The Iliad*, Homer wrote of the Trojan War and of its heroes. According to Shay (1994), one hero, Achilles, was described by Homer as suffering a form of traumatic grief reaction in response to the death of his friend, Patroclos, for which he felt some culpability. In Homer's story, the assault on Troy had slowed and, indeed, the Greeks were being driven back to their ships. The greatest of the Greek heroes, Achilles, had refused to continue to fight because he felt he had been insulted by the Greek king Agamemnon. Finally, as a means of rallying the Greek army, Achilles's friend Patroclos agreed to wear his friend's armor and fight as if he were Achilles. Initially, the strategy worked, but the Trojan hero Hector soon met the impostor in battle and killed him. When Achilles learned of his friend's death, he was overwhelmed with grief, anger, and guilt. "Sorrow fell on Achilles like a cloud. He swept up the dust with both hands, and poured it over his head and smirched his handsome face. . . . He tore his hair and fell flat in the dust. . . . Antilochos had taken the hands of Achilles . . . for he feared Achilles might put the steel to his own throat" (Homer, 1999, p. 216). Achilles was so distraught that he entered into battle, even though he had been told by the gods that if he did so, he would be killed. Achilles cried, "Quick let me die, since it seems my friend was killed and I was not there to help him! He perished far from his native land, and I was not there to defend him!" (Homer, 1999, p. 218). Emotionally overwhelmed, Achilles entered the battle, slew Hector, who killed Patroclos, and at a later time died as Paris's arrow struck him in his only vulnerable point, his heel.

The syndrome of psychological angst described by Homer, which arguably led to the death of Achilles, albeit indirectly, seems consistent with a posttraumatic stress reaction as we now know it.

According to Trimble (1981), more modern accounts of posttraumatic psychological symptoms were first associated with physical injuries to the spinal column and were noticed as early as the mid–18th century. Spinal concussion was even viewed as a cause of the traumatic neuroses. As the 18th century progressed, spinal concussions became closely associated with traumatic incidents within the railroad industry. The term "railway spine" emerged to reflect this close association and reflected a syndrome of neurological and psychological symptoms that are consistent with posttraumatic distress as we understand it. In 1865, Charles Dickens appeared to develop posttraumatic distress in response to a railway accident in Kent. He later wrote that he was "curiously weak," experiencing intrusive memories of the accident and an avoidance of traveling by train.

Although posttraumatic reactions, such as "soldier's heart" were recorded as a result of the American Civil War, not much relative emphasis was placed on those accounts in the history of medicine. That would have to wait until World War I.

Early Diagnostic Formulations

World War I was supposed to be the great war to end all wars. Initially, it was seen as a glorious escapade by many. As the battle lines seemed to stagnate in France, trench warfare emerged. Shouts of "over the top" usually heralded a virtually suicidal advance into barbed wire, exploding cannon shells, machine gun fire, poisonous gases, and in closest quarters, sharpened bayonets. Terms such as *shell shock, battle fatigue,* and *soldier's heart* were the diagnostic labels applied to those who developed incapacitating posttraumatic reactions.

According to Wilson (1995), the work of Sigmund Freud greatly influenced the understanding of posttraumatic stress. But Freud was known to have been influenced by Janet (1919/1976), who identified dissociative reactions as a splitting of unconscious and conscious processes in response to an event the mind simply could not integrate. Janet was also the first to hint at the role that interpretational mechanisms might play in psychotraumatogenesis. Nevertheless, Wilson (1995) argued that Freud recognized that the traumatic neuroses were engendered as a result of an overwhelmingly powerful external agent that distorted normal ego functioning, causing a fixation on the theme of mastery. Freud further postulated that there were discrete symptom clusters, a recognition that predated the official taxonomy by 70 years.

World War II and the Korean War yielded additional manifestations of posttraumatic dysphoria. As a result, the first edition of the *Diagnostic and Statistical Manual of Mental Disorders* (American Psychiatric Association, 1952) listed Gross Stress Reaction as a diagnostic category to capture the disordered variation of the human response to trauma. The second edition of the *Diagnostic and Statistical Manual of Mental Disorders* (American Psychiatric Association, 1968) used a category called Adjustment Reaction to Adult Life to capture the same syndrome. Both of these diagnostic formulations emphasized the transient nature of the dysphoric reaction. If the symptoms were seen to persist in the absence of the psychotraumatogenetic stressor, another psychiatric disorder was to be considered, however.

PTSD in *DSM–III*

As noted earlier, PTSD emerged as an anxiety disorder in 1980 within the *DSM–III* (American Psychiatric Association, 1980). According to Summerfield (2001), "Early proponents of the diagnosis of post-traumatic stress disorder were part of the antiwar movement in the United States. . . . The new diagnosis was meant to shift the focus of attention from the details of a soldier's background and psyche to the fundamentally traumatogenic nature of war. This was a powerful and essentially political transformation. . . . Post-traumatic stress disorder legitimised their 'victimhood' " (p. 95). In doing so, it served as a political condemnation of the Vietnam War.

The *DSM–III* defined a traumatic stressor as "a recognizable stressor that would evoke significant symptoms of distress in almost everyone" (p. 238). Three subsequent symptom clusters were then delineated. Thus, the *DSM–III* formulated PTSD as

A. Exposure to a recognizable stressor;
B. Reexperiencing the trauma (one of three symptoms within symptom cluster B);
C. Numbing of responsiveness (one of three within symptom cluster C); and
D. Other symptoms not present before the trauma (two of six within symptom cluster D), which included sleep disturbance, hyperalertness, exaggerated startle, guilt, memory impairment, and others.

The *DSM–III* further noted that "symptoms may begin immediately or soon after the trauma. It is not unusual, however, for the symptoms to emerge after a latency period of months or years following the trauma" (American Psychiatric Association, 1980, p. 237).

PTSD in *DSM–III–R*

The *DSM–III–R* was published in 1987 (American Psychiatric Association, 1987). PTSD remained within the taxonomy as an anxiety disorder, but greater refinement was offered. The nature of the traumatic event was redefined in the *DSM–III–R*, which noted, "The person has experienced an event that is outside the range of usual human experience and that would be markedly distressing to almost anyone" (p. 250). This broadened definition embraced the notion of vicarious, or secondary traumatization, more so than did the definition in the *DSM–III*.

Diagnostic categories were expanded to five:

A. Exposure;
B. Reexperiencing (one of four symptoms in symptom cluster B);

C. Avoidance/numbing (three of seven symptoms in cluster C);
D. Increased arousal (two of six symptoms of largely sympathetic nervous system activity within cluster D); and
E. A symptom duration of one month or longer.

(The latter was included as an attempt to differentiate PTSD from transient grief or adjustment reactions.)

PTSD in DSM–IV

In 1994, the DSM was once again revised. PTSD was retained as an anxiety disorder in the DSM–IV (American Psychiatric Association, 1994). The DSM–IV criteria (see Exhibit 2.1) represented major alterations in the official criteria for PTSD, and even recognized a more acute variant of the posttraumatic syndrome, acute stress disorder (ASD; see Exhibit 2.2).

There were three major changes in the DSM–IV formulation of PTSD:

First, the DSM–IV reformulated the definition of the traumatic event. Although the DSM–III and DSM–III–R defined the traumatic stressor as an unusually distressing event, the DSM–IV actually restricted the nature of the stressor by limiting it to events that involve actual or threatened death or serious injury to oneself or others. The DSM–III–R stressor of sudden destruction to one's home or community, in the absence of injury or death, was omitted. This restriction in the nature of the traumatic stressor has not been well received by many individuals who work in mass disaster venues and believe that a mass disaster in and of itself is psychotraumatogenetic.

Second, although restricting one aspect of the traumatic criterion (criterion A, 1), the DSM–IV actually broadened another aspect of the traumatic stressor by including the notion of subjective appraisal. The A(2) criterion of the DSM–IV noted that the individual's response to the traumatic event must involve "intense fear, helplessness, or horror." Fear, helplessness, and horror are obviously subjective states that are the result of a process of subjective appraisal. Thus, an important shift was realized. The DSM–III and DSM–III–R placed the greatest etiological weight on the traumatic event. The DSM–IV now placed the diagnostic emphasis on the reaction of the individual to the traumatic event. Implicit in this shift is the inclusion of the inherent meaning, perception, or interpretation assigned to the traumatic event by the individual experiencing the traumatic event.

Figure 2.1 represents a phenomenological algorithm that functionally integrates the core elements of the posttraumatic stress response, taking into consideration the role of subjective interpretation. Figure 2.1 also illustrates that numerous psychological disorders (PTSD, ASD, dissociative identity disorders, major depression, panic disorder, phobic avoidance, sub-

EXHIBIT 2.1
DSM–IV (1994) Diagnostic Criteria for Posttraumatic Stress Disorder

A. The person has been exposed to a traumatic event in which both of the following were present:
   (1) Event or events that involved actual or threatened death or serious injury, or a threat to the physical integrity of self or others
   (2) The person's response involved intense fear, helplessness, or horror. **Note:** In children, this may be expressed instead by disorganized or agitated behavior

B. The traumatic event is persistently reexperienced in one (or more) of the following ways:
   (1) Recurrent and intrusive distressing recollections of the event, including images, thoughts, or perceptions. **Note:** In young children, repetitive play may occur in which themes or aspects of the trauma are expressed
   (2) Recurrent distressing dreams of the event. **Note:** In children, there may be frightening dreams without recognizable content
   (3) Acting or feeling as if the traumatic event were recurring (includes a sense of reliving the experience, illusions, hallucinations, and dissociative flashback episodes, including those that occur on awakening or when intoxicated). **Note:** In young children, trauma-specific reenactment may occur
   (4) Intense psychological distress at exposure to internal or external cues that symbolize or resemble an aspect of the traumatic event
   (5) Physiological reactivity on exposure to internal or external cues that symbolize or resemble an aspect of the traumatic event

C. Persistent avoidance of stimuli associated with the trauma and numbing of general responsiveness (not present before the trauma), as indicated by three (or more) of the following:
   (1) Efforts to avoid thoughts, feelings, or conversations associated with the trauma
   (2) Efforts to avoid activities, places, or people that arouse recollections of the trauma
   (3) Inability to recall an important aspect of the trauma
   (4) Markedly diminished interest or participation in significant activities
   (5) Feeling of detachment or estrangement from others
   (6) Restricted range of affect (e.g. unable to have loving feelings)
   (7) Sense of a foreshortened future (e.g., does not expect to have a career, marriage, children, or a normal life span)

D. Persistent symptoms of increased arousal (not present before the trauma), as indicated by two (or more) of the following:
   (1) Difficulty falling or staying asleep
   (2) Irritability or outbursts of anger
   (3) Difficulty concentrating
   (4) Hypervigilance
   (5) Exaggerated startle response

E. Duration of the disturbance (symptoms in Criteria B, C, and D) is more than 1 month.

F. The disturbance causes clinically significant distress or impairment in social occupational, or other important areas of functioning.

Specify if:
   Acute: if duration of symptoms is less than 3 months
   Chronic: if duration of symptoms is 3 months or more

Specify if:
   With Delayed Onset: if onset of symptoms is at least 6 months after the stressor

---

Note. Reprinted with permission from *Diagnostic and Statistical Manual of Mental Disorders*, Fourth Edition. Copyright 2000 American Psychiatric Association.

EXHIBIT 2.2
DSM–IV (1994) Diagnostic Criteria for Acute Stress Disorder

A. The person has been exposed to a traumatic event in which both of the following were present:
   (1) the person experienced, witnessed, or was confronted with an event or events that involved actual or threatened death or serious injury, or a threat to the physical integrity of self or others
   (2) the person's response involved intense fear, helplessness, or horror
B. Either while experiencing or after experiencing the distressing event, the individual has three (or more) of the following dissociative symptoms:
   (1) a subjective sense of numbing, detachment, or absence of emotional responsiveness
   (2) a reduction in awareness of his or her surroundings (e.g., "being in a daze")
   (3) derealization
   (4) depersonalization
   (5) dissociative amnesia (i.e., inability to recall an important aspect of the trauma)
C. The traumatic event is persistently reexperienced in at least one of the following ways: recurrent images, thoughts, dreams, illusions, flashback episodes, or a sense of reliving the experience; or distress on exposure to reminders of the traumatic event
D. Marked avoidance of stimuli that arouse recollections of the trauma (e.g., thoughts, feelings, conversations, activities, places, people)
E. Marked symptoms of anxiety or increased arousal (e.g., difficulty sleeping, irritability, poor concentration, hypervigilance, exaggerated startle response, motor restlessness)
F. The disturbance causes clinically significant distress or impairment in social, occupational, or other important areas of functioning or impairs the individual's ability to pursue some necessary task, such as obtaining necessary assistance or mobilizing personal resources by telling family members about the traumatic experience
G. The disturbance lasts for a minimum of 2 days and a maximum of 4 weeks and occurs within 4 weeks of the traumatic event
H. The disturbance is not due to the direct physiological effects of a substance (e.g., a drug of abuse, a medication) or a general medical condition, is not better accounted for by Brief Psychotic Disorder, and is not merely an exacerbation of a preexisting Axis I or Axis II disorder

Note. Reprinted with permission from *Diagnostic and Statistical Manual of Mental Disorders*, Fourth Edition. Copyright 2000 American Psychiatric Association.

stance abuse, even brief psychotic reactions, to name a few) may be attributable to traumatic exposure. These disorders are not even limited to major psychiatric syndromes but may be manifest as personality disorders (see chapter 12) and stress-related physical diseases. The neurobiology and efferent neuroendocrine and endocrine mechanisms are presented in Figure 2.2.

As the algorithm in Figure 2.1 indicates, posttraumatic stress represents a dynamic "process" rather than a monothetic formulation. A review of Figure 2.1 reveals that the sine qua non of PTSD is a qualifying traumatic event. However, Figure 2.1 also indicates, given the polythetic nature of PTSD, that the interpretation, or meaning, that the individual assigns to

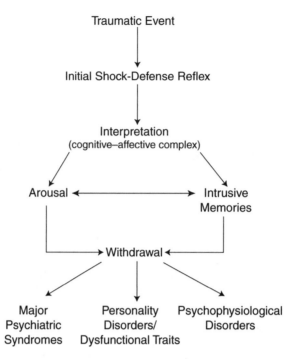

Traumatic Event

↓

Initial Shock-Defense Reflex

↓

Interpretation
(cognitive–affective complex)

Arousal ⟷ Intrusive Memories

Withdrawal

Major Psychiatric Syndromes   Personality Disorders/ Dysfunctional Traits   Psychophysiological Disorders

Figure 2.1. A model of posttraumatic stress. From *Psychotraumatology: Key Papers and Core Concepts in Post-traumatic Stress* (p. 45), by G. S. Everly, Jr., and J. M. Lating, 1995. New York: Plenum Press. Copyright 1995 by Plenum Press. Adapted with permission.

the event may greatly affect the manifest severity of the subsequent symptoms. This alteration, made to consider the subjective appraisal of the traumatic event, has engendered some concern from victims' advocacy groups in that acknowledgment of the subjective aspects of the traumatic stressor may lead to a "blame the victim" attitude. Yehuda (1999) raised this issue and notes that in the *DSM–IV*, individuals must experience an adverse subjective response to the traumatic event, thus the study of risk factors becomes necessary rather than inappropriate (Yehuda, 1999). However, the *DSM–IV* does recognize that the severity of the traumatic event may correlate with the severity of manifest symptoms. As noted previously, the nature and degree of manifest posttraumatic symptomatology is a function of the nature of the traumatic event and the individual experiencing the event. To avoid misinterpreting this concept as reason to "blame the victim," Figure 2.3 portrays the role of the victim's subjective interpretation in overall event potency (severity). Traumatic events will vary in their normative severity, or potency. This is called stimulus response seterotypy and simply means that "mild" stressors usually engender mild responses and "Severe" stressors usually engender severe responses. Automobile accidents

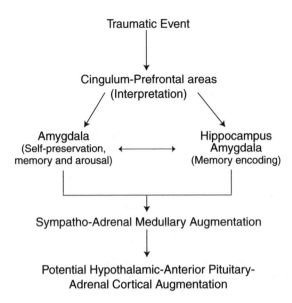

Figure 2.2. Neurobiology of PTSD. From *Psychotraumatology: Key Papers and Core Concepts in Post-traumatic Stress* (p. 42), by G. S. Everly, Jr., and J. M. Lating, 1995. New York: Plenum Press. Copyright 1995 by Plenum Press. Adapted with permission.

are less severe than torture. Thus, as the norm-referenced severity of the stressor event increases, the less a role subjective interpretation, called individual response specificity, plays in determining the severity of the manifest symptom response. Thus, subjective interpretation plays less of a role in shaping the traumatic response to torture than it might compared with an automobile accident.

Figure 2.3 addresses this issue by illustrating that although interpretation of the traumatic event is an important aspect of the PTSD picture, traumatic events in and of themselves carry a certain degree of inherent potency.

It should also be noted that Figure 2.1 suggests that much of the depressive avoidance, numbing, and withdrawal that is replete in the posttraumatic stress constellation may be but a second-order symptom manifestation engendered as a result of the increase arousal and intrusive recollective ideation—a notion not embraced by the psychological community at large.

A third change in the *DSM–IV* formulation of PTSD was that there was a new criterion added, criterion F: "The disturbance causes clinically significant distress or impairment in social, occupational, or other important areas of functioning" (American Psychiatric Association, 1994, p. 429). Thus, the mere presence of manifest symptomatology is insufficient to warrant the diagnosis of the disorder. Rather, the amplitude of the symptoms must be considered, as well.

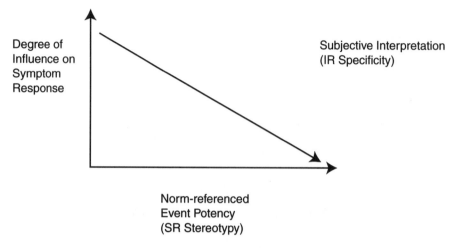

Degree of
Influence on
Symptom
Response

Subjective Interpretation
(IR Specificity)

Norm-referenced
Event Potency
(SR Stereotypy)

Figure 2.3. Subjective interpretation and event potency. From *A Clinical Guide to the Treatment of the Human Stress Response* (2nd ed., p. 324), by G. S. Everly, Jr., and J. M. Lating, 2002. New York: Kluwer/Plenum Press. Reprinted with permisison.

Finally, although not a major change in the diagnostic criteria themselves, the *DSM–IV* acknowledged the potential for PTSD to be associated with "a change from the individual's previous personality characteristics" (American Psychiatric Association, 1994, p. 425). In recognizing that PTSD could alter something as concretized as personality, a new realm of psychological and biological phenomenological possibilities emerges.

PTSD in *ICD–10*

The *International Classification of Disease, 10th Edition (ICD–10)*, published by the World Health Organization (WHO; 1990, 1992), serves as the current international nosological compendium of disease. The *ICD–10 Classification of Mental and Behavioural Disorders* (WHO, 1992) contains a category called "Reaction to severe stress, and adjustment disorders" (F43). PTSD (F43.1) is contained within that category. The *ICD–10* stated that PTSD

> arises as a . . . response to a stressful event or situation . . . of an exceptionally threatening or catastrophic nature, which is likely to cause pervasive distress in almost anyone (e.g., natural or man-made disaster, combat, serious accident, witnessing the violent death of others, or being the victim of torture, terrorism, rape, or other crime). (WHO, 1992, p. 148)

Diagnostically, in addition to the aforementioned trauma, there must be evidence of intrusive recollections of the event. Emotional detachment and numbing are often present but they are not essential constituents for the diagnosis. Finally, autonomic, mood, and behavioral disturbances clearly round out the diagnostic picture but are not of prime importance from the perspective of the *ICD–10*. Thus, the *ICD–10* contains a construction for PTSD that is somewhat similar to that contained within the *DSM–IV*, but is less rigid with regard to the nature of the stressor and the nature of the resultant symptom patterns.

The *ICD–10* appears to have a greater sensitivity to the long-term ramifications of psychological trauma. The *ICD–10* contains a formal diagnostic category titled "Enduring personality change after catastrophic experience" (F62.0). In an appreciation of the potentially profound effect that psychological traumatization may exert, this category states, "Enduring personality change may follow the experience of catastrophic stress. . . . Posttraumatic stress disorder (F43.1) may precede this type of personality change, which may then be seen as a chronic irreversible sequel of stress disorder" (WHO, 1992, p. 209).

PREVALENCE OF PTSD

Having reviewed PTSD as it appears in the official nosological compendia, let us examine its prevalence. It may be argued that adverse posttraumatic stress reactions represent a clear and present public health challenge (Everly & Mitchell, 1999). Although it is to be expected that those exposed to a traumatic event will develop some form of posttraumatic dysphoria, the prevalence with which such dysphoria reaches the proportions of a psychiatric "disorder" wherein it interferes with social or occupational functioning is alarming. Consider the following:

1. The adult (ages 18–45) lifetime prevalence for exposure to one or more traumatic events (as defined by the *DSM–IV*) has been estimated to be more than 89% in an urban community area investigation (Breslau et al., 1998).
2. "Overall, among those exposed to extreme trauma, about 9 percent ultimately develop post-traumatic stress disorder" (U.S. DHHS, 1999, p. 237). That estimate has been posited elsewhere to be higher (Yehuda, 1999).
3. In the general adult population, the lifetime prevalence of PTSD in the United States has been estimated to range between 1.3% (Davidson, Hughes, & Blazer, 1991) and 8% (American Psychiatric Association, 1994).
4. Given the especially severe forms of traumatic stressors, the risk of developing PTSD was found to be about 34% (current

prevalence) in response to mass disasters (North et al., 1999), about 49% in response to rape, and about 53% (lifetime prevalence) in response to captivity, kidnapping, or torture (Breslau et al., 1998).

5. The prevalence of posttraumatic stress disorder ranged from 15% to 31% for samples of urban firefighters based on a traumatic exposure prevalence ranging from 85% to 91% (Beaton, Murphy, & Corneil, 1996);

6. The current prevalence of PTSD was psychometrically estimated to be about 18% in a random sample of Kuwaiti firefighters (Al-Naser & Everly, 1999).

7. The current prevalence of PTSD was psychometrically estimated to be about 13% in a sample of suburban police officers (H. Robinson, Sigman, & Wilson, 1997).

8. The current prevalence of PTSD among Vietnam War veterans was estimated to be about 15%, and the lifetime prevalence was estimated to be about 30% (Kulka et al., 1990)

9. In a survey of PTSD, it was found that 74% of cases lasted more than six months (Breslau et al., 1998).

10. Symptoms of distress and PTSD are positively correlated with exposure to traumatic stressors (Wee, Mills, & Koelher, 1999; Weiss, Marmar, Metzler, & Ronfeldt, 1995) in a virtual dose–response relationship.

Clearly, posttraumatic stress appears to be reaching almost epidemic proportions in the Unites States (and perhaps elsewhere). It may be argued that it represents a public health challenge that should not be ignored.

A TWO-FACTOR MODEL OF POSTTRAUMATIC STRESS

Young (1995) has declared that PTSD does not warrant the status of a formalized psychiatric disorder. He has argued that the disorder does not possess an intrinsic unity. We disagree with this assessment. The variability with respect to (a) what individuals develop the disorder and (b) what symptomatology becomes manifest argues less for its apocryphal nature and more for its polythetic phenomenology. More specifically, we consider posttraumatic stress as a spectrum disorder, somewhat similar to the pluralistic formulation of depression described by Klerman, Weissman, Rousaville, and Chevron (1984)—that is, the qualitative and quantitative nature of the symptoms of the disorder will vary according to the overall severity of the disorder. Figure 2.4 presents posttraumatic stress as a spectrum disorder.

Despite the aforementioned variability, we believe that there are two unifying core factors, often latent, of the disorder that are reliable across

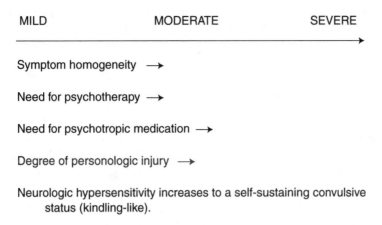

SEVERITY

MILD   MODERATE   SEVERE

Symptom homogeneity →

Need for psychotherapy →

Need for psychotropic medication →

Degree of personologic injury →

Neurologic hypersensitivity increases to a self-sustaining convulsive
     status (kindling-like).

Figure 2.4. Posttraumatic stress as a spectrum disorder.

the presentation spectrum and that warrant consideration in treatment planning. This formulation we refer to as the *two-factor model of posttraumatic stress* (Everly, 1989, 1993a, 1993b, 1994).

The components of the two-factor model are

1. A psychological hypersensitivity; and
2. A neurological hypersensitivity.

A close examination of the factors involved in PTSD suggests a virtual neuropersonologic phenomenology. Let us examine the two-factor model in greater detail.

Psychologic Hypersensitivity

The first factor in the two-factor formulation of PTSD we refer to as psychologic hypersensitivity and recognize its foundations as personologic. As noted in chapter 1, we believe PTSD arises because of a direct assault on, and resultant injury to, the structural and functional integrity of one's personality structure. More specifically, the term *psychologic hypersensitivity* reflects a violation of some deeply held explanatory belief, an essential thread in the fabric of human personality. This core belief is referred to as an assumptive explanatory worldview, or *Weltanschauung* (Everly, 1993a, 1993b, 1994, 1995). These assumptive worldviews are not just important, they are imperative to adaptive functioning. They serve to provide meaning, order, and safety to one's environment. Thus, a traumatic event, according to this perspective, is predicated on some situation that is perceived as violating this deeply held and imperative worldview. Most commonly, we think of the traumatic event as being a life-threatening event—thus a violation to the assumption of safety discussed by writers such as Maslow (1970). But it appears as if these explanatory worldviews may be even more far-reaching. We shall explore them in greater detail later in this volume.

Neurologic Hypersensitivity

The second factor in the two-factor formulation of PTSD is a neurologic hypersensitivity. The neurologic hypersensitivity is thought to consist of a lowered functional depolarization threshold within the amygdaloid posterior hypothalamic efferent pathways, as well as other limbic-related structures such as the anterior pituitary. This functional hypersensitivity is thought to give rise to a potential overreactive cascade of neurological, neuroendocrine, and systemic hormonal phenomena, as well as behavioral impulsivity, irritability, and a propensity for violence or isolating avoidance. The limbic hypersensitivity itself appears to result from a potential myriad of physiological mechanisms that may have the potential to reach convulsive proportions and to become virtually self-perpetuating, perhaps over the course of a lifetime. These mechanisms may even accrue a toxic nature. We shall review the anatomy and physiology of the posttraumatic stress response in far greater detail in chapter 4.

KEY POINT SUMMARY

1. Although PTSD first appeared in the *DSM–III* in 1980 as an official psychiatric disorder, the posttraumatic stress syndrome has been known since the time of Homer and the ancient Greeks.

2. The most current formulation of PTSD appears in the *DSM–IV*, published in 1994. The *DSM–IV* is a departure from earlier formulations in that it recognizes the role that subjective appraisal plays in the etiology of the disorder but restricts the definition of the traumatic stressor to those things that involve actual, or threatened, death or serious injury. The *DSM–IV* also added an additional diagnostic criterion (F) that dictates that the posttraumatic syndrome must cause clinically significant distress or impairment.

3. The international classification system, the *ICD–10*, views PTSD less restrictively, but does specifically describe a condition wherein extreme trauma may permanently alter the victim's personality.

4. PTSD may be viewed pluralistically as a spectrum disorder, suggesting that the symptom profiles, their underlying substrates, may vary with their increasing severity.

5. The prevalence of PTSD has been estimated at about 1 to 8% in the general population, with anywhere from 9% to 25% of those exposed to a traumatic stressor actually developing PTSD.

6. Phenomenologically, PTSD may be viewed as consisting of two factors: a psychological hypersensitivity and a neurological hypersensitivity. The psychological component is thought to reflect a condition wherein the traumatic event represents an assault on the individual's core explanatory worldview—in other words, a deeply held imperative belief that is a component within the constituency of the personality structure. The neurologic hypersensitivity appears to represent an increased sensitivity, or neural irritability, of key central nervous system structures yielding hyperexcitability, impulsiveness, violent inclinations, and exaggerated startle reactions.

7. PTSD is but only one of the syndromes of posttraumatic distress. It seems clear that major depressive episodes, personality dysfunction, phobic formation, panic disorder, dissociative disorders, substance abuse, and even psychotic manifestations may result from exposure to traumatic events.

8. Finally, PTSD may be an ideal candidate for a personality-guided psychotherapeutic approach, perhaps more so than other *DSM–IV*, Axis I syndromes, in that PTSD arises from an assault on, or injury to, the functional and structural integrity of the personality itself.

3

THE DEFINING MOMENT OF PSYCHOLOGICAL TRAUMA: WHAT MAKES A TRAUMATIC EVENT TRAUMATIC?

Why is it that, overall, we expect about 9 to 25% of individuals exposed to a traumatic event to develop posttraumatic stress disorder (PTSD; U.S. DHHS, 1999)? Why isn't it 100%? Given these statistics, why is it that we expect about 30 to 40% of individuals who are directly exposed to a mass disaster to develop PTSD? Why isn't it 9 to 25%?

The issue at hand is paramount for anyone treating PTSD. It seems clear that exposure to a traumatic event is a necessary but not sufficient criterion for the development of PTSD. How can we attempt to treat PTSD without some fundamental understanding of the genesis and phenomenological nature of the disorder itself? Thus, we ask, "What is the essence of psychological trauma and the posttraumatic stress response?" In the next two chapters, we shall offer an answer to that question by expanding the two-factor model of posttraumatic stress introduced in chapter 2. More specifically, in this chapter, we examine the role of key psychological variables in psychotraumatogenesis. In the next chapter, we review key biological features of the posttraumatic stress response.

THE ROLE OF SUBJECTIVE INTERPRETATION: GENERAL CONSIDERATIONS

The greatest endocrinologist of his time, as well as the founder of the "stress" concept, Hans Selye, once noted, "It is not what happens to you that matters, but how you take it" (conference comments). Perhaps the most acclaimed pioneer in the field of psychosomatic medicine, Stuart Wolf, once said, "It is evident from the idiosyncratic nature of interpreting experience that to understand the impact of an event, the focus of inquiry must be the individual" (conference comments). The philosopher Epictetus once wrote that people are disturbed, not by things, but by the views that they take of them. Even Shakespeare once wrote, "For there are no things good nor bad, but thinking makes them so" (*Hamlet*, 1999). Finally, it may be that stressors, like beauty, lie in the eye of the beholder. Although clearly avoiding a "blame the victim" scenario, one point does emerge that is worthy of consideration. Much of the difference between an event that results in acute distress with regard to an event that results in chronic PTSD appears to lie in the subjective severity of the event—in other words, how the two events are differentially interpreted by the individuals who actually experience them (there are notable exceptions to the principle—e.g., torture, death or serious injury of a child, especially one's own).

Based on the work of Lazarus (1966; Lazarus & Folkman, 1984) and Selye (1976), Everly (1989) constructed a phenomenological model of the human stress response (see Figure 3.1).

Consistent with the more recent *DSM–IV* (American Psychiatric Association, 1994), a pivotal element of that model was the subjective interpretation of real, imagined, or anticipated stressor events. Everly proposed that the amplitude and chronicity of the human stress response was largely dictated by the nature of the subjective interpretational process in the wake of exposure to a traumatic, or otherwise distressing, event. Some years later, Smith, Everly, and Johns (1993), using mathematical modeling procedures, tested the plausibility of the model developed by Everly. In a large-scale investigation of the stressor-to-disease process in a sample of more than 1,500 research participants, it was discovered that the subjective interpretation of work-related stressors played a more significant role in the development of stress-related disease than did exposure to the actual work-related stressor itself.

Stressor ⟶ Cognitive ⟶ Affective ⟶ Neurologic ⟶ Enhanced ⟶ Target ⟶ + Coping ⟶ Attenuated Arousal
Interpretation Integration Tone Stress Arousal Organ
Enhanced Arousal ⟶ – Coping ⟶ Sustained Arousal

Figure 3.1. A model of the human stress response.

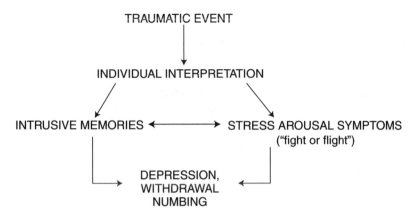

TRAUMATIC EVENT

INDIVIDUAL INTERPRETATION

INTRUSIVE MEMORIES ←——————→ STRESS AROUSAL SYMPTOMS
("fight or flight")

DEPRESSION,
WITHDRAWAL
NUMBING

Figure 3.2. Posttraumatic stress disorder. From *Psychotraumatology: Key Papers and Core Concepts in Post-traumatic Stress* (p. 28), by G. S. Everly, Jr., and J. M. Lating, 1995. New York: Plenum Press. Copyright 1995 by Plenum Press. Adapted with permission.

Later, in a continuation of his efforts to create phenomenological models of the human stress response, Everly (1989, 1993a, 1994) constructed a model of the posttraumatic stress process. Once again, the subjective interpretation was to play a key deterministic role in posttraumatic phenomenology (see Figure 3.2). As described by Everly and Lating (1995), the manifestation of the three symptom clusters consisting of intrusive memories, stress arousal symptoms, and withdrawal, depression, and numbing are predicated on a complete interaction between the traumatic event and the individual experiencing the event.

Everly proposed that subjective interpretation of the traumatic event was the defining moment of psychotraumatogenesis. Consistent with this formulation, in 1994, the official nosological compendium of psychiatric disorders, the *Diagnostic and Statistical Manual of Mental Disorders*, Fourth Edition (*DSM–IV*; American Psychiatric Association, 1994), dramatically altered its definition of a traumatic event and seemed to acknowledge the role of subjective interpretation in psychotraumatogenesis. The *DSM–IV* stated that to be considered a traumatic event, the event must engender "fear, helplessness, or horror" (American Psychiatric Association, 1994, p. 428). Clearly, fear, helplessness, or horror are all states of subjective interpretation.

To review, it seems reasonable to assume that everything that we consciously perceive undergoes a process of psychological filtering. Using a biological metaphor, these filters act as a form of protective psychological "immune system." Conceptually speaking, an event that becomes a trauma is an event that breaches one's protective psychological filtering mechanisms. Returning to the biological metaphor, a traumatic event is a pathogen that overwhelms one's psychological "immune system."

Many authors (Girdano, Everly, & Dusek, 2001; Rahe, 1974, 1976) concede that these psychological filters typically consist of factors such as personality traits, culture, previous related experiences, self-concept, and certainly one's coping mechanisms and resources. But some writers of recent research point to a far more specific factor when asking what makes a traumatic event traumatic: The factor is that of one's personologic schemas, or belief systems. In chapter 1 we mentioned two types of personologic schemas, or belief systems, that were important in the treatment planning for PTSD:

1. Personality-specific thematic beliefs; and
2. Overarching imperative explanatory assumptive worldviews.

We will see that the personality-specific thematic beliefs are important to consider when initially formulating the therapeutic alliance with the trauma patient. But, as suggested in chapter 2, it is the explanatory assumptive worldviews that hold the answer to trauma resolution. From this perspective, a traumatic event is one that violates, or destroys, the assumptive worldview about oneself or one's world (Everly, 1993a, 1994; J. Frank & Frank, 1991). Trauma resolution means successfully addressing this issue. This chapter examines the assumptive explanatory worldviews.

THE ASSUMPTIVE WORLDVIEWS

In an excellent volume on psychotherapy, titled *Persuasion and Healing*, J. Frank and Frank (1991) expand the notion undergirding Cantril's term *assumptive world*. They stated, "Leading a successful life, even surviving, depends on the ability to predict future events from present ones, or at least the belief that one can do so. . . . Since prediction is based on understanding, the need to make sense of events is as fundamental as the need for food or water" (J. Frank & Frank, 1991, p. 24). They cite neuropsychological investigations that suggest that there exists a biological mandate, existing within the dominant hemisphere, to interpret and otherwise create a meaningful world. They go on to discuss what may be the most salient point within this context.

> To deal with the world and enjoy life, a person's assumptive world must correspond more or less closely to conditions as they actually are. . . . Thus, everyone is strongly motivated to monitor the validity of his or her assumptions. . . . If an act fails to produce predicted consequences, the person is in trouble. (J. Frank & Frank, 1991, p. 26)

These assumptions are so important that they are encoded as part of the fabric of the personality itself. Experiences that challenge, threaten, or invalidate core assumptions serve as the potential foundations for posttraumatic dysphoria or maladaptive coping patterns. They assault the fundamental construction of one's personality.

EXPLANATORY WORLDVIEWS (WELTANSHAUUNG)

Continuing this theme of pivotal assumptions, Everly (1993a, 1994) noted that human beings require, and therefore they create, explanatory worldviews concerning themselves and their respective environments. Everly (1993a, 1994, 1995), borrowing from the field of rhetoric, has referred to these deeply held belief systems as *Weltanschauung* (from the German *welt*—meaning "world" and *anschauung*—meaning "perspective"). These beliefs serve as important assumptive models, or explanatory worldviews, that bring order to what may be an otherwise chaotic environment. These Weltanschauung not only serve as explanatory constructs with anxiolytic properties, but at the same time, potential diatheses, or psychological vulnerabilities, if threatened or destroyed.

Based on a review of relevant literature, there appears to be at least five core assumptive explanatory worldviews that are threads in the fabric of personality and that have relevance in understanding psychological trauma:

1. The belief in a fair and just world;
2. The need for attachment to, and trust in, others;
3. The need for physical safety;
4. The need for a positive self-identity and view of oneself—in other words, self-esteem, self-efficacy; and
5. The belief in some overarching meaning or order to life—for example, religion, spirituality, or faith in a defining order, unifying paradigm, and so forth.

Using these worldviews as foundation, then we see that events that threaten, violate, or destroy one or more of these worldviews serve as the psychological basis for the creation of a traumatic event. More specifically, traumatic events may be created on the basis of events that are extremely distressing and involve the following:

1. Violation to the assumption that justice and fairness must prevail (e.g., a significant injustice—death or injury of a child—a criminal escaping justice, bad things happening to good people, evil conquering over good);
2. Abandonment, treachery, betrayal, especially if perpetrated by a trusted person, organization, or institution;

3. Threats to, or violations of, the physical safety of oneself or others (especially if involving children, loved ones, or people with which there is a personal identification); this condition is made worse if the threats are unpredictable;
4. Contradiction to the view of oneself in a positive, self-efficacious perspective (e.g., guilt is a common psychotraumatologic theme based on (a) doing something one should not have done, (b) not doing something one should have done that ultimately resulted in a significant problem, injury, loss, catastrophe, etc., or (c) an association with survival, i.e., "survivor guilt"); and
5. A disruption to, or violation of, some deeply held overarching assumption about life and perhaps death. For example, a "crisis of faith," or some chaotic, unpredictable adversity without some explanation, rationale, meaning, or overarching explanatory schema may result in a crisis of faith or religion, or an existential crisis.

Similar themes such as the violation of the need for safety, the violation of trust, a threat to one's self-esteem, the disruption of the need for intimacy, and the need for control have been postulated as themes that may undergird the process of vicarious traumatization, especially among helping professionals (McCann & Pearlman, 1990; Rosenbloom, Pratt, & Pearlman, 1995).

Why are these personal beliefs so critical to maintaining psychological well-being? And why, if violated, do they create such havoc within one's psyche? The answer appears to be two-fold: First, as noted in chapter 1, these personal beliefs serve to reduce anxiety and uncertainty in a world where much must be taken for granted. Second, these worldviews serve as substitutes for actual physical and behavioral protection mechanisms, thus their extreme importance ontogenetically. This notion is consistent with the existence of a biological mandate to "make sense" of the world.

Without understanding how the person views any given traumatic event (i.e., the meaning attached to the traumatic event), we cannot fully understand the nature of the trauma, the phenomenological course of the posttraumatic reaction, nor can we begin to formulate the best therapeutic intervention for that individual. In the final analysis, the defining moment of the traumatic event resides in its assigned meaning.

Let us take a closer look at putative assumptive explanatory worldviews.

JUST WORLD BELIEFS

According to Melvin J. Lerner (1980), the "belief in a just world" refers to assumptions that people have so that they can plan, work for, and obtain desired outcomes while avoiding fearful or frightening situations. Within Western society, a "just world" is predicated on the notion that people "get what they deserve." This sense of entitlement or deserving is grounded in one's behavior and one's attributes. For example, behaviors ranging from neglect to friendliness are deserving of different outcomes. Attributes, such as different physical appearances, intelligence, and even membership in a certain segment of society may be considered to result in different fates. Lerner (1980) suggested that people will use various mechanisms to construe events to fit their beliefs. For example, one may use generalizations from past experiences, which include an amalgam of (a) personal observation, often viewed with a healthy dose of selective attention; (b) cultural wisdom and morality tales, which includes religious convictions as well as media portrayals of heroes and villains; (c) a conceptual belief that this is how our minds work, in other words we create a balance or homeostasis of the causal order of positive and negative events (our brains, then, use this compartmentalization to maintain harmony by suggesting that any imbalance is merely temporary); and (d) that it is a functional part of the person's motives and goals. More explicitly, "People want to and have to believe they live in a just world so that they can go about their daily lives with a sense of trust, hope, and confidence in the future. If it is true that people want or need to believe that they live in a world where people get what they deserve, then it is not surprising that they will find ways, other things being equal, to interpret events to fit this belief" (Lerner, 1980, p. 14).

Lerner (1980) also recognized that cultural norms influence just-world beliefs. These norms may occur at an individual level, at a group level, and at the generic or general cultural themes level (e.g., belonging to Western societies or having various and distinct political ideologies). Maturation within a culture also provides a means for modification or an appreciation of the proposed stages of just-world beliefs. According to Rubin and Peplau (1975),

> While most people probably believe in a just world during at least part of their childhood, they come to question this belief as they grow older. This questioning may be fostered by personal experiences of injustice and by the attainment of a principled view of mortality that transcends obedience to conventional standards and authorities. (p. 76)

Lerner (1980) argued, however, that most people do not give up the belief that we get what we deserve; it is just too intrinsic. Instead, he suggested that we modify this belief as we get older "to make it less vulnerable to threats from disqualifying experiences" (p. 156). In other words, belief in a just world may no longer serve as profound a foundation for our sense of "security" as it did in childhood. We do not need to construct and maintain elaborate defenses to protect the belief. Instead, we move beyond the need for security and find a way to create for ourselves meaningful patterns of our experiences and, in turn, less vulnerable forms of the belief. According to Lerner (1980),

> We do act as fairly objective processors of the best information available, and, when confronted with evidence of an injustice, we see it, and adjust our reactions, including the relevant beliefs in the way our world works, to accommodate the information. It also seems, however, that there is a constant monitoring of this process which sees to it that the "underpinnings" or is it "overarching construction" of our world view is not threatened by the consequences of this information processing. The content of the monitor's agenda certainly can vary greatly from person to person, but an essential constant can be portrayed as a belief in a Just World—a world in which I can and do get what I deserve. (p. 159)

In a recent compendium of just-world research, Lerner (1998) acknowledged and reviewed contemporary theoretical models of processing information (Epstein, Lipson, Holstein, & Hub, 1992; Shweder & Haidt 1993) and offered his own with regard to adult information processing. In essence, Lerner distinguished between "experiential" and "rational" processes when considering just-world beliefs. As Lerner summarized,

> As a result most adults live with two systems of morality. One is the underlying, vestigial, pre-conscious "justice motive" that operates according to relatively simple, cognitively primitive, rules of association and organization. These preconscious processes are "introspectively opaque," and often associated with emotional reactions of anger, shame, guilt, etc. The second moral system, superimposed on the earlier one, consists of the consciously available conventional, rational rules of moral judgments and reasoning. Both systems can and do involve issues of deserving and justice; however the intuitive preconscious processes follow radically different, counter normative rules. (p. 267)

Lerner also indicated that beliefs in a just world are vulnerable to modification by real-world experiences. Janoff-Bulman (1992, 1995) has written extensively on the effects of how victimization (e.g., rape, robbery, assault, sexual abuse, natural disasters) may disrupt and strongly threaten core assumptions we have about the world and our invulnerability. Janoff-Bulman (1992) has suggested that we have the following three assumptions related to our fundamental perceptions of invulnerability:

1. The world is benevolent, which suggests that not only do good things happen, but people are also good;
2. Events in the world are meaningful, or that they are predictable and that an outcome contingency is perceived; and

3. That we are positive and worthy, meaning that we are decent people deserving of a good outcome.

ATTACHMENT/TRUST

It may be argued that mammals have thrived, if not survived, largely because they live in groups. The human neonate is incapable of self-care, thus survival itself is predicated on allowing someone else to care for you and having someone else so-motivated to care for you. These aspects of interpersonal attachment are too vital to be left to chance, and thus there exists, we believe, a biologically hard-wired system to attend to these processes. Let us take a closer look at attachment and trust.

Developmentalist John Bowlby (1969) has suggested that there are two different facets to attachment. The one facet is positive; infants, for example, enjoy being with and reciprocally interacting with a caregiver. The other facet of attachment is more negative; there is an inherent fear of the unknown that leaves one feeling vulnerable and eager to become attached to and stay close to a familiar object. Bowlby suggested that these inherent, unspecific fears serve as a survival mechanism, particularly in infants. Thus, distressed children will seek proximity to caregivers; however, if caregivers are unable (or unwilling) to provide a sense of safety and security, a sense of abandonment and mistrust may be engendered. Ainsworth (1989), who collaborated with Bowlby for more than 40 years, has suggested that attachment theory is applicable throughout life and has described the nature of affectional bonds in later life, including friendships and kinships.

Janoff-Bulman (1995) has described how individuals victimized by people they know (e.g., a date, spouse, parent, friend) suffer tremendous difficulty establishing a sense of trust in subsequent relationships. Herman (1992) noted that "a secure sense of connection with caring people is the foundation of personality development. When this connection is shattered, the traumatized person loses her basic sense of self" (p. 52).

Catherall (1989) has proposed a modified object relations theory that suggests that impaired psychological functioning may occur when the attachment belief in "cultural selfobjects" is challenged concurrently with ego disruption. An example of this phenomenon may be seen in chronic PTSD war veterans who have experienced a failed self–selfobject relationship between themselves and their country. Pomeroy (1995) has presented a model of the relationship between trauma and violence that emphasizes three resources to ensure survival: a relational level, where connectedness and trust are key issues, a limbic level, which focuses on fight and flight responses, and the shock-reflex level, which addresses symptoms such as rage and avoidance.

Van der Kolk (1988, 1996) has described how disruptions in attachment bonds provide insight into the biological nature and psychological response to trauma. In subhuman primates, disruption in attachment yields reactions of distress that appear to be primitive variants of the posttraumatic distress syndrome (a more generic form of PTSD) in humans.

In a questionnaire sample of attributional style and dysfunctional beliefs in 43 survivors of child sexual abuse, Wenninger and Ehlers (1998) have reported high correlations between beliefs of trust, safety, and intimacy and posttraumatic symptoms.

A survey of Kuwaiti citizens after the Iraqi invasion of Kuwait indicated that treachery and betrayal were key psychological themes associated with symptoms of posttraumatic distress (Al-Naser, Everly, & Al-Khulaifi, 2001). Courtois (2000) has offered a sequenced treatment model of complex PTSD in the wake of sexual abuse that includes a focus on developing a sense of safety in relationships and increased trust in others.

Hedges (2000) recently addressed how the aftermath of childhood trauma specifically affects the survivor's ability to form a therapeutic attachment. A preponderance of the struggle involves the paradox of desperately seeking attachment while reliving their experience of connection as one of violation. This problem is relevant to a therapist, because the therapeutic alliance is being formed. It is also relevant to relationships outside of the therapeutic process.

Bowlby has placed additional emphasis on an individual's need to create working models of the environment (known as the environmental model) and of one's self (i.e., one's own skills, resources, etc., known as the organismic model). The achievement of life's goals, including a sense of security and attachment, requires a functional environmental model continually interacting with an organismic model. He noted,

> To be useful both working models must be kept up-to-date. As a rule this requires only a continuous feeding in of small modifications, usually a process so gradual that it is hardly noticeable. Occasionally, however, some major change in environment or organism occurs. . . . At those times radical changes in the model are called for. Clinical evidence suggests that the necessary revisions of the model are not always easy to achieve. Usually, they are completed but only slowly, often they are done imperfectly, and sometimes done not at all. (Bowlby, 1969, p. 82)

Using different terminology, Bowlby described the essence of psychological trauma: the contradiction of extant environmental or organismic (self-perception) *Weltanschauung* and the often laborious road to reintegration and recovery.

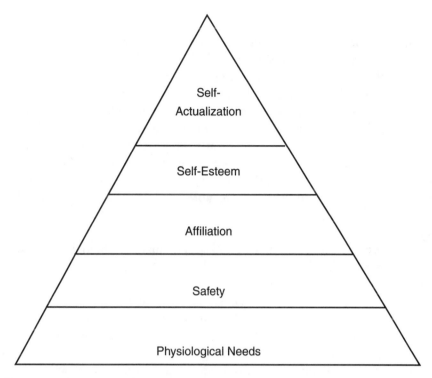

Figure 3.3. Maslow's hierarchy of human needs. From *Psychotraumatology: Key Papers and Core Concepts in Post-traumatic Stress* (p. 39), by G. S. Everly, Jr., and J. M. Lating, 1995. New York: Plenum Press. Copyright 1995 by Plenum Press. Adapted with permission.

SAFETY

In 1943, Abraham Maslow proposed a theory of personality and human motivation that was a blending of the functionalist tradition of James with the holism of Werthemier and the dynamicism of Freud, Adler, and Jung. Maslow (1943, 1970) referred to his theory as a holistic–dynamic theory; it was based on a hierarchy of human needs (see Figure 3.3).

As Figure 3.3 indicates, Maslow constructed a hierarchy of human needs that serves as a means of understanding human motivation. At the absolute foundation of all motivation is the need to satisfy basic physiological needs; second only to this drive is the psychological need for safety. Safety was defined by Maslow as having security, protection, stability, structure, and freedom from fear.

Maslow's hierarchy of needs was completed by the addition of the need to belong and be loved, the need for self-esteem, and finally self-actualization, or total self-fulfillment of one's capabilities or potential.

D. Williams and Page (1989) developed measures relevant for the safety, belonging, and esteem levels of the hierarchy. In particular, they assessed the need for gratification, need importance, need salience, and self-concept.

Maslow referred to the first four basic needs as deficiency needs or D-needs. He believed that satisfying these lower order needs would allow one to avoid physical sickness or psychological maladjustment (Maslow, 1968). Maslow found support for his theory in the influential work of Walter Cannon's (1932) theory of homeostasis, or processes whereby the body automatically attempts to maintain physiological equilibrium. Maslow stated that one cannot progress up the hierarchy until one has satisfied a lower need. Therefore, lower order needs are more urgently demanding than higher order needs. It is possible, therefore, that some individuals may "get stuck" and spend a lifetime pursuing a rudimentary need.

Trauma is the antithesis of safety. No matter which higher order Maslovian need level one has attained before being traumatized, trauma automatically drops one back to a quest for the lower order need for safety.

Thus, to review, Maslow has stated that human beings focus their energies on the task of satisfying the most fundamental needs first. The physiological needs that serve to sustain life are the most fundamental and serve to motivate behavior until the need is satisfied. Satisfied needs no longer serve to motivate. The most fundamental of all psychological needs is the need for safety. Until lower order needs are satisfied, one cannot and will not progress up the hierarchy to higher order needs. If one's safety and protection are challenged, we find that the quest for safety becomes the dominating goal and "a strong determinant not only of (one's) current world outlook and philosophy but also of (one's) philosophy of the future . . . a man in this state, if it is extreme enough and chronic enough, may be characterized as living almost for safety alone" (Maslow, 1970, p. 39). Maslow added that the persistent inhibition, or even the threat of inhibition, of the fundamental needs serves as the basis for psychopathology. In effect, if the attainment and maintenance of the most fundamental of needs becomes thwarted, a potential pathognomonic psychological and behavioral fixation occurs around the theme of that fundamental need attainment.

"Trauma represents a violation or contradiction to one's quest for safety. Trauma is the antithesis of order, protection, and security. Trauma represents a contradiction to the quest for safety and thereby stifles any further personality growth until the safety need is, indeed, satisfied" (Everly, 1993a, pp. 275–276). The victim of psychological traumatization, in Maslovian terms, has become fixated in the quest to attain the psychological goal of safety. The quest to satisfy the psychological need for safety becomes the dominant theme in the patient's life, consuming virtually all available resources, and may persist for the remainder of one's life.

The current literature is replete with implications of how safety assumes a major role in traumatic stress and its recovery. Stein (1997), for example, provides a phenomenological psychoanalytical perspective on the unconscious response to the Oklahoma City bombing in 1995, and describes how the trauma served as a violation of many peoples' "stimulus barrier" and symbolic boundary of safety. The need for safety has also been a particular emphasis in the development and recovery of posttraumatic stress in children (Monahon, 1997; Olafson & Boat, 2000; Pynoos, Steinberg, Ornitz, & Goenjian, 1997) and families (Catherall, 1998). Also, Copeland and Harris (2000) have addressed the primary need for safety in their workbook designed to help women recover from sexual, emotional, or physical abuse. The integrated treatment of the concomitance between posttraumatic stress reactions and chemical dependency has relied heavily on the therapeutic principle and strategy of safety first (Hiebert-Murphy & Woytkiw, 2000; Najavits, Weiss, Shaw, & Muenz, 1998; Sullivan & Evans, 1996). Herman (1992) has argued that recovery from trauma is predicated on establishing or reestablishing a basic sense of safety. In fact, in her description of the three stages of trauma recovery, she has stated that "the central task of the first stage is the establishment of safety" (p. 155). The other two stages involve remembrance and mourning and reconnection with ordinary life.

SELF-EFFICACY AND SELF-ESTEEM

Alfred Adler (1929) suggested more than 70 years ago that the desire to make decisions and affect outcomes—in other words, to enact control— is a basic tenet of human behavior. It is the construct of cognitive control that is typically considered to have the most impact on the stress response (Cohen, Evans, Stokols, & Krantz, 1980; Sarafino, 1998; Thompson, 1981). A hallmark of the traumatic event is the usurping of the sense of self-efficacy, self-control.

Martin Seligman and his colleagues' theory of learned helplessness (Overmier & Seligman, 1967; Seligman & Maier, 1967) is often acknowledged as a progenitor of the cognitive-control focus. Using an experimental design known as triadic, their seminal animal research typically consisted of three groups of dogs receiving different types of pretreatments. The first group (the escape group) was given a controllable event (an outcome influenced by some response), the second group (the helplessness group) was yoked to the first (i.e., they received the same event as the first group; however, it was now uncontrollable), and the third group (naive group) received no pretreatment. The dogs in the first two groups were then exposed to electric shock. The difference between the groups was that the dogs in the escape group were trained to turn the shock off (e.g., pressing a panel located on either side of their heads with their noses), whereas the responses of the dogs in the yoked group had no effect. The dogs in the naive group received no shock.

After 24 hours, all three groups received 10 trials of signaled escape–avoidance training in a shuttle box in which jumping over a shoulder-high barrier within 10 seconds of a discriminant signal (e.g., lights dimming) would prevent the shock. Failure to jump led to a shock that continued until the dog jumped or for the duration of 60 seconds. The escape group and the naive group jumped the barrier readily; however, the yoked group initiated few escape attempts. Moreover, when they did respond successfully, they did so inconsistently. In fact, the preponderance of these dogs laid down and did not react emotionally while being shocked. Seligman and his colleagues (Overmier & Seligman, 1967; Seligman & Maier, 1967) described that these laboratory experiments produced deficits in the yoked dogs in three distinct domains: (a) motivation to respond, (b) decreased ability to learn that responding had an impact, and (c) emotional disturbance, primarily anxiety or depression. It is interesting to note that Hiroto (1974) replicated these findings, fairly precisely, on college students in an experiment in which unsignaled loud noise served as the stimulus and moving a lever from one side of a box to another served to eliminate the noise.

The learned helplessness model formulated by Seligman and his colleagues has had a tremendous impact on the theoretical development in psychology of the effects of uncontrollable outcomes and their impact on symptoms associated with depression and anxiety.

Abramson, Metalsky, and Alloy (1989) proposed the hopelessness theory of depression as a distinct clinical subtype of depression. According to this theory, the perception of hopelessness is considered a sufficient cause of depression and low self-esteem, rather than being considered a particular symptom.

Albert Bandura (1977, 1982, 1997), renowned for his social–cognitive theory of human behavior, focused on a cognitive locus of appraisal to help account for maladaptive stimulus–response interactions. A major construct in his more than 20 years of work is the concept of self-efficacy that he defines as "beliefs in one's capabilities to organize and execute the courses of action required to produce given attainments" (Bandura, 1997, p. 3). Thus, efficacy beliefs or appraisals of competence and control influence behaviors, thoughts, feelings, and emotions. Individuals possessing a high sense of self-efficacy are often task-oriented and use multifaceted and integrative problem-solving skills to enhance successful outcomes when dealing with psychosocial stressors. Conversely, people with limited self-efficacy may perceive psychosocial stressors as unmanageable and are more likely to dwell on perceived deficiencies, which in turn generates increased stress and diminishes potential problem-solving energy, lowers aspirations, and weakens commitments.

Bandura (1977, 1997) has posited that people's beliefs concerning their efficacy are determined by four principal influences:

1. Enactive attainment—in other words, enactive mastery experiences or performance accomplishments are considered the most powerful source of self-efficacy because mastery is based on actual success.
2. Vicarious mastery—in other words, vicarious positive experiences (observational learning, modeling, imitation) increase confidence by observing behaviors of others, noting contingencies of behavior, and then using this information to form expectancies of their own behavior. An observer's perception of characteristic similarity between him- or herself and the model is an important factor in vicarious mastery experiences.
3. Verbal persuasion or social persuasion uses expressions of faith in one's competence. The impact of verbal persuasion is less profound than the previous two sources; however, when applied in combination with vicarious and enactive techniques, the influence of self-efficacy is more effective.
4. Finally, physiological and affective states influence self-efficacy in that comfortable physiological sensations and positive affect are likely to enhance one's confidence in a given situation.

Extremely powerful, overwhelming events (e.g., traumatic events) are more likely to be associated with appraisals of profound inefficacy, even hopelessness. Traumatic events are likely to directly attack self-efficacy:

1. Because they are experiences that represent actual, or perceived, failure;
2. Represent vicarious threats, injury, or failure;
3. Are often associated with verbalizations that ascribe the role of a "helpless victim"; and
4. Are commonly associated with states of physiologic dysregulation and loss of physiologic control (e.g., panic, dissociation, loss of neuromuscular control, acute loss of bladder or bowel control), which may further engender a sense of hopelessness.

SPIRITUAL BELIEFS/FAITH/MEANINGFULNESS

Existentialist Viktor Frankl (1959), a concentration camp survivor and founder of logotherapy, or meaning therapy, has argued that failure to find meaning and a sense of responsibility in one's life lies at the root of psychopathology. Frankl quoted Nietzsche, who said, "He who has a why to live can bear with almost any how." Yet as Frankl explained in his treatise on logotherapy, he who loses the why to live may lose the how to live as well. "Man's search for meaning is the primary force in his life and not a 'secondary rationalization' of instinctual drives. This meaning is unique and specific in that it must and can be fulfilled by him alone," noted Frankl (1959, p. 99). He added, "The way in which a man accepts his fate and all the suffering it entails, the way in which he takes up his cross, gives ample opportunity—even under the most difficult circumstances—to add a deeper meaning to his life" (Frankl, 1959, pp. 106–107).

Perhaps the most common source by which individuals find an overarching sense of meaning in life and death, especially when there are no other sources of explanation, is a superordinate faith or religion.

The trauma literature has often included spiritual/religious issues as an important aspect in the development and treatment of posttraumatic stress (Carmil & Breznitz, 1991; Dyregrove & Mitchell, 1992; Everly, 2000c, 2000d; Jaffe, 1985; Pearlman & Saakvitne, 1995; Wilson, 1989). As alluded to earlier in this chapter, Lerner's (1980) description of ultimate justice and Janoff-Bulman's (1992) tenets of shattered assumptions imply that traumatic events, although affecting the physical and psychological well-being of victims, may also produce a pervasive state of dispiritedness among survivors. According to Wilson and Moran (1998), "Religious faith and spirituality are integral aspects of personality and essential components of one's identity" (p. 168). The term *faith* has many connotations, but in general it underscores concepts of conviction, commitment, meaning, relevance, coherence, and trust that provides the believer with feelings of congruence, optimism, and hope (Meissner, 1987). Faith is probably best considered as an active, fluid process ascending and transforming itself over time.

> As it matures, spiritual faith carries one beyond the imaginative spirituality of childhood and the conforming spirituality of adolescence to the examined and self-less commitments of adult spirituality. It is this uninterrupted, constant, and maturing faith that offers one vitality, meaning, and purpose in life. (Wilson & Moran, 1998, p. 17)

If a traumatic event challenges or destroys one's overarching spiritual or religious belief system, we refer to the reaction as a "crisis of faith."

Judith Herman (1992) has suggested that "events which produce traumatic responses shatter one's faith in 'the natural or divine order' and plunge the believer into a debilitating state of 'existential crisis' " (p. 51). Furthermore, she asserted that the psychological impact of trauma "pervades every relationship, from the most intimate familial bonds to the most abstract affiliations of community and religion (Herman, 1992, p. 52). Therefore, trauma may result in pervasive feelings of confusion, bitterness, disillusionment, and anger as one evaluates and reevaluates his or her spiritual beliefs and faith in terms of meaning and purpose. Decker (1993) has proposed that even in the absence of PTSD symptoms traumatized individuals will necessarily seek inspiration and meaning in life through spiritual development. According to Decker (1993), "regardless of how one might respond to trauma, there is a spiritual evolvement occurring—trauma may be viewed as demanding a conscious shift in awareness toward greater meaning and an expanded purpose" (p. 42). He has further noted that "it is our ordinary ideas regarding life that betray our need for meaning. The occurrence of trauma means that regular ideas and expectations and ordinary ways of pacifying ourselves will no longer suffice" (Decker, 1993, p. 43).

Therefore, developing a holistic model of treatment, which includes acknowledging and including a spiritual component, may positively influence trauma recovery. Wilson and Moran (1998), while recognizing that clinicians do not need to be or become pastoral counselors or clergy members, suggest the following guidelines in incorporating spiritual beliefs into treatment:

1. Given the possibility of patient reluctance, the therapist may consider initiating discussion of religious faith.
2. Consider an exploration of pretrauma religious history as well as changes in spiritual belief in the wake of the trauma.
3. Be aware that some patients may consider that their feelings of anger and bitterness directed at God or their Higher Power may be perceived as irrational.
4. Be sensitive to the possibility individuals with survivor guilt may feel that expressing their thoughts and feelings will result in the therapist confirming that the magnitude of their perceived sins are not worthy of divine forgiveness.
5. Be aware that some people may assign the therapist the role of "heavenly judge."
6. Some individuals who have been severely traumatized have been left feeling disconnected from the Divine and unprotected. Expect to encounter those feelings of alienation.

Although trauma survivors search for individual meaning regarding matters of spirituality and faith, it is imperative that therapists, pastoral counselors, and clergy facilitate rather than direct the process (Decker, 1993). Wilson and Moran concluded that "the goal of spiritual direction or counseling with the survivor of trauma is to unfold, clarify, transform, renew, and rebuild a viable and fulfilling relationship with a complex God who cannot be experienced fully or comprehended totally" (p. 175).

KEY POINT SUMMARY

1. An essential thread within the fabric of human personality is the constellation of core psychological beliefs.
2. We believe that there exist five core beliefs:
   a. The belief in a fair and just world;
   b. The need for attachment to, and trust in, other persons;
   c. The need for physical safety;
   d. The need for a positive self-identity, view of oneself—in other words, self-esteem, self-efficacy; and
   e. The belief in some overarching order to life—e.g., religion, spirituality, or faith in a defining order, unifying paradigm, etc.
3. We believe that it is this personologic substrate that is attacked during exposure to a traumatic event.
4. Thus, traumatic events engender posttraumatic symptom patterns to the degree that they involve:
   a. Violation to the assumption that justice and fairness must prevail. For example, a significant injustice (death or injury of a child), a criminal escaping justice, bad things happening to good people, evil conquering over good all represent potential traumatic events;
   b. Abandonment, treachery, betrayal, especially if perpetrated by a trusted person, organization, or institution;
   c. Threats to, or violations of, the physical safety of oneself or others (especially if involving children, loved ones, or people with which there is a personal identification); this condition is made worse if the threats are unpredictable;
   d. Contradiction to the view of oneself in a positive, self-efficacious manner; especially if the event involved acting in a manner so as to cause harm to others or the failure to act in such a manner so as to protect others; survivor guilt is also known to exist;
   e. A disruption to, or violation of, some deeply held overarching assumption about life, and perhaps death. For example, some chaotic, unpredictable adversity without some explanation, rationale, meaning, or overarching explanatory schema may result in a crisis of faith or religion, or an existential crisis.
5. In summarizing the five core psychological themes that undergird posttraumatic stress disorder, we see from the various perspectives that human beings need (and therefore create) a sense of justice, an attachment to others, a need for physical

safety, a desire to be self-efficacious, a need for meaning, and spiritual belief. These goals are achieved through the use of working models, assumptions about the world and oneself, and other explanatory processes. Psychological traumatization serves to contradict or shatter the very foundations of what makes the world safe and secure and the very nature of self.

4

BIOLOGICAL FOUNDATIONS OF POSTTRAUMATIC STRESS DISORDER

In a previous chapter we argued that posttraumatic stress disorder (PTSD) possesses a two-factor phenomenological core: (a) a pathognomonic violation or contradiction to some deeply held and psychologically necessary belief system—in other words, an assumptive and explanatory worldview; and (b) a pathognomonic hypersensitivity for, or status of, neural excitability within the subcortical limbic structures. In chapter 3, we discussed the defining moment of trauma—the violated worldview. In this chapter, we review the biological consequences of that pathogenic psychology. In doing so we present the biological foundations of PTSD.

PTSD AS A DISORDER OF AROUSAL

PTSD represents a brain out of control at the most rudimentary levels of function.

Kardiner's Physioneurosis

Kardiner (1941) conceptualized posttraumatic syndromes as variations on a theme of "physioneurosis." This term is indicative of the notion that posttraumatic syndromes reflect an inextricable combination of biological and psychological substrates. Kardiner recognized five consistent clinical features of the posttraumatic syndromes:

1. Exaggerated startle response and irritability;
2. Atypical dream experiences;
3. A propensity for explosive and aggressive reactions;
4. Psychic fixation on the traumatic experience; and
5. Constriction of personality functioning.

The essential feature of Kardiner's exposition was the notion of a psychiatric disorder within which the biological features were intertwined in such a way so as to actually define—not merely reflect symptomatically—the disorder.

Everly and Benson's Disorders of Arousal

Van der Kolk (1988) recognized PTSD as a pathognomonic inability to modulate arousal. Consistent with this conclusion, Everly (1990) proposed that PTSD was best understood as a psychologically engendered "disorder of arousal," as described by Everly and Benson (1989).

The disorders of arousal formulation serves as a taxonomic formulation that is based not on florid symptom presentations but rather on more salient, often latent, phenomenological mechanisms.

Traditionally, science has classified diseases on the basis of their cause or their end-organ symptoms or signs. The American Psychiatric Association's *Diagnostic and Statistical Manual of Mental Disorders* (DSM–IV, 1994) is replete with examples of both. Regarding classification by "cause," for example, adjustment disorders are caused by the inability to adjust to new situations. Regarding classification by symptoms, on the other hand, mood disorders are characterized by affective symptom complexes, and anxiety disorders are characterized by anxious symptomatology. PTSD is uniquely classified by its cause (trauma), the time of its emergence (posttraumatic), and its response (stress).

Seldom in our nosological efforts, however, do we bother to consider other, less obvious, taxonomic criteria, even though these latent taxa might be far more utilitarian. Such a taxonomic consideration is derived from the work of Meehl (1973). Based on an integration of the work of Selye (1976), Gellhorn (1967), Gray (1982), and Post (Post & Ballenger, 1981), it has been proposed that various anxiety and stress-related diseases be viewed in light of a new taxonomic perspective (Everly, 1990; Everly & Benson, 1989). Evidence indicates that numerous psychiatric and somatic stress-related diseases possess a common denominator that serves as a homogenizing, but latent, taxonomic criterion—"latent taxon" for short. It has been proposed that this latent taxon is pathognomonic arousal. Such disorders may be referred to collectively as disorders of arousal (Everly, 1989; Everly & Benson, 1989). Therefore, despite a wide variety of symptomatic responses and an even wider variety of stressor stimuli, these disorders are best seen as but variations on a theme of a pathognomonic neurologic hypersensitivity. More specifically, the "disorders of arousal" concept is based on a corpus of evidence indicating that a major homogenizing phenomenological constituent of these disorders is a limbic system-based neurologic hypersensitivity—that is, a lowered threshold for excitation or a pathognomonic status of excessive (potentially convulsive) arousal within the limbic circuitry and its neurological, neuroendocrine, or endocrine efferent limbs. This neurologic hypersensitivity may, in extreme instances, achieve subcortical convulsive proportions capable of giving rise to a host of seizure-like syndromes—for example, complex partial seizures, narcoleptic syndromes, bipolar affective presentations, seemingly uncontrollable violent tirades, amnestic syndromes, and panic-like convulsive manifestations.

Everly (1990) has argued that PTSD is a virtual prototypic example of the disorders of arousal taxonomy. As such, the disorders of arousal formulation serves to provide insight into a host of affective and ictal signs and symptoms that not only covary with PTSD but also serve to define its biology.

ANATOMICAL FOUNDATIONS

Let us now examine the anatomical bases of postraumatic stress.

The Limbic System

The search for the anatomical foundations of the neurologic hypesensitivity characteristic of PTSD must begin in the subcortical limbic system. The limbic system represents an aggregation of paleocortical structures, first boldly delineated by Papez (1937) as an integrated neural circuit implicated in emotional expression. "Papez's circuit," as it would come to be known, consisted of the mammillary bodies, fornix, hippocampus, cingulated cortex, and anterior thalamic nuclei. The boundaries of this circuit would be expanded some years later by Paul MacLean (1949) to include the amygdala, septum, and associated hypothalamic areas. MacLean recognized that this circuit functioned as a system, hence the term *limbic system*. This system serves as the hub of the central nervous system replete with efferent and afferent pathways (MacLean, 1949; Weil, 1974). MacLean (1949) wrote, "This region of the brain appears to be so strategically situated as to be able to correlate every form of internal and external perception. And . . . has many strong connections with the hypothalamus for discharging its impression" (p. 351). But of greatest interest to the study of PTSD are

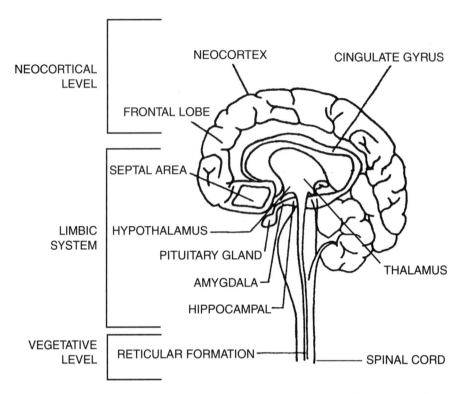

Figure 4.1. The human brain. From *Psychotraumatology: Key Papers and Core Concepts in Post-traumatic Stress* (p. 21), by G. S. Everly, Jr., and J. M. Lating, 1995. New York: Plenum Press. Copyright 1995 by Plenum Press. Adapted with permission.

the amygdaloid and hippocampal formations within the limbic circuitry (see Figure 4.1; Everly, 1993a, 1993b).

Amygdaloid Complex

Henry and Stephens (1977) and MacLean (1949) viewed the amygdaloid complex as the origins of the posterior hypothalamic–sympathetic– adrenal medullary emergency response complex, sometimes referred to as Cannon's (1929, 1932) fight or flight response. This efferent axis clearly represents the most fundamental of all manifestations of the human stress response. In addition, the startle reflex is born of this mechanism, because the central amygdala sends projections that mediate the startle reflex (LeDoux, 1992). Behaviors such as aggression, violence, and rage also seem to be related to this efferent response mechanism (Henry & Stephens, 1977). There has even been discussion that the amygdaloid formations represent a unique encoding mechanism for survival-related memories. Memories encoded via this mechanism appear to be immune to extinction and destined to a reiterative course over the life of the individual (LeDoux, 1992). This view is consistent with earlier formulations of Henry and Stephens (1977) wherein the amygdaloid complex was seen to modulate the aggression response with regard to the fear response through complex mechanisms capable of appraising the magnitude of threat posed within both novel and confrontational situations. See Everly (1989, 1990, 1993a, 1993b, 1995) for a review of these issues. Thus, many of the prime characteristics of PTSD seem consistent with known amygdaloid mechanisms.

Most persuasively, however, recent work by Rauch and his colleagues (Rauch et al., 2000) have shown an exaggerated amygdaloid response in combat veterans diagnosed with PTSD.

Finally, Huber (2001) used positron emission tomography to compare same-subject brain activation during acute periods of traumatic flashbacks compared to acute periods of fearful but nontraumatic memory activation. Results indicated that right lingual gyrus, right thalamo-mamillary pathways, and the right cerebellum were differentially activated, indicative of hyper-activation of thalamo-cortical closed-loop networks.

Hippocampal Formations

The anatomy of PTSD appears to be more complicated than merely the anatomy of the amygdaloid complex, as described previously. The hippocampus also appears to be involved. The hippocampal formations (dentate gyrus, Ammon's horn, subicular complex, and the entorhinal area) appear to be intimately involved in sensory and immediate memory consolidation, as well as amnestic phenomena (Swanson, 1983). They also appear to be involved in the reorganization of memory traces drawn from their primary cortical storage areas. Everly and Horton (1989) first found neuropsychological evidence suggestive of hippocampal dysfunction in PTSD patients. Such evidence appeared as difficulty in immediate to short-term memory consolidation as well as difficulty in concentration. The hippocampal formations are replete with glutamate and aspartate chemistries (Wieraszko, 1983) and may be vulnerable to glutamic and aspartic initiated excitotoxic phenomena. Concentrational difficulties, amnestic dysfunction, and even neuronal death are possible problems associated with overstimulation of the hippocampal formations.

Most important to our understanding of PTSD and related posttraumatic syndromes, however, is the view that much of the neurological integration that is thought to occur in the limbic system actually occurs in, or by way of, the hippocampal structures. Weil (1974) provided a putative map for the flow of impulses through the limbic system. He noted that prefrontal cortical, amygdaloid, and cingulate impulses may converge in the hippocampus. According to Swanson (1983), the hippocampus integrates information from all primary sensory areas, emotional mechanisms, cognitive mechanisms, and even somatosensory mechanisms. The views of Weil and Swanson are in concert with the conclusions of Gray. Gray (1982, 1985) concluded that prefrontal, cingulate, and amygdaloid impulses must pass through a form of hippocampal gating mechanism. This hippocampal gate appears to serve as a form of regulator, or "governor," that serves to arrange, prioritize, and modulate information from virtually all aspects of the nervous system.

But even more important to the study of PTSD, Gray suggested that these hippocampal mechanisms, specifically septo-hippocampal mechanisms, act as a form of "comparator." Gray noted, "The central task of this overall system is to compare, quite generally, actual with expected stimuli" (Gray, 1985, p. 8). Consistent with formulations presented in the previous chapter, one's worldviews and core assumptions about life itself represent the most fundamental of all expectations. In the previous chapter, it was suggested that there was a biological basis, if not mandate, for the construction of assumptive worldviews. Although initially proposed to be in the left neocortical hemisphere, it seems that Gray's functional analysis of the hippocampus is worthy of serious consideration.

In situations where there is discordance between expected versus experienced realities, a mismatch of sorts is created. If these mismatched realities have relevance to protection of one's young, one's own survival, or some other critical worldview, it is likely that a neural overload condition might be created in the hippocampus, with a resultant myriad of stress and anxiety-like presentations including enhanced physiological effector mechanisms, consistent with Selye's (1956, 1976) notions of the human stress response. Reiman et al. (1986), using PET scan technology, found the hippocampus to play an active role in heightened anxiety.

Peripheral Efferent Projections

Finally, the peripheral efferent pathways that find their origins in the amygdaloid and hippocampal formations must certainly be involved in the anatomy of PTSD. Based on the work of Mason (1968a, 1968b, 1968c), Levi (1972), and Selye (1956), Everly (1989) described three primary efferent axes by which the excitation within the limbic circuitry may express itself.

The most rapid of the primary efferent chains is commonly referred to as the *neural axis* and consists of three pathways. The first neural pathway that is implicated in the traumatic stress response consists of extraordinary excitation within the amygdaloid–posterior hypothalamic–sympathetic nervous system. It is responsible for activation of organs within the human body that are innervated by the sympathetic nervous system. A second neural pathway that is extraordinarily activated in traumatic stress is the

EXHIBIT 4.1
Peripheral Efferent Mechanisms in Traumatic Stress

I. NEURAL AXIS:
   A. Sympathetic nervous system
   B. Neuromuscular nervous system
   C. Parasympathetic nervous system

II. NEUROENDOCRINE AXIS:
   A. Enhanced sympatho–adrenal medullary release: epinephrine
   B. Enhanced sympatho–adrenal medullary release: norepinephrine

III. ENDOCRINE AXIS:
   A. Enhanced/altered HPAC release: Glucocorticiods—e.g., cortisol
   B. Enhanced HPAC release: Mineralocorticoids—e.g., aldosterone
   C. Enhanced HPAC release: Beta Lipotropin—e.g., endogenous opioids
   D. Altered HPAC release: human growth hormone
   E. Enhanced HPAC release: testosterone
   F. Altered HPAC release: estrogen and progesterone

neuromuscular system. Excessive activation within this pathway may result in muscle spasms, neuromuscular tension headaches, and related syndromes. Finally, the third neural pathway consists of extraordinary activation of the anterior hypothalamic–parasympathetic nervous system. This pathway consists of extraordinary activation of the organs within the human body that are innervated by the parasympathetic nervous system. This efferent pathway is not commonly activated as part of the traumatic stress response, but when in evidence often reflects extreme neurological excitation.

The second primary efferent axis that is extraordinarily activated as part of the traumatic stress response is actually a continuation of the sympathetic nervous system and is referred to as the *neuroendocrine axis*. The components of the axis consist of the amygdala, posterior hypothalamus, sympathetic nervous system, and the adrenal medullae. From the adrenal medullary bodies, the hormones epinephrine and norepinephrine are secreted into the systemic circulation and serve to continue the extraordinary activation of the sympathetic nervous system.

The final primary efferent axis that is extraordinarily activated in traumatic stress is commonly referred to as the *endocrine axis*. This is the most complex of the efferent pathways. Extraordinary activation of the hypothalamic–anterior pituitary–adrenal cortical (HPAC) system may lead to alterations in levels of the following releasing factors and hormones: adrenocorticotropic hormone, cortisol, endogenous opioids, testosterone, estrogen, progesterone, human growth hormone, and aldosterone. Everly (1989) provided a detailed analysis of such putative efferent mechanisms that are summarized in Exhibit 4.1.

PHYSIOLOGICAL FOUNDATIONS

The concepts of tuning, charging, and kindling help us to better understand the physiological foundation of PTSD.

Gellhorn's Ergotropic Tuning

We must begin our search for the physiology of PTSD with one of the greatest of the applied physiologists, Ernst Gellhorn. The work of Gellhorn not only documented the existence of a complex autonomic nervous system–neocortical–limbic–somatic integration (Gellhorn, 1957, 1967), but later served as one of the most cogent explanations of the pathophysiological arousal that has been described in this chapter.

Almost 40 years ago, Gellhorn described a hypothalamically based ergotropic tuning process as the neurophysiological basis for affective lability, autonomic nervous system hyperfunction, anxiety, stress arousal, and related emotional disorders (Gellhorn, 1965, 1967; Gellhorn & Loofbourrow, 1963). Gellhorn stated,

> It is a matter of everyday experience that a person's reaction to a given situation depends very much upon his own mental, physical, and emotional state. One might be said to be "set" to respond in a given manner. In the same fashion the autonomic response to a given stimulus may at one time be predominantly sympathetic and may at another time be predominantly parasympathetic . . . the sensitization of autonomic centers has been designated "tuning" and we speak of sympathetic tuning and parasympathetic tuning . . . and refers merely to the "sensitization" or "facilitation" of particular centers of the brain. (Gellhorn & Loofbourrow, 1963, pp. 90–91)

Gellhorn chose the term *ergotropic tuning* to describe a preferential pattern of sympathetic nervous system responsiveness and hyperresponsiveness. Such a neurologic hypersensitivity could then serve as the basis for a host of disorders, including PTSD. Etiologically, Gellhorn (1965) stated, "In the waking state the ergotropic division of the autonomic is dominant and responds primarily to environmental stimuli. If these stimuli are very strong . . . the tone and reactivity of the sympathetic system increases" (pp. 494–495). Thus, extremely intense, traumatic stimulation could then serve to create a condition of pathognomonic ergotropic neurologic hypersensitivity.

Several mechanisms may engender and sustain the ergotropically tuned status. Gellhorn (1964) provided evidence that discharge from limbic centers sends neural impulses in two simultaneous directions: (a) to neocortical targets and (b) to the skeletal musculature via pyramidal and extra pyramidal projections (see also Gellhorn & Loofbourrow, 1963). The neocortical centers then send impulses back to the limbic areas and to the locus ceruleus by way of noradrenergic and other pathways, thus sustaining limbic activity. Simultaneously, neuromuscular proprioceptive impulses (indicative of neuromuscular status) from afferent muscle spindle projections ascend primarily via the dorsal nerve root within the spinal column and reticular activating system, ultimately projecting not only to cerebellar targets but to limbic and neocortical targets as well. Such proprioceptive bombardment further excites target areas and sets into motion a complex mechanism of positive neurological feedback, sustaining, and potentially intensifying, ergotropic tone (Gellhorn, 1964, 1965, 1967).

Thus, we see that Gellhorn has proposed a model of neural hypersensitivity and empirically demonstrated that intimate neocortical hypothalamic somatic relationships exist using the limbic system as (a) a central "hub" for efferent projections to the neocortex and somatic musculature, as well as (b) an afferent target for neocortical, proprioceptive, interoceptive, and brain-stem impulses. This configuration creates functional, potentially self-sustaining mechanisms of affective and ergotropic arousal. It certainly seems reasonable and is highly likely that such a mechanism could play an important role in manifesting, and even sustaining, posttraumatic symptomatology.

Weil's Neurologic Reverberation and Charging

Weil (1974) developed a model somewhat similar to that of Gellhorn. In fact, Weil made brief reference to the work of Gellhorn in the construction of a neurophysiological model of emotional behavior.

Weil noted, in agreement with Gellhom, that the activation threshold of the autonomic nervous system (particularly hypothalamic nuclei), as well as limbic centers, can be altered. Instead of the concepts of sympathetic and parasympathetic systems, Weil used a parallel but broader construction, that of arousal and tranquilizing systems, respectively. He called the facilitation of activation within these systems "charging." With regard to the concept of neurological hypersensitivity, Weil agreed with Gellhorn that high intensity, traumatic stimulation could charge the arousal system within the human being. Weil argued that a cascade of high-intensity environmental stimuli could serve to create a condition of self-sustaining subcortical reverberation. This reverberating circuit exists largely because of the reciprocal association that exists between higher cortical centers responsible for cognition, hypothalamic nuclei, affectively charged limbic pathways, and even the thalamic reticular formation.

Thus, we have seen that the models constructed by both Gellhorn (ergotropic tuning of nerve cells) and Weil (arousal-oriented charging of nerve cells) represent physiological templates that help us understand both the initiation and, most important, the recalcitrant potentially self-sustaining pathophysiologic mechanisms inherent in PTSD.

Models of Neuronal Plasticity, Kindling, and Sensitization

In an attempt to understand the phenomenon of neurological hypersensitivity at the most basic structural levels, in this section we review popular models of neuronal plasticity, kindling, and sensitization.

The concept of kindling represents one of the most popular models of plasticity and neurological hypersensitivity in clinical literature. *Kindling* is a term originally conceived of to identify the process by which repeated or highly intense neural stimulation of limbic structures leads to a lowered convulsive threshold (limbic seizure threshold) and to a condition of spontaneous activation of such structures, with resultant affective lability, violent aggressive tirades, exaggerated startle responsiveness, general autonomic nervous system hyperfunction, and behavioral disturbances (Goddard, McIntyre, & Leech, 1969; Joy, 1985; Post, 1985; Post, Uhde, Putnam, Ballenger, & Berrettini, 1982). Kindling-like processes have been implicated in a host of behavioral and psychopathological conditions (Monroe, 1970, 1982; Post & Ballenger, 1981).

Shader (1984) has stated, "With regard to anxiety disorders, one might speculate that kindling processes could increase attack-like firing from a source such as the locus ceruleus" (p. 14). Redmond and Huang (1979) have supported such a conclusion by suggesting that panic disorders are predicated on a lowered firing threshold at the locus ceruleus. Such discharge could then arouse limbic and cortical structures on the basis of ventral and dorsal adrenergic efferent projections arising from the locus ceruleus. Monroe (1982) speculated that certain episodic behavioral disorders may be based on a kindling-like limbic ictus. He noted, "As it is known that environmental events can induce synchronized electrical activity within the limbic system, this also provides an explanation of why environmental stress[ors] might sensitize patients to acute exacerbations of an ictal illness" (p. 713). Monroe (1970, 1982) implicated explosive behavioral tirades, impulsively destructive behavior, extreme affective lability, and episodic psychotic behavior in such a neurologic dysfunction. According to van der Kolk, Greenberg, Boyd, and Krystal (1985), "Long-term augmentation of LC (locus ceruleus) pathways following trauma underlies the repetitive intrusive recollections and nightmares that plague patients with PTSD (posttraumatic stress disorder)" (p. 318).

Post et al. (1982) extended the kindling model and stated, "Kindling and related sensitization models may also be useful conceptual approaches to understanding the development of psychopathology in the absence of seizure discharges" (p. 719). They suggested that adrenergic and dopaminergic agonists may sensitize animals and humans to behavioral hyperactivity and especially affective disorders. They referred to this phenomenon as "behavioral sensitisation" rather than kindling because no ictal status is obtained as an end point. Rather, the achieved end point represents the defining property of limbic neurologic hypersensitivity—in other words, a lowered depolarization threshold and an increased propensity for spontaneous activation of limbic and related circuitry. The behavioral sensitization model appears to have particular relevance to the phenomenology of PTSD and may serve as a primary pre-ictal explanatory model.

Lynch and his colleagues at the University of California sought to clarify the micromorphology of this mechanism. They identified postsynaptic processes as the likely target area. Their research in long-term neuronal potentiation revealed a functional augmentation in the dendritic spines of highly stimulated neuronal pathways. More specifically, such changes included a 33% increase in synaptic contacts, as well as a decrease in the length and width variation of the dendritic spines (Deadwyler, Gribkoff, Cotman, & Lynch, 1976; Fifkova & van Harreveld, 1977; Lee, Schottler, Oliver, & Lynch, 1980). Delanoy, Tucci, and Gold (1983) pharmacologically stimulated the dentate granule cells in rats and found a kindling-like neurologic hypersensitivity to result.

Joy's superb review (1985) of the nature and effects of kindling summarizes the potential alterations in biologic substrata that may be involved in the kindling phenomenon. He noted that "kindling produces important changes in neuronal function and connectivity" (p. 46).

Whatever the biological alteration underlying the neuronal plasticity associated with limbic system neurological hypersensitivity, the phenomenon:

1. Appears to be inducible on the basis of high intensity (traumatic) stimulation;
2. Appears to last for hours, days, and even months (Deadwyler et al., 1976; Fifkova & van Harreveld, 1977; Goddard & Douglas, 1976; Monroe 1982);
3. Appears to show at least some tendency to decay over a period of days or months in the absence of continued stimulation if the initial stimulation was insufficient to cause permanent alteration (Fifkova & van Harreveld, 1977; Joy, 1985); and
4. Appears to be inducible on the basis of environmental, psychosocial, pharmacological, or electrical stimulation (I. Black et al., 1987; Doane, 1986; Monroe, 1970; Post, 1986).

In summary, the preceding has suggested that PTSD may be classified within a group of disorders that share as a core and defining characteristic a pathognomonic neurologic hypersensitivity and sustained status of excitation residing primarily within the limbic circuitry. The specific putative etiological and sustaining mechanisms of this limbic *neurologic* hypersensitivity may be summarized into six basic categories:

1. Increased excitatory neurotransmitter activity within the limbic circuitry (I. Black et al., 1987; Mefferd, 1979; Post, 1985; Post & Ballenger, 1981; Post, Rubinow, & Ballenger, 1986; Sorg & Kalivas, 1995);
2. Declination of inhibitory neurotransmitters or receptors (Cain, 1992);
3. Augmentation of micromorphologic structures (especially amygdaloid and hippocampal dendritic branching (Cain, 1992; Post, Weiss, & Smith, 1995);
4. Changes in the biochemical bases of neuronal activation—for example, augmentation of phosphoproteins or changes in the transduction mechanism c-fos to alter the genetic message within the neuron's nucleus (Cain, 1992; Post, 1992; Sorg & Kalivas, 1995);
5. Increased arousal of neuromuscular efferents with resultant increased proprioceptive bombardment of the limbic system (Gellhorn, 1958a; 1964, 1968; Malmo, 1975; Weil, 1974); and
6. Repetitive cognitive excitation, such as obsessional thoughts, intrusive reiterative recollections, and flashbacks (Gellhorn, 1964, 1968; Gellhorn & Loofbourrow, 1963).

EXCITATORY TOXICITY, NEURAL DEATH, AND GENETIC ALTERATION: POTENTIAL CONSEQUENCES OF TRAUMATIC STRESS

Olney (1978) and McGeer and McGeer (1988) documented that excessively intense stimulation of central nervous mechanisms could be toxic to neural substrates. McGeer and McGeer (1988) implicated glutamate and aspartate as excitotoxins capable of inducing neural lesions through an excitotoxic mechanism. The putative mechanism involves a potentially lethal drain on mitochondria within affected cellular nuclei. Similarly, high-amplitude cascades of glucocorticoids (e.g., cortisol) have been found to be associated with lesions in the highly plastic areas of the limbic system, such as the hippocampal formations (Sapolsky, Uno, Rebert, & Finch, 1990).

Consistent with the work of Sapolsky, Bremner (1999) found, via magnetic resonance imaging (MRI), reduced hippocampal volume in patients with PTSD and in patients with histories of child abuse. The reduced hippocampal volume is consistent with what one might expect as a result of an excitotoxic hippocampal lesioning process as speculated by Everly and his colleagues.

Finally, Yehuda (1999) has raised the issue of the genetic transmission of PTSD-like symptoms. Such conclusions are confounded by the shared familial environments of the second generation cohort. However, in a relevant yet provocative paper, Post (1992) provided indirect support for the inheritability of affective disorders with implications for PTSD. He noted that the genetic transcription factor c-fos may be physiologically altered by intense neurochemical stimulation. He specifically implicated noradrenergic, dopaminergic, glutaminergic, and aspartaminergic neurochemical processes, all known to be highly active in posttraumatic stress.

RELATED DISORDERS

As noted in the previous chapter, PTSD is not the only syndrome that may result from exposure to a traumatic event. Psychological trauma may manifest itself in the form(s) of other psychiatric or somatic problems or comorbidities including, but not limited to, depression, dissociative disorders, numerous and varied anxiety disorders, complex partial seizures, psychotic manifestations, and potentially any of the somatic disorders of arousal as described by Everly and Benson (1989), including but not limited to cardiovascular disorders, gastrointestinal disorders, and immunologic dysfunctions.

KEY POINT SUMMARY

1. It may be that Kardiner (1941) best captured the essence of PTSD when he described posttraumtic syndromes within the context of a "physioneurosis." Consistent with Kardiner's formulation, Everly (1990) proposed that PTSD may be understood as a disorder of arousal. That is, PTSD represents a disorder wherein there exists a pathognomonic neurologic hypersensitivity. This sensitivity may be understood as a neural irritability, or lowered threshold for excitation.
2. Anatomically, we believe that PTSD resides within the limbic circuitry, a highly sensitive subcortical system intimately involved in emotion and survival.
3. More specifically, we believe the primary anatomical centers for PTSD are the amygdaloid nuclei and the hippocampal structures (the locus coeruleus, posterior hypothalamus, anterior hypothalamus, and the prefrontal cortex appear to be similarly involved).

4. Physiologically, there is evidence that norepinephrine, endogenous opioids, serotonin, dopamine, glutamate, aspartate, and corticotrpin releasing factor (and cortisol) may all play important roles in the phenomenology of posttraumatic stress. Animal models implicate diminished levels of gamma amino butyric acid and messenger RNA.

5. It is believed that traumatic activation of the central nervous system mechanism then possesses the ability to activate peripheral mechanisms that may exert effects on the entire human body. These peripheral mechanisms are thought to consist of a neurological axis (sympathetic, parasympathetic, and neuromuscular nervous systems), a neuroendocrine axis (the augmented release of systemic epinephrine and norepinephrine), and an endocrine axis (altered activity of the anterior pituitary and its efferent pathways).

6. Physiologically, we believe, as noted earlier, that the nervous system of the individual suffering from PTSD has become exquisitely sensitive to dysfunctional activation. Gellhorn referred to the sensitization of the nervous systems as ergotropic tuning. Weil used a similar construction but referred to the mechanism as a reverberating circuit. Based on research with cocaine, Post and his colleagues used the concept of behavioral sensitization to describe the nervous system that has become dysfunctionally irritable. The formulations of Gellhorn, Weil, and Post may provide some insight into the physiologic mechanisms that undergird PTSD. Indeed, the nervous system of an individual diagnosed with PTSD is characterized by an inability to regulate excitation. Putative mechanisms that may sustain neural hypersensitivity include (a) increased excitatory neurotransmitter activity within the limbic circuitry (I. Black et al., 1987; Mefferd, 1979; Post, 1985; Post & Ballenger, 1981; Post et al.; Sorg & Kalivas, 1995); (b) declination of inhibitory neurotransmitters and receptors (Cain, 1992); (c) augmentation of micromorphologic structures (especially amygdaloid and hippocampal dendritic branching (Cain, 1992; Post, Weiss, & Smith, 1995); (d) changes in the biochemical bases of neuronal activation—for example, augmentation of phosphoproteins or changes in the transduction mechanism c-fos to alter the genetic message within the neuron's nucleus (Cain, 1992; Post, 1992; Sorg & Kalivas, 1995); (e) increased arousal of neuromuscular efferents with resultant increased proprioceptive bombardment of the limbic system (Gellhorn, 1958a,

1964, 1968; Malmo, 1975; Weil, 1974); and (f) repetitive cognitive excitation, such as obsessional thoughts, intrusive reiterative recollections, and flashbacks (Gellhorn, 1964, 1968; Gellhorn & Loofbourrow, 1963; Horowitz, 1997).

7. Recent evidence suggests that neural death may be a potential end point in a dramatic cascade of neural overstimulation. Dramatic overstimulation may exhaust mitochondria within the nuclei of affected cells, causing their demise. Indirect support for such a hypothesis may be derived from radiologic studies indicating smaller hippocampal formations in traumatized individuals.

8. Posttraumatic stress may manifest itself not only as PTSD but as a wide variety of psychiatric and somatic disease manifestations.

9. Speculation has focused on the ability of traumatic physiology to induce genetic alterations. Although no direct evidence exists at this time to support such a conclusion, mechanisms, potentially capable of inducing such alterations, may well exist and appear to be consistent with the physiology of PTSD, as we currently understand it. Post (1992) has speculated that intense cascades of norepinephrine, dopamine, glutamate, and opioids may induce transcription errors adversely affecting messenger RNA.

10. Ivan Pavlov once noted that the strength of the nervous system resides in its ability to inhibit arousal. The inability to regulate and otherwise inhibit arousal is a cornerstone of PTSD.

II

ASSESSMENT OF POSTTRAUMATIC STRESS

INTRODUCTION: ASSESSMENT OF POSTTRAUMATIC STRESS

In Part II, we address the third component of a clinical science: assessment. The study of posttraumatic stress disorder (PTSD), as an endeavor, has yielded an immense proliferation in quantifiable assessment data over the past 22 years. Although the increase in the number of standardized assessment instruments has greatly facilitated the rapid accumulation of empirical data within the field, several practical issues persist. For example, there remains a lack of consensus regarding the parameters of what constitutes a traumatic event, considerable comorbidity also exists between PTSD and other disorders such as depression and substance abuse, and unresolved issues persist regarding response biases (faking good or bad; Keane & Kaloupek, 1997; Weathers & Keane, 1999). Not surprisingly, these unresolved methodological issues, combined with the propagation of numerous assessment instruments, have resulted in a clear lack of consensus regarding what a core PTSD assessment battery should entail. The purpose of the two chapters within this section is not to attempt to resolve these complex issues. Instead, our goal is to provide the reader who is doing personality-guided therapy of PTSD with a brief overview of the psychological, psychophysiological, neurological, and neuropsychological instruments most commonly used in the assessment of PTSD. We appreciate that most clinicians doing personality-guided therapy may find that the use of more personality-based (most likely projective) and the recently introduced worldview measures of PTSD may be most consistent with the perspectives and inherent themes of this volume. However, we would be remiss if we did not address the advancements and use of many of the current standardized instruments in the field. This two-chapter overview may, therefore, serve as a helpful, condensed reference guide of the current PTSD assessment lexicon. The reader is referred to more comprehensive textbooks for a complete review of these topics (see, e.g., Briere, 1997; Saigh & Bremner, 1999).

5

PSYCHOLOGICAL AND PSYCHOPHYSIOLOGICAL ASSESSMENT OF POSTTRAUMATIC STRESS

In this chapter we review the more common approaches to the psychological and psychophysiological assessment of posttraumatic stress disorder (PTSD). More specifically, we review (a) structured diagnostic interviews, traditional objective and projective measures, self-report PTSD and trauma measures, and worldview measures; and (b) psychophysiological assessment methods, such as heart rate, blood pressure, and skin conductance.

STRUCTURED DIAGNOSTIC INTERVIEWS

Structured Clinical Interview for DSM–IV (SCID)

The SCID, which is modeled after a clinical interview and used to assess Axis I and Axis II psychiatric disorders, allows the interviewer to use symptom-specific questions and clinical judgment to determine whether the interviewee meets diagnostic criteria for a disorder. When used with a trauma population, in addition to the specific PTSD module, it may also be worthwhile to assess for frequently comorbid conditions by presenting the anxiety disorder, affective disorder, and substance abuse disorder modules, along with the screen for psychotic symptoms (Keane & Kaloupek, 2002). For the PTSD module, each symptom is assessed by a standard prompt question, and the interviewer then rates each symptom as either inadequate, absent, subthreshold, or threshold. Only symptoms receiving the latter rating are considered to be present.

Although there are limited data on the psychometric properties of the SCID for the *DSM–IV* (American Psychiatric Association, 1994), the PTSD module of the SCID for *DSM–III–R* (American Psychiatric Association, 1987) has demonstrated adequate reliability and validity. For example, in the National Vietnam Veterans Readjustment Study (NVVRS), Kulka and his colleagues (Kulka et al., 1991) reported a kappa coefficient of .93 when they compared independently scored audiotapes of the SCID interview. Also, a kappa of .68 was reported by Keane and his associates (Keane et al., 1998) when the SCID was administered on two separate occasions by independent clinicians. Moreover, Resnick, Kilpatrick, and Lipovsky (1991) identified the SCID as an instrument of choice in the assessment of PTSD following rape. A primary limitation of the SCID is that the item scoring provides only dichotomous data regarding item presence and symptom severity. In general, clinicians believe that psychological symptoms are more dimensional than dichotomous (either present or absent), so in this respect the SCID appears restrictive.

PTSD Symptom Scale–Interviewer Version (PSS–I)

Although initially developed for sexual assault victims using *DSM–III–R* criteria, according to Foa and Tolin (2000), the PSS–I (Foa, Riggs, Dancu, & Rothbaum, 1993) is a semistructured interview designed to assess *DSM–IV* PTSD symptoms. The PSS–I, which takes approximately 20 to 30 minutes to complete, consists of 17 items rated on a 0 (not at all) to 3 (five or more times per week/very much) scale by the interviewer in response to the participant's answer to a brief question. The PSS–I yields a total severity PTSD score that is the sum of the raw item scores, as well as reexperiencing, avoidance, and arousal subscores. For diagnostic purposes, a symptom is considered present if it is rated at 1 or higher. Foa and her colleagues (1993) reported impressive psychometric properties for the PSS–I. More specifically, an alpha coefficient of .85 was reported for all items, test–retest reliability was .80 for the total score, and when compared to a SCID-based diagnosis, the PSS–I had a sensitivity of .88 and a specificity of .96.

Structured Interview for PTSD (SIP)

The original SIP was introduced by Davidson, Smith, and Kudler (1989) using *DSM–III* (American Psychiatric Association, 1980) criteria;

however, a newer 17-item version exists that uses *DSM–III–R* criteria (Davidson, Kudler, & Smith, 1990). The SIP was designed to assess information about symptom presence or absence as well as severity of symptoms using initial prompts and then behavioral example questions as clarifying follow-ups. The severity of each symptom is rated on a 5-point scale, both for the past month and for the worst period since experiencing the trauma. The ratings in general follow the pattern of 0 = none, 1 = mild, 2 = moderate, 3 = severe, 4 = extremely severe. To be considered as meeting PTSD criteria, the symptom must be rated at a 2 or higher; a total score is obtained by adding the ratings for the 17 items. A Chronbach's alpha of .94 for the total score has been reported as evidence of internal consistency, and a two-week test–retest reliability score of .71 has also been reported (Davidson et al., 1989). When compared to the SCID, the SIP evidenced a sensitivity rate of .96 and a specificity rate of .80 (Davidson et al., 1989).

The psychometric properties of the SIP have been evaluated since the introduction of *DSM–IV* (Davidson, Malik, & Travers, 1997). These data reveal a Chronbach's alpha of .80, four-week test–retest reliability of .89, and interrater reliability at baseline of $r = 0.90$. Compared to the SCID, and using a cutoff score of 15, the SIP had a sensitivity value of 100% and a specificity value of 88%. At a cutoff score of 20 on the SCID, the SIP's sensitivity and specificity values were both at 100%.

PTSD–INTERVIEW (PTSD–I)

The PTSD–I, developed by Watson, Juba, Manifold, Kucala, and Anderson (1991), consists of items that closely reflect *DSM–III–R* criteria. The first question inquires whether the interviewee has experienced an event that the *DSM–III–R* would classify as a trauma. The remaining items, which are scored on a Likert rating scale ranging from 1 (no or never) to 7 (extremely or always), address the PTSD symptoms of reexperiencing, avoidance, arousal, and duration. A rating of 4 on the scale, which corresponds to a self-rating of "somewhat" or "commonly," is used to signify the presence of a symptom. A summary section is then completed by the interviewer and a frequency/severity score is calculated. Watson and associates (1991), in a sample of 31 Vietnam War veterans, reported high ratings of internal consistency (alpha = .92) and impressive test–retest reliability for a one-week interval ($r = .95$). In a sample of 61 Vietnam War veterans, Watson and colleagues (1991) reported that the PTSD–I had a sensitivity of .89, a specificity of .94, and an overall hit rate of 91.8% using the Diagnostic Interview Schedule (DIS; Robins & Helzer, 1985) as a criterion. The mean PTSD–I total score for the stress group was 58.2 ($SD = 14.5$).

There is currently no literature to suggest that the PTSD–I has been modified for *DSM–IV* criteria.

Clinician Administered PTSD Scale (CAPS)

The CAPS (Blake et al., 1990, 1995) was developed at the National Center for PTSD in Boston to provide continuous measurement of PTSD symptomatology and to determine the extent of social and vocational impairment attributable to the symptom clusters that make up the PTSD condition. The CAPS is a semistructured interview that measures the 17 core symptoms of PTSD on two 0 to 4 scales by assessing the frequency (never to daily or almost daily) and intensity (none to extreme) of each item. Follow-up questions are then asked to clarify the response and determine its validity. A frequency rating of at least 1 (once or twice within the past month) and a severity rating of at least 2 (moderate) are needed for symptom endorsement. Of note, there are other more conservative scoring approaches to symptom endorsement on the CAPS (e.g., sum of frequency and intensity scales is 4 or greater). The CAPS also assesses for lifetime prevalence of PTSD. In a sample of 123 Vietnam veterans (Weathers et al., 1992), test–retest reliabilities ranged from .90 to .98 for different pairs of raters, and internal consistency was .94 for the total score. Moreover, a CAPS severity score of 65 was found to have 95% specificity, 84% sensitivity, and a kappa coefficient of .78 when compared with the SCID.

The CAPS has undergone a revision specifically for *DSM–IV* criteria. The most conspicuous changes include adding an assessment protocol for Criterion A, a requirement that interviewers rate the link between a specified trauma and a symptom as either unlikely, probable, or definite, adding items that assess the dissociative symptoms of acute stress disorder, and clarifying how the rating scale anchors are to be used (Weathers & Keane, 1999). Moreover, the version of the CAPS that assesses current and lifetime diagnoses is now known as the CAPS–DX, and the one-week symptom version is now known as the CAPS–SX (Weathers & Keane, 1999). Although generally highly regarded, the one significant drawback to the CAPS is that it may take as long as 60 to 90 minutes to complete (Newman, Kaloupek, & Keane, 1996; Solomon, Keane, Newman, & Kaloupek, 1996).

Traditional Objective and Projective Measures

The Minnesota Multiphasic Personality Inventory (MMPI) and the MMPI–2

The MMPI (Hathaway & McKinley, 1951) and now the MMPI–2 (Butcher, Dahlstrom, Graham, Tellegen, & Kaemmer, 1989) have been used in the assessment of PTSD. Although there is considerable overlap between the two tests, there are differences that should be highlighted when assessing clinical profiles and subscales for PTSD.

Keane, Malloy, and Fairbank (1984) noted a consistent 8–2/2–8 high point profile on the MMPI. High scores on scale 2 (Depression) reflect symptomatic depression and are considered to be associated with the negative symptoms of PTSD (avoidance, dysphoria, withdrawal), whereas elevations on scale 8 (Schizophrenia) reflect the possibility of the positive symptoms of the disorder (reexperiencing or dissociation). As the MMPI–2 was developed, items were added, changed, or deleted from the original MMPI. Also, the MMPI–2 norms were based on a more representative sample of the U.S. population and not on a clinical sample, as in the MMPI. Because of these new normative data, the calculation of the T scores was amended, and these changes have resulted in somewhat different profiles than the original MMPI (Lyons & Wheeler-Cox, 1999).

Although the scores on the MMPI and MMPI–2 remain highly correlated, comparison studies between the two measures (Albrecht et al., 1994; Litz et al., 1991; Wetter, Baer, Berry, Robinson, & Sumpter, 1993) have suggested that the 2–8/8–2 code type may not be protypical of PTSD on the MMPI–2. In particular, the frequent elevation of scale 7 (Psychasthenia) relative to scales 2 and 8 provides enough recurrent data to suggest that the 8/7 profile warrants future research consideration as a possible PTSD profile (Lyons & Wheeler-Cox, 1999). Lyons and Wheeler-Cox (1999) also noted, however, that the MMPI may be better suited if the primary objective of testing is to make a differential diagnosis. Glen et al. (2002) recently reported on MMPI–2 profile differences between Vietnam veterans and Gulf War veterans. Using parametric analyses, Vietnam veterans had a mean 8–2 MMPI–2 code type, whereas Gulf War veterans had a mean 8–1 MMPI–2 code type (indicative of additional emphasis on somatic concerns). Using descriptive techniques, an examination of frequency counts revealed that the most common two-point clinical code type among Vietnam veterans was 7–8/8–7 (16.4%), whereas for the Gulf War veterans it was 6–8/8–6 (23.7%).

In addition to the use of the clinical scales of the MMPI to assess for PTSD, there have been two other scales derived from item analyses. The first, and most heavily researched of the two, is the PK scale developed by Keane, Malloy, and Fairbank (1984). The original scale consisted of 49 items, and a cutoff score of 30 correctly classified 82% of Vietnam War veterans in a validation and cross-validation sample. In an effort to validate and cross-validate the PK scale on an accident–disaster sample, Koretsky and Peck (1990) correctly classified 87% of validation participants and 88% of cross-validation participants using a cutoff score of 19 in a total sample of 69 participants. Watson (1990), in a review of PTSD measurement studies, suggested a cutoff of about 25 may yield the best balance between sensitivity and specificity.

When the MMPI–2 was published, the PK scale was amended by dropping three items and rewording another. For the normative sample of the MMPI–2, the revised 46-item PK scale demonstrated alphas of .85 for men and .87 for women and equally impressive test–retest reliabilities (Lyons & Keane, 1992). Lyons and Keane (1992) suggested that a raw score cutoff of 28 be used for the MMPI–2 PK scale. Recent data (Scheibe, Bagby, Miller, & Dorian, 2001) suggest, however, that the MMPI–2 clinical scales of Psychasthenia and Schizophrenia and the content scales of Anxiety and Anger may be more effective predictors of the presence of PTSD than the PK scale in civilian populations. Clearly, additional studies are needed.

The other PTSD scale, the PS scale, was developed from the MMPI–2 (Schlenger & Kulka, 1989). The PS scale contains 60 items; these include the 46 PK items in addition to 14 additional items that were shown to best differentiate non–treatment-seeking Vietnam War veterans with PTSD from non–treatment-seeking Vietnam War veterans without PTSD (Kulka et al., 1988). The MMPI–2 manual (Butcher et al., 1989) indicates that a cutoff of 26 should be used for women and 23 for men. Litz and colleagues (1991) have suggested that the PS scale may be more applicable to community samples that may not be seeking treatment, whereas the PK scale may be more applicable to treatment-seeking groups.

Gaston, Brunet, Koszycki, and Bradwejn (1998) introduced an MMPI Acute PTSD scale (32 items) and a MMPI Chronic PTSD scale (41 items) for diagnosis of civilians exposed to traumatic events (e.g., armed robbery, physical or sexual assault, hostage-taking, or serious death threats). Using the MMPI–R, which contains only 399 items, a cutoff score of $\geq$ 19 for the Acute PTSD scale resulted in sensitivity of 80%, specificity of 86%, and an overall hit rate of 83% when discriminating between a validation sample of acute PTSD patients (having the disorder for less than six months) and panic disorder patients. For the Chronic PTSD scale, a cutoff score of $\geq$ 21 resulted in sensitivity of 80%, specificity of 70%, and an overall hit rate of 75% in discriminating between a validation sample of chronic PTSD patients (having the disorder for more than six months) and panic disorder patients. Using a cutoff score of 25 improved the hit rate to 80%. The MMPI–R items that make up the scales and discriminate between acute and chronic PTSD and panic disorder are identified in the article.

Forbes and his colleagues (2002) recently used the MMPI–2, along with other assessment instruments, to examine the impact of personality factors on symptom change for 141 Vietnam War veterans with chronic PTSD. Using partial correlations and linear multivariate regression, their results revealed that the MMPI–2 dimensional measure of borderline personality (Morey, Waugh, & Blashfield, 1985) served as the strongest predictor of negative outcome. They considered the features of "alienation, negative emotionality, anger dysregulation, and substance abuse (possibly self-medication)" (p. 330) as negatively affecting treatment. Moreover, regression analyses of the most salient scales revealed the following five items (and how they were endorsed) to be predictive of negative treatment outcome:

Q410: I am often so annoyed when someone tries to get ahead of me in a line of people that I speak to that person about it (true); Q429; Except by Doctors orders, I never take drugs or sleeping pills (false); Q276; I love my mother, or (if your mother is dead) I loved my mother (true); Q134; At times I feel like picking a fist fight with someone (true); Q291; I have never been in love with anyone (true). (p. 329)

Clearly, the negative relationship between symptom improvement and endorsement of a loving relationship with one's mother requires additional exploration; however, the authors propose that the veterans' relationship with their mothers may have been (or was) "idealized, interfering with the development of healthy, adaptive, and loving relationships with others" (p. 331).

MCMI

The original Millon Clinical Multiaxial Inventory (MCMI; Millon, 1983), the MCMI–II (Millon, 1987), and now the MCMI–III (Millon, 1994) are among the most widely used personality tests. The MCMI is grounded in Millon's biosocial learning theory, yet its revisions and modifications are intended to reflect the current theoretical, clinical, and research acumen in the domain of personality. In this regard, the MCMI–III is aligned with the taxonomy of *DSM–IV*, and 95 new items were selected to replace 95 items from the MCMI–II, which had the *DSM–III–R* as its taxonomic structure. Moreover, a 16-item PTSD scale, the R scale, has been added to the Clinical Syndromes group in the MCMI–III. A review of these items reveals, however, that only six of them are related to *DSM–IV* PTSD criteria (mostly intrusive recollections). The preponderance of the items are related to symptoms of depression that are not a part of the current PTSD diagnosis.

Before the introduction of the PTSD scale in the MCMI–III, the studies that did investigate the relationship between traumatic events and responses on the MCMI typically revealed elevations on the personality scales of Avoidant, Dependent, Passive–Aggressive, and Borderline, and on the syndrome scales of Anxiety, Somatoform, Delusion Disorder, Major Depression, and Thought Disorder (Briere, 1997; Bryer, Nelson, Miller, & Krol, 1987). According to the *MCMI–III Manual* (Millon, 1994), the PTSD scale is reliable, with a test–retest of .94 and an alpha of .89. It also has a correlation of .61 with the Impact of Events Scale (Millon, 1994). The

MCMI–III scale (R) purports to assess PTSD with a 53% sensitivity and a positive predictive power of 73%.

But the MCMI–III (and MCMI–II) aggregate configural profile may take on several forms and may be more valuable in the personologic insight that may be provided. Three primary trauma profiles appear to emerge from the MCMI:

1. Aggregate elevations on Schizoid, Avoidant, and Negativistic (passive–aggressive) scales are often viewed as the withdrawing flight variant of the MCMI posttraumatic stress profile;

2. Aggregate elevations on the Narcissistic, Aggressive, and Antisocial scales may be viewed as the aggressive fight variant of the MCMI posttraumatic stress profile; and

3. Aggregate elevations on the Negativistic, Self-defeating, Schizoid/Avoidant, Aggressive, and Borderline scales may be viewed as the affectively labile profile that is often characteristic of "complex PTSD"—in other words, indicative of early developmental trauma, abuse, or neglect.

Rorschach

The utility of the Rorschach in traumatized populations has been investigated in more than 20 published studies (e.g., Bersoff, 1970; Frank, 1992; Sloan, Arsenault, Hilsenroth, Harvill, & Handler, 1995). The advantage, of course, of using this type of unstructured projective technique is that it allows a clinician to examine the world from the patient's perspective. Using the Rorschach with PTSD patients, van der Kolk and Ducey (1989) confirmed the failure of the patients to assimilate the traumatic event into some meaningful schema or worldview. This theme, it will be recalled, is consistent with the perspective undergirding the personality-guided approach espoused within this volume. Levin and Reis (1997) have nicely summarized these concepts:

> Trauma sequelae, as described by Rorschach studies, may serve an adaptive defensive function, seen in the attempt to limit affective involvement as a safeguard to the flooded affect and precarious controls that predominate. A mantle of interpersonal distance, guardedness, and hypervigilance to further feared threat are all defensive protections that may serve the trauma survivor in the struggle to regain equilibrium. (p. 540)

Of the published Rorschach studies, the most consistent scoring result for patients with posttraumatic states has been the increased number of inanimate movement responses (*m*; Levin & Reis, 1997). Another recurrent finding has been the use of diffuse shadowing (*y*), which purportedly taps into the concepts of anxiety and hopelessness and the predominant use of unstructured color, which is thought to be related to unmodulated affect (Levin & Reis, 1997; van der Kolk, 1994). Moreover, Armstrong and Loewenstein (1990) developed the Trauma Content Index (TC/R) in an attempt to identify traumatized individuals, including those with dissociative identity disorder. The index consists of the totaling of the sex, blood, and anatomy content scores in addition to the aggressive and morbid special scores divided by the total number of responses.

Symptom Checklist–90–Revised (SCL–90–R)

The SCL–90–R (Derogatis, 1983), although developed as a general symptom checklist, has been used extensively in PTSD assessments. Not surprisingly, researchers have attempted to develop subscales of the SCL–90–R designed specifically to assess PTSD. Saunders, Arata, and Kilpatrick (1990) developed a 28-item scale that discriminated PTSD in a sample of 355 female crime victims. This Crime-Related PTSD Scale (CR–PTSD), although not meant to be administered independently of the SCL–90–R, has very good internal consistency (alpha = .93) and effectively classified 89% of the sample. Similarly, Weathers and colleagues (1996) developed a 25-item scale (fewer than half of the items are on the CR–PTSD scale) know as the War-Zone-Related PTSD Scale (WZ–PTSD) that discriminated PTSD in combat veterans.

SELF-REPORT PTSD AND TRAUMA MEASURES

Impact of Event Scale (IES) and Impact of Event Scale–Revised (IES–R)

The IES (Horowitz, Wilner, & Alvarez, 1979), although developed before the advent of the *DSM–III* and the formal diagnosis of PTSD, still became one of the most widely used standardized measures of posttraumatic symptomatology. The IES is a 15-item scale used to assess current subjective distress caused by any life event, and its items are theoretically related to the view of stress responses initially posited by Horowitz and his colleagues (1976). The 15 items provide data on the symptoms of intrusive thinking (7 items) and avoidance (8 items) in addition to a total score.

Within the past five years, the IES was revised (Weiss & Marmar, 1997) to include six items of hyperarousal and one item assessing dissociative reexperiencing, thus making its items more consistent with the *DSM–IV* diagnosis of PTSD. Recent data on the 22–item IES–R in a sample of 429 emergency workers yielded coefficient alphas of .85 for intrusion, .85 for avoidance, and .79 for hyperarousal (Weiss, 1996; Weiss & Marmar, 1997).

Penn Inventory for PTSD

The Penn Inventory (Hammarberg, 1992), which measures the severity of a traumatic event, is a 26-item scaled-sentences inventory with three options per statement, as in the Beck Depression Inventory (BDI; Beck & Steer, 1987). The Penn Inventory is based on *DSM–III* and *DSM–III–R* criteria and provides a continuous total score that ranges from 0 to 78. It lacks, however, items that specifically address physiological reactivity, hypervigilance, and effortful avoidance. The mean score on the Penn Inventory for patients with PTSD has ranged from 48.8 to 55.2 (*SD* = 7.6 to 12.3), whereas the mean score in samples of non-PTSD participants ranged from 15.3 to 15.5 (*SD* = 8.9; Hammarberg, 1996). In a series of samples of trauma survivors, a cutoff score of 35 on the Penn Inventory has yielded an overall hit rate of 93% (Hammarberg, 1992, 1996; Hammarberg & Silver, 1994).

Mississippi Scale for Combat-Related PTSD

The Mississippi Scale (Keane, Caddell, & Taylor, 1988) is a 35-item scale based on *DSM–III* criteria. It was developed specifically to assess for PTSD in war veterans, and a 5-point Likert scale (from 1 = never to 5 = always true) is used by the examiner to rate each item, for a total score ranging from 35 to 175. A validation study on a sample of 92 combat veterans revealed that a cutoff score of 107 correctly identified 90% of participants as either PTSD or non-PTSD. Keane and his colleagues (1988) reported an alpha level of .94 and test–retest reliability of .97.

A civilian version of the Mississippi Scale (CMS), which modified military terminology, is now available (Vreven, Gudanowsi, King, & King, 1995). This scale contains 11 items each relating to withdrawal/numbing, reexperiencing and avoidance, 8 arousal items, and 5 guilt and suicidality items. Norris and Perilla (1996) have developed a revised version of the civilian scale by retaining 28 items from the original CMS and adding two items from the Traumatic Stress Schedule (Norris, 1990). Evidence of internal consistency include alpha scores of .86 and .88, and test–retest reliability was .84 (Norris & Perilla, 1996).

Posttraumatic Stress Diagnostic Scale (PDS)

The PDS (Foa, 1995) is a 49-item, four-part severity rating scale of PTSD. The most distinctive feature of this scale is that it assesses all the *DSM–IV* criteria of PTSD. Part 1 of the PDS surveys exposure to various traumatic events, as well as a chance to identify an event. Part 2 assesses the characteristics of the event identified in Part 1 to help determine if it meets the *DSM–IV* definition of Criterion A. Part 3 lists and then assesses on a 4-point scale (0 = not at all or only one time to 3 = five or more times a week/almost always) the 17 specific symptoms identified in PTSD over the past month. A symptom is considered present if it scores a 1 or higher. Part 4 gauges symptom impact on daily, social, and occupational functioning. Evidence of internal consistency includes a Cronbach's alpha value of .92 for the total score, and reliability correlation of .83 was reported for a two- to three-week test–retest. When compared with the SCID, the PDS evidenced a sensitivity rate of .89 and a specificity rate of .75 (Foa, Cashman, Jaycox, & Perry, 1997).

Davidson Trauma Scale (DTS)

The DTS (Davidson, 1996) is a 17-item scale that assesses *DSM–IV* PTSD symptoms. After identifying a traumatic event, the respondent rates the frequency (0 = not at all to 4 = every day) and severity (0 = not at all distressing to 4 = extremely distressing) of accompanying PTSD symptoms. A table included in the manual that relies on ratios and target population base rates may then be used to determine if the total DTS score (which may range from 0 to 136) converts into a PTSD diagnosis (Weathers & Keane, 1999). Evidence of internal consistency includes Cronbach's alpha scores of .99 for the total score, .97 for the frequency items, and .98 for the severity items (Davidson et al., 1997). Test–retest scores in the same sample yielded a reliability coefficient of .86 for the total score. When using the SCID as the criterion, the DTS with a total cutoff score of 40 yielded a sensitivity rate of .69 and a specificity rate of .95 (Davidson et al., 1997).

PTSD Symptom Scale–Self-Report (PSS–SR) and Modified PTSD Symptom Scale–Self-Report (MPSS–SR)

The PSS–SR (Foa et al., 1993) is a 17-item self-report measure that complements the PSS–I, reviewed previously. In a sample of 44 rape victims, Foa and colleagues (1993) reported test–retest reliability of .74 over a one-month interval for the total severity score. Using a SCID–based PTSD diagnosis, the PSS–SR evidenced a sensitivity of .62, specificity of 1.00, and an efficiency of .86.

The MPSS–SR (Falsetti, Resnick, Resnick, & Kilpatrick, 1993) was developed for use with other trauma populations by rewording six items from the PSS–SR. Also, the MPSS–SR added a 4-point rating scale to assess the frequency of PTSD symptoms (0 = not at all to 3 = five or more times per week). Falsetti and her colleagues (1993) reported internal consistency alphas of .96 for a treatment sample and .97 for a community sample. Moreover, in a treatment sample, the MPSS–SR had a sensitivity rate of .93 and a specificity rate of .62 when compared with the SCID (Falsetti, Resick, Resnick, & Kilpatrick, 1997).

WORLDVIEW SCALES

Considering the importance we placed on the proposed belief systems reviewed in chapter 3, we will review the extant scales that assess assumptions and worldview beliefs.

Belief in a Just World Scale (BJWS)

The BJWS (Rubin & Peplau, 1975) is a 20-item scale that assesses beliefs on a 6-point continuum. Half of the items refer to the perception that the world is just and people get what they deserve, whereas the other items refer to an unjust world where good deeds and bad deeds are in essence rewarded equally. Despite its frequent use, Lerner (1980) suggested that the scale might be a better indicator of how people maintain a just world belief rather than an independent measure of the degree to which people believe in a just world. Cronbach alphas for the scale have ranged from 0.67 to 0.78 (Ma & Smith, 1986; Smith & Green, 1984).

World Assumptions Scale (WAS)

The WAS, which is based on the theoretical insights of Janoff-Bulman (1992), is a 32-item questionnaire that incorporates a 6-point Likert scale to assess the subscales of benevolence of the world, the meaningfulness of the world, and self-worth. The WAS, which is not limited to use with trauma populations, has reliabilities of .87, .76, and .80 for the subscales of benevolence of the world, meaningfulness of the world, and self-worth, respectively (Janoff-Bulman, 1996).

World View Scale (WVS)

The WVS (Fletcher, 1996) is a 75-item self-report regarding current beliefs following a traumatic event. The scale allows for the formation of five scales: (a) assumption of safety, security, and enjoyability of the world; (b) assumption of predictability, orderliness, justness, understandability, certainty, and controllability of the world; (c) assumption of self-worth; (d) trustworthiness of others; and (e) the possibility that a positive belief may occur from the exposure to stress. There are limited psychometric data on this scale.

PSYCHOPHYSIOLOGICAL ASSESSMENT

The interest in assessing the psychophysiological responses to trauma can be traced to Kardiner (1941) who, more than 60 years ago when describing the sequelae of war, identified the physioneurotic features of increased startle, irritability, fixation on the trauma, an atypical dream life, and an explosive anger reaction. Wenger (1948) is often credited with the first controlled investigation of physiological responses associated with what came to be known as PTSD when he reported physiological differences between World War II combat flyers who were recovering from "operation fatigue" with different comparison groups.

In another of the seminal studies of psychophysiological assessment of traumatic stress symptoms, Dobbs and Wilson (1960) compared heart rate, electroencephalographic (EEG), and respiration responses of three diverse groups (8 "decompensated" World War II combat veterans, 13 "compensated" war veterans, and 10 students who served as a control group). After a 5- to 7-minute baseline period, the research participants were told that a tape recording of a combat noise would be played and that it would be discontinued at any time if they chose. The participants were then exposed to approximately 8 minutes of audiotaped sounds of an artillery barrage, small arms fire, and aerial bombardment. During the second half of the recording, synchronized single light flashes from a photic stimulator were presented to intensify the stimulation; however, they had minimal effect.

The mean pulse rate and respiration responses to the combat recording were significantly greater in the compensated group than in the student group. Moreover, because of the decompensated participants' behavioral agitation during the presentation of the combat stimuli, physiological measures could not be reliably attained. Dobbs and Wilson (1960) reported that five of the decompensated veterans were unable to listen to the full length of the recording, turning it off after periods ranging from a few seconds to 4 minutes.

CURRENT RESEARCH

From a review of the recent literature, the most frequently measured PTSD psychophysiological response has been heart rate (HR). Other measured responses include blood pressure, skin conductance (SC), electromyographic (EMG) activity, and skin temperature.

According to Keane and his colleagues (1998), the contemporary research in the area of psychophysiological assessment began with two independent studies in the early 1980s. In the first study, Blanchard, Kolb, Pallmeyer, and Gerardi (1982) replicated the work of Dobbs and Wilson with several methodological changes. For example, the diagnostic criteria for patients with PTSD were made more explicit by using *DSM–III*, the nonveteran control group was matched for age with the veteran combat group, and a "neutral" stressor (strident music) was added to the combat sounds. The study compared psychophysiological reactivity of 11 male Vietnam War veterans with 11 age- and sex-matched nonveterans with no psychiatric diagnoses. Skin resistance level, blood pressure, heart rate, skin temperature, and forehead EMG were recorded during five trials, each consisting of mental arithmetic followed by a 6-minute return to baseline, 30 seconds of music, 30 seconds of silence, and 30 seconds of combat sounds. Over the course of the five trials, the volume of the music and combat noise gradually increased from 42 to 82 dB. Last, the participants were exposed to another combat tape that lasted for 8 minutes and gradually increased in intensity from 41 to 78 dB.

The results revealed that the control and PTSD groups both evidenced increased heart rate and systolic blood pressure during mental arithmetic. Only the PTSD veterans, however, had significantly greater increased systolic blood pressure, heart rate, and forehead EMG during the combat sounds. A discriminant function analysis revealed that nearly 96% of participants could be correctly classified by heart rate measures alone. Although these results are compelling, the lack of a non-PTSD combat veteran group made it difficult to determine whether the outcome was attributable to PTSD or whether the differences were caused by combat exposure (Lyons, Gerardi, Wolfe, & Keane, 1988).

The second study, by Malloy, Fairbank, and Keane (1983), directly addressed this question when they administered an audiovisual protocol and collected heart rate and skin resistance on 10 Vietnam War veterans with PTSD, 10 combat veterans without a psychiatric diagnosis, and 10 noncombat psychiatric patients who were screened to rule out combat exposure, psychosis, and organicity. While listening to relevant sounds (e.g., car noises, crowd noises), participants were first shown a series of neutral photographs of a couple embarking on a trip to a shopping mall. They were then shown pictures of combat scenes of a platoon loading onto helicopters and flying over rice paddies; these scenes were accompanied by engine noises and sounds of machine gun fire. Each videotape segment lasted 60 seconds, with an accompanying sound level increase in 10 dB increments to a maximum of 80 dB.

Psychophysiological results of the PTSD, normal, and psychiatric groups revealed no significant differences in heart rate or skin resistance data during either of the baseline periods preceding the videos. Unlike the other groups, however, the PTSD group increased their mean heart rate from 93 bpm during the neutral tape to 104 bpm during the combat tape. In addition, 8 of the 10 PTSD participants, but none of the veterans without PTSD, chose to terminate the combat scene.

Subsequent studies have refined the methodology used in the psycho-physiological assessment of PTSD (Blanchard, Kolb, Gerardi, Ryan, & Pallmeyer, 1986; Pallmeyer, Blanchard, & Kolb, 1986), with one of the most highly touted methodological innovations being the implementation of audiotaped descriptions of idiosyncratic trauma experiences (Pitman, Orr, Forgue, de Jong, & Claiborn (1987). Blanchard and Buckley (1999), in a review of the psychophysiological assessment of PTSD, reported that "based on personal experience we would endorse the use of idiosyncratic audiotapes as the preferred stimulus presentation method" (pp. 261–262).

In the largest known sample-size study to date, Keane and his colleagues (1998) investigated the utility of psychophysiological measurement in the diagnosis of PTSD in a multisite clinical trial of 1,168 participants with current, lifetime, or no diagnosis of PTSD. The procedure included the use of mental arithmetic, standardized audiovisual scripts (a still image with background soundtrack), and idiographic imagery scripts (the two most personally stressful combat experiences from the Vietnam War era) while physiological measures (heart rate, skin conductance, electomyogram, systolic blood pressure, and diastolic blood pressure) and subjective units of distress were assessed.

The results revealed that the participants with current PTSD had a higher mean heart rate baseline score (74 beats/min) when compared to the lifetime prevalence (70.7 beats/min) or no PTSD (70.5 beats/min) groups. In response to the mental arithmetic challenge, all three groups demonstrated a pattern of change; however, the current PTSD group showed less overall response than the lifetime or no PTSD groups. The major focus of the study was to determine whether physiological responses between the groups differed to the audiovisual scenes or to the imagery scripts. As expected, the current PTSD group demonstrated a greater response for heart rate, skin conductance, diastolic blood pressure, and subjective unit of distress when compared to the no PTSD sample for both audiovisual and imagery formats. Greater EMG responding occurred only for the imagery scripts. When compared to the lifetime PTSD group, the current PTSD group showed statistically significant greater responses in heart rate and skin conductance during the audiovisual presentation. Also, when compared to the never PTSD group, the lifetime group showed statistically greater differences in heart rate and EMG during the imagery scripts. Moreover, a regression equation, which was tested and cross-validated, demonstrated physiologically based classification rates of 69% and 64%, respectively.

Another important advancement in PTSD research has been the expansion of sample populations to include more women and civilians, primarily sexual assault and motor vehicle accident victims (Blanchard, Hickling, Taylor, Loos, & Girardi, 1994; Griffin, Resick, & Mechanic, 1994). For example, a recent psychophysiological study by Wolfe and her colleagues (2000) was completed on women who worked primarily as nurses or medical assistants and experienced Vietnam War-zone trauma (e.g., direct mortar attack, handling dead or maimed bodies). The results of this study revealed differences in reaction to trauma cues for skin conductance and systolic blood pressure for those with PTSD compared to those without.

KEY POINT SUMMARY

1. This chapter began with conceptual overviews and presented the psychometric properties of structured diagnostic interviews, including the Structured Clinical Interview for *DSM–IV* (SCID), the PTSD Symptom Scale–Interview Version (PSS–I), the Structured Interview for PTSD (SIP), the PTSD–Interview (PTSD–I), and the Clinician Administered PTSD Scale (CAPS).
2. We reviewed the traditional objective and projective measures of the MMPI, MMPI–2, MCMI, Rorschach, and Symptom Checklist 90–Revised (SCL–90–R), providing profile and item considerations where possible.
3. Self-report PTSD and trauma measures, including the Impact of Events Scale (IES), the Impact of Events Scale–Revised (IES–R), the Penn Inventory for Posttraumatic Stress Disorder (Penn Inventory), the Mississippi Scale for Combat-related PTSD, the Posttraumatic Stress Diagnostic Scale (PDS), the Davidson Trauma Scale (DTS), and the PTSD Symptom Scale–Self-Report (PSS–SR) and Modified PTSD Symptom Scale–Self-Report (MPSS–SR) were reviewed.
4. Given the underlying premise of this volume, the available worldview scales of Belief in a Just World Scale (BJWS), World Assumptions Scale (WAS), and World View Scale (WVS) were summarized.
5. A brief historical perspective of the psychophysiological assessment of PTSD was then offered. A review of more current research demonstrated the use of heart rate, blood pressure, skin conductance, electromyographic, and skin temperature measures as promising avenues of additional refinement in psychophysiological methodology when assessing PTSD.
6. It may well be that recovery from PTSD is only achieved when the worldviews are functionally integrated and there is no longer evidence of neurological hypersensitivity.

6

NEUROPSYCHOLOGICAL ASSESSMENT AND POSTTRAUMATIC STRESS

No personality-guided psychotherapeutic formulation of posttraumatic stress would be complete without some consideration of the functional, as well as organic, neuropsychological aspects of the disorder. As presented in chapter 5, as well as in chapter 2, there is increased recognition and acceptance regarding the complex phenomenological nature of posttraumatic stress. As newer etiological, diagnostic, and treatment models of posttraumatic stress and posttraumatic stress disorder (PTSD) reflect the growing interest of information-processing factors and cortically mediated functions, the use of neuropsychological assessment becomes increasingly valuable. Therefore, despite the relative dearth of formal neuropsychological assessment studies in the area of PTSD, understanding the etiology and neurocognitive concomitants associated with traumatic stress have emerged as concepts worthy of increased methodological investigation. From a personality-guided psychotherapeutic perspective, neuropsychological assessment offers unique insight into the functional, and possible organic, foundations of posttraumatic symptomatology, especially those that seem most enduring and intractable to treatment. This chapter reviews the neuropsychological assessment of posttraumatic stress and PTSD.

EARLY FORMULATIONS

Kolb (1987) is often credited with one of the most well-articulated rationales for the connection between PTSD and neuropsychology. His work was predicated on the notion that the conditioned fear and hyperarousal responses typically observed in animals who had been repeatedly shocked is quite comparable to the behavioral and physiological symptoms associated with PTSD. Wolfe and Charney (1991) concurred with the classical conditioning phenomenon of stress triggering and emotional response offered by Kolb, and expanded this notion to suggest that neurotransmitters and neuropeptide systems (e.g., noradrenergic, dopaminergic, serotonergic, opioid, and benzodiazepine) are also likely included. As noted in chapter 4, Everly (1990, 1995), in a reformulation of Kolb's perspective, suggested a "neurological hypersensitivity phenomeonon" in which high-intensity neural stimulation leads to hyperarousal for neurological stimulation within the limbic system. This hypersensitivity would be consistent with deficits in memory associated with the hippocampus (located within the limbic system). Other neuropsychological deficits identified by PTSD patients would likely be in the areas of attention and executive functioning (Knight, 1997).

Considering the various functional neurocognitive deficits thought to be related to PTSD, several different instruments have been proposed for inclusion in a comprehensive assessment battery (Horton, 1995; Wolfe & Charney, 1991). For example, the Wisconsin Card Sorting Test (Lezak, 1983), which is often used to measure nonverbal concept formation; the Trail Making Test (TMT; Reitan, 1958, 1993), which is used to assess visual scanning, perceptual ability, motor functioning, and the ability to rapidly shift cognitive sets; and the Stroop Color Word Test (Golden, 1976), which is used to assess cognitive flexibility, are frequently administered as part of a neuropsychological screening battery. The Paced Auditory Serial Addition Task (Gronwall, 1977) is a particularly sensitive measurement of attention and concentration that may also be effectively used.

Moreover, memory testing that assesses short- and long-term recall and recognition abilities is an extremely relevant part of a neuropsychological assessment, as is the more recent innovative formats designed to assess aspects of explicit versus implicit memory (Schacter, 1992). Explicit memory involves intentional and conscious recollection and retention of information that can be assessed using traditional tests such as free recall, cued recall, and recognition. Tests such as the Wechsler Memory Scale (WMS; Wechsler, 1945), the Wechsler Memory Scale–Revised (WMS–R; Wechsler, 1987), the Wechsler Memory Scale–Third Edition (WMSIII, Wechsler, 1997), and the California Verbal Learning Test (CVLT; Delis, Freeland, Kramer, Kaplan, & Ober, 1987) are generally thought to assess this type of memory. Implicit memory, on the other hand, is an unintentional, unconscious form of recollection that, in effect, does not depend on the awareness of the individual that he or she has the memory. Implicit memory is frequently assessed via indirect memory tasks such as word-stem completion and perceptual identification. Because a core pathogenic feature of PTSD involves a reexperiencing of the traumatic event in the form of nightmares, flashbacks, and intrusive images, researchers suggest that this idiographic processing and preservation of trauma-relevant information may occur automatically and thus be consistent with implicit memory (Amir, McNally, Riemann, & Clements, 1996; Amir, McNally, & Wiegartz, 1996).

In addition to specific assessment instruments, Wolfe and Charney (1991) cogently articulated a series of relevant application considerations for conducting neuropsychological assessments with PTSD patients. First, they suggested determining whether cognitive dysfunction can be demonstrated in PTSD patients and how it is characteristically different from other affective disorders (i.e., depression and anxiety) with similar clinical presentations. Second, they suggested considering under what circumstances (i.e., behavioral, environmental, or biological) information processing changes will appear and how psychological sequela will be assessed if there happens to be an identified organic injury. Third, they suggested considering if particular PTSD symptoms result in specific cognitive performance deficits. Fourth, they suggested considering the connection between changes in mental processing and the diagnosis of PTSD. More recently, Knight (1997) suggested that sleep patterns and quality, residual effects of physical damage, medication and substance use, compensation, and secondary gain issues are all additional relevant interpretive concerns that should be considered when neuropsychological assessment is performed on PTSD patients. With these concepts in mind, we will review briefly some of the neuropsychological studies in the area of PTSD assessment. Although we recognize the content and functional overlap between the following domains, we separated the studies into the categories of attention and concentration and memory for organizational purposes.

ATTENTION AND CONCENTRATION

Dalton, Pederson, and Ryan (1989), in one of the first formerly identified studies of neuropsychological assessment and PTSD, reported test data from 100 Vietnam War veteran inpatients who received a myriad of assessments. Included in the battery were either the majority of subtests or a complete Wechsler Adult Intelligence Scale–Revised (WAIS–R; Wechsler, 1981), the Trail Making Test (Parts A & B; Reitan, 1958), the Stroop Color-Word Naming Test (Golden, 1978), the Rey Auditory Verbal Learning Test (Schmidt, 1996), the Shipley Institute of Living Scale (SILS; Shipley, 1940),

Serial Digit Learning (Benton, Hamsher, Varney, & Spreen, 1983), and Temporal Orientation (Benton et al., 1993). Overall, the data resembled normative scores from nonclinical samples. The tests where the veterans scored lower were the Stroop Color-Word Naming Test, the Benton Visual Retention Test (Benton, 1974), and Trails B, although the authors acknowledged that these deficits may have been a result of the anxiety effects often seen in psychiatric inpatients.

In another early investigation, Everly and Horton (1989) assessed attention and short-term memory in 14 patients clinically assessed as meeting criteria for PTSD. The test they administered was the four-word short-term memory test (Ryan & Butters, 1980) that "requires the examiner to read four unrelated words and then say a three-digit number. The patient counts backward by 3s from the three-digit number for an interval of 15 or 30 seconds. At the end of the interval, the patient repeats the to-be-remembered material" (Everly & Horton, 1989, p. 808). The results suggested possible neuropsychological impairment in 12 of 14 patients. Such impairment was consistent with hippocampal damage.

Beckham, Crawford, and Feldman (1998) investigated performance on Parts A and B of the Trail Making Test in 90 combat veterans, 45 of whom had a diagnosis of PTSD. The data revealed that the combat veterans with PTSD demonstrated significantly poorer performance on both parts of the TMT when compared to the non-PTSD veterans. Specifically, the combat veterans with PTSD had a mean performance of 47.6 (SD = 20.9) and 100.8 (SD = 45.2) on Parts A and B, respectively. Moreover, when compared to normative data from a sample of average intelligence psychiatric inpatients (Hays, 1995), the sample of combat veterans with PTSD scored at the 25th percentile on Trails A and B.

In a comprehensive investigation of a sample of 43 Operation Desert Storm veterans, 19 of whom met SCID diagnostic criteria of PTSD, Vasterling, Brailey, Constans, and Sutker (1998) reported significant differences on tasks of concentration. More specifically, the PTSD participants responded to more distractor items than the non-PTSD participants, suggesting that the former group had difficulty limiting their responses. However, although the PTSD participants had deficits on measures of sustained attention and mental manipulation, they did not demonstrate comparable problems on measures of selective attention or cognitive flexibility.

In a more recent investigation of 31 rape survivors (15 of whom had a diagnosis of PTSD) and 16 control participants, Jenkins, Langlais, Delis, and Cohen (2000) assessed aspects of sustained attention and concentration using the Continuous Performance Test (CPT; Loong, 1988), the Paced Auditory Serial Addition Task (PASAT; Gronwall, 1977), Digit Span and Digit Symbol from the WAIS–R (Wechsler, 1981), the Posner Visual Selective Attention Task (Posner, Walker, Friedrich, & Rafal, 1984) that measures covert shifting of attention, and the Trail Making Test (Parts A & B; Reitan, 1993). After covarying out the effects of higher depression scores for the PTSD group, these participants performed poorer than the non-PTSD and control groups on measures of sustained attention for auditory (PASAT, Digit Span) and visual (CPT, Digit Symbol, Trails B) stimuli, but not on a measure of visuospatial selective attention (Posner Task). These data support the conclusions of Vasterling and her colleagues (1998), and are consistent with the neurobiological models of PTSD that emphasize how the brain areas responsible for sustained attention are affected by stress-related hyperarousal (Everly, 1993b, 1995; Friedman, Charney, & Deutch, 1995).

MEMORY

The preponderance of the studies examining neuropsychological deficits and PTSD have investigated various aspects of memory functioning. Uddo, Vasterling, Brailey, and Sutker (1993) compared a sample of PTSD veterans (n = 16) with a sample of non-PTSD National Guard enlistees (n = 15) on a series of memory and attention/concentration measures. After ruling out premorbid neurological disorders, the authors reported that the PTSD participants scored lower than the controls on measures assessing acquisition of new material, immediate recall, and delayed verbal and visual recall.

Bremner and his colleagues (1993) examined the difference in intelligence and immediate and delayed recall between 26 Vietnam War combat veterans with PTSD and 15 controls matched for demographic characteristics, including socioeconomic status and alcohol use. For this study, intelligence was assessed by the vocabulary, arithmetic, picture arrangement, and block design tests of the WAIS-R, and memory was assessed by the logical and figural memory subtests of the WMS-R, and the verbal and visual components of the Selective Reminding Test (Buschke, 1973). The groups did not differ in estimated intelligence; however, compared to the control group, the PTSD participants scored 44% lower on immediate recall and 55% lower on delayed recall as assessed by the logical (verbal) memory portion of the WMS. Moreover, the PTSD patients scored significantly lower on the verbal and visual parts of the Selective Reminding Test than did the comparison group. Commenting on the performance of the PTSD participants, Bremner and associates (1993) stated that "the PTSD patients in our study displayed memory problems comparable to those of other clinical populations with clearly documented temporal lobe damage and hippocampal involvement" (p. 1018).

Thrasher, Dalgleish, and Yule (1994) investigated the conceptualized effects of unprocessed trauma-related information in memory by assessing 33 survivors of the Zeebrugge ferry disaster, 13 of whom met diagnostic criteria for PTSD. A control group of 12 participants was also assessed. The participants were given the emotional Stroop task, in which five sets of 20 colored cards (red, blue, yellow, or green) were presented, and the total time it took the participants to name the colors for each set was assessed. The target words consisted of the following categories: semantically unrelated neutral words, semantically related neutral words, positive emotional words, threat words (such as *tense, scared,* or *anxious*), and disaster-related words (taken from transcripts of survivors' accounts of the ferry disaster such as *water, bodies, sinking,* or *trapped*). The results showed that the participants with PTSD symptomatology exhibited a selective processing bias (longer mean response time to name the colors) for the disaster-related words. In fact, their reaction time to the disaster words not only exceeded their times on the neutral and positive words but was also significantly greater than their reaction time to the threat words. This effect was not observed for the Zeebrugge survivors without PTSD symptomatology or the control group.

Yehuda and her associates (1995) evaluated intelligence, learning, and memory in 20 male combat veterans diagnosed with PTSD compared to 12 matched controls. Although the groups did not differ in estimated intelligence on the WAIS–R as assessed by the vocabulary and block design subtests or on letter fluency or category fluency, they did differ on their performance on the CVLT. Although the groups demonstrated comparable initial attention, immediate memory, cumulative learning, and interference from previous learning abilities, there was a striking difference in retention following the presentation of an intervening word list. The PTSD group demonstrated significantly poorer performance than the comparison group in both short-delay free recall and long-delay free recall. This notion of "forgetting" explicit, not personally relevant information is an important aspect of PTSD memory deficits.

McNally, Lasko, Macklin, and Pitman (1995) expanded this line of research by assessing explicit memory disturbances for personally relevant and specific autobiographical material in 19 Vietnam combat veterans with PTSD compared to 13 Vietnam combat veterans without PTSD. The participants were shown 20 words printed on separate index cards, 10 were positive cue words (e.g., *friendly, loyal, humorous*) and 10 were negative cue words (e.g., *lazy, selfish, cruel*). Participants were then asked to report a specific personal memory (i.e., a time when they displayed the trait) for each word. The results showed that the PTSD participants had more difficulty retrieving specific autobiographical memories than those without PTSD. This effect was more pronounced when retrieving positive traits. An additional interesting finding of this study was that disturbances in autobiographical memory were most evident in the seven PTSD participants who wore Vietnam War regalia (e.g., fatigues and medals) during the session. These participants, when compared to the healthy combat veterans and to the PTSD participants not wearing the regalia, shared fewer recent memories overall and more readily retrieved memories that were at least 10 years old. These findings regarding explicit, declarative memory certainly warrant replication with an increased sample size; however, they support McNally and his colleagues' (1995) contention that "preoccupation with intrusive memories of memories of trauma may consume cognitive resources, rendering it difficult for traumatized persons to use memory in a specific adaptive fashion" (pp. 619–620).

Compared to the methodological procedure described by McNally and his colleagues in which specific voluntary aspects of autobiographical memory were assessed, the PTSD symptoms of intrusive memories and flashbacks may be described as involuntary accessing of autobiographical memories of traumatic events. Thus, these idiographic intrusions are considered to be implicit or nondeclarative in nature. Amir et al. (1996) used a noise-judgment task to assess if there was an implicit bias for threat in 14 Vietnam combat veterans with PTSD compared to 14 Vietnam combat veterans without PTSD. The noise judgment task consisted of the 28 participants initially hearing and repeating 24 sentences (12 related to combat— "The chopper landed in the hot LZ," and 12 neutral—"The shiny apple sat on the table") presented in a random counterbalanced order. Participants then heard and repeated nine other neutral sentences that were presented with three different background noise volumes (low, medium, and high). They then rated the noise volume on a 5-point scale. The participants then heard and repeated 48 sentences (24 of which they heard and repeated initially) while the three different background noise volumes occurred. Participants rated the noise volume and, because their responses were audiotaped, accuracy of their responses could be determined. The results evidenced that when compared to the controls, PTSD patients rated the background noise accompanying the "old" or initially heard combat-related sentences as lower than the noise accompanying the 24 new combat-related sentences. This occurred at the high-noise volume and implies an implicit memory bias for threat such that "cognitive structures relevant to threat were easily primed for PTSD patients" (p. 633).

Krikorian and Layton (1998) reported the case of a healthy 53-year-old man with no history of neurological or psychiatric problems who was buried under 5.5 meters of sand for 15 minutes as the result of a construction accident. This isolated traumatic incident led to the occurrence of PTSD along with amnesia for the event caused by anoxic encephalopathy. After four years of treatment, including an amobarbital interview and a visit to the site of the accident, the patient maintained that he did not remember the event. Despite this contention, he suffered from recurrent intrusive thoughts of being buried alive and suffocating, avoidance of construction sites, sleep disturbance, and an exaggerated startle response. The authors suggested the role of implicit or nondeclarative memory in PTSD. More specifically, they argued that

> although the emotional trauma must have been experienced consciously (because it occurred before he succumbed to the anoxia), the neurophysiological effects of the anoxia rendered the experience inaccessible as an episodic memory. However, certain aspects of the event, in particular the excessive fear and associated sensory images, not only were registered, but also must have been consolidated and remained accessible to one or more non-declarative systems. (p. 361)

Collectively, neuropsychological research demonstrates that individuals with PTSD process information differently than non-PTSD participants. Although no definitive profile for PTSD has become apparent, several studies have found consistently poor performance on attention–concentration, short-term verbal memory, and increased retroactive interference (Golier & Yehuda, 2002). Accumulating data have also recently focused on the proposed tenet that selective information processing may be a characteristic feature of those who are more susceptible to developing PTSD. Support for this contention is the work of McNally, Kaspi, Riemann, and Zeitlin (1990), who noted that among veterans, the interference of processing trauma-relevant information appears to be consistently correlated with severity of PTSD rather than combat exposure. Additional cross-sectional and longitudinal investigations are needed to examine the possible pretraumatic risk factors and posttraumatic cognitive decline in response to trauma (Golier & Yehuda, 2002). Mediating variables, such as personality diatheses, intensity and duration of trauma exposure, previous traumatic experiences (Breslau, Chilcoat, Kessler, & Davis, 1999), personal or family history of psychopathology, and lower education and intelligence all warrant additional investigation when considering the development of PTSD.

With regard to neuropsychological test performance, recent results have suggested that lower precombat intelligence may be a risk factor for developing PTSD in combat veterans (Macklin et al., 1998). The authors, in a unique prospective study, obtained preexposure intelligence, as assessed by the Armed Forces Qualification Test (AFQT; Maier, 1993), which has a mean score of 100 and a standard deviation of 20, and found that preexposure intelligence predicated later development of PTSD symptoms (assessed by the Clinician Administered PTSD Scale; CAPS; Blake et al., 1990, 1995). Moreover, when controlling for precombat intelligence and later combat exposure, current intelligence was no longer correlated with PTSD. Also of note is that the precombat mean IQ of the 59 PTSD veterans was in the average range (106.3; the 31 healthy veterans had a mean IQ of 119).

Therefore, although comparative lower IQ predicted PTSD, it is important to acknowledge that the PTSD veterans did not have low intelligence.

Other current data offer support for neurological soft signs, which are "nonspecific indicators of impairment that typically do not allow localization of central nervous system lesions" (Gurvits et al., 2000, p. 181), in PTSD patients. In a sample of Vietnam veterans and sexually abused women, copying two- and three-dimensional figures and performing rhythmic sequential movements best discriminated between those with and without PTSD. Moreover, the neurological soft signs were associated with lower IQ and neurodevelopmental problems in both samples.

NEUROLOGICAL FINDINGS: NEUROIMAGING, EEG, AND EVENT-RELATED POTENTIALS

Orr and Kaloupek (1997), in a review of psychophysiological studies of PTSD, suggest that "the critical element appears to be activation of the memory network in which the traumatic event is encoded. Once a memory is activated, emotions that are associatively linked with it also become activated along with their accompanying physiological responses" (p. 71). Bremner and his colleagues (1997) have suggested that certain brain structures involved in memory are likely abnormal in PTSD patients. More specifically, the amygdala, which mediates the startle response and other emotional responses to traumatic cues, and the hippocampus, which is essential for short-term recall and is involved in the emotions of fear and anxiety, are considered to be the structures most primarily affected. Recent neuroimaging data have also suggested that there is a decrease in volume of the hippocampus that may be related to the neuronal damage that could occur from excessive levels of glucocorticoids associated with traumatic stress (Bremner et al., 1995; Bremner et al., 1997). Moreover, studies that have used script-driven imagery of traumatic events in comparing responses of PTSD and control participants have shown a difference in regional cerebral blood flow (rCBF) with the use of positron emission tomography (PET). Relative to control participants, individuals with PTSD in the traumatic imagery condition show increased rCBF in the right-sided limbic, paralimbic, and visual areas, including the amygdala. Furthermore, there was a concurrent decrease in rCBF in Broca's area (Rauch et al., 1996).

Other data suggest that an exaggerated startle response (larger magnitude eye-blink EMG) when exposed to intense auditory stimuli occurs in individuals with PTSD compared to individuals without PTSD (Morgan, Grillon, Southwick, Davis, & Charney, 1995; Orr, Lasko, Shalev, & Pitman, 1995). Also, as mentioned previously, there has been a notable increase in electrophysiological brain activity measurement as a psychophysiological assessment tool in PTSD. Essentially, what has been measured is EEG brain wave activity (e.g., alpha and theta) and event-related potentials (ERPs), which essentially reflects one's ability to filter or process stimulus information. When measuring ERPs, Orr and Kaloupek (1997) noted that:

> ERPs are obtained from the electroencephalographic scalp potentials that are generated by presentations of discrete stimuli (such as tones). The characteristic waveforms usually become apparent only when averaged over multiple trials. These waveforms are analyzed in terms of amplitude and latency of characteristic components that are designated by their positive or negative electrical potential and the timing of their onset after stimulus presentation. For example, N200 refers to a negative-going response 200 ms after the stimulus, whereas P300 refers to a positive response at about 300ms. (p. 78)

The data obtained from ERP studies have been associated with various sensory and informational processing to both internal and external events. P300, for example, has been associated with stimulus meaningfulness and N100 has been associated with attention. Paige, Reid, Allen, and Newton (1990) are usually credited with the first study examining the effects of ERPs in PTSD patients. In their study, they report that 9 of 12 PTSD veterans had heightened central nervous system sensitivity as evidenced by a decrease in P200 amplitude when responding to increased tone intensities. The opposite effect was found in five of the six non-PTSD veterans. Other ERP studies (Charles et al., 1995; McFarlane, Weber, & Clark, 1993) support the notion that PTSD individuals have a longer N200 latency and prolonged P300 responses to distracting tones, suggesting processing disturbances (e.g., concentration, memory, and selective attention). More recently, P300 data suggest that combat veterans with PTSD have heightened orientation responses or increased attention to new, distracting stimuli that may be indicative of a processing bias toward information that may be interpreted as emotionally meaningful (Blomhoff, Reivang, & Malt, 1998) or as vague or potentially threatening (Kimble, Kaloupek, Kaufman, & Deldin, 2000).

KEY POINT SUMMARY

1. Traditional assessment of PTSD has relied on diagnostic interviews, standardized psychometrics, and psychophysiological assessments. The addition of neuropsychological assessment technologies are relatively new.
2. From a personality-guided psychotherapeutic perspective, neuropsychological assessment provides insight into functional neuropsychological foundations of PTSD symptomatology.

3. Neuropsychological assessment may also provide insight into possible organic foundations (e.g., cognitive and neurodevelopmental risk factors) of PTSD symptomatology. Such insight may provide additional elucidation about the role that organic factors may play not only in the emergence of PTSD but also in enduring and recalcitrant symptomatology.
4. Accumulating evidence suggests that there is functional and structural damage residing within the more severe PTSD presentations.
5. Currently, evidence suggests that those with PTSD are also likely to exhibit attentional, concentrational, short-term, and nondeclarative memory deficits.
6. Some of these deficits are consistent with temporal lobe or hippocampal damage or functional insufficiency.
7. If, indeed, evidence of deficits emerge from neuropsychological assessments, appropriate rehabilitation strategies may now be included in the overall synergistic personality-guided treatment plan as recommended by Millon et al. (1999).

III
THERAPEUTIC
INTERVENTION

INTRODUCTION: THERAPEUTIC
INTERVENTION

According to Millon, the fourth and final element of a clinical science is therapeutic intervention. Within this the third and final section within this volume, we address personality-guided therapeutic intervention with posttraumatic stress disorder.

As the title of this book indicates, we take a personality-guided approach to the treatment of posttraumatic distress. Based on the tenets of Millon's personality-guided therapy, we not only argue that as the severity of posttraumatic distress increases the need for a personality-guided approach also increases, but we also embrace the notion that a synergistic therapeutic stance should be taken. Recall from chapter 1 that synergistic psychotherapy entails using a combination of psychotherapeutic interventions, specifically selected from an even broader array of therapeutic techniques, designed to meet the idiosyncratic personologic and psychotherapeutic needs of an individual patient at a given point in time. According to Millon, "The palette of methods and techniques available to the therapist must be commensurate with the idiographic heterogeneity of the patient for whom the methods and techniques are intended" (Millon et al., 1999, p. 145). Thus, synergistic psychotherapy is the application of multiple intervention techniques, either simultaneously (potentiated pairings) or serially (catalytic sequences) in a tailored manner to specifically address the essential phenomenological elements of the extant disorder and the unique persono-logic elements of individual patient, in a combinatorial manner.

PRINCIPLES OF RECOVERY AND RESTORATION

A two-factor conceptualization has guided our understanding of the phenomenology of PTSD, and thus will serve as the overarching strategic formulation for the treatment of PTSD and related syndromes of posttrau-matic distress. This strategic formulation will be the context within which the synergistic, personality-guided therapeutic approach to the treatment of PTSD will be structured.

Pierre Janet (1919/1976) appeared to advocate a two-pronged approach to the treatment of psychological trauma:

1. Regulating intense arousal; and
2. Making intellectual sense out of the traumatic experience.

This approach is consistent with Everly's (1989, 1993a, 1993b, 1994, 1995) neurocognitive approach to the treatment of posttraumatic distress and is similarly consistent with Millon's (Millon et al., 1999) synergistic personal-ity-guided therapy recommendations. Everly has advocated a two-factor strategic formulation wherein the therapist:

1. Uses methods for neurologic desensitization; and
2. Attempts to reintegrate a functional worldview.

We use an integration of these principles in the following chapters on therapeutic intervention.

In chapters 7 and 8, we discuss what is an essential element to psycho-therapeutic improvement, especially in the treatment of the trauma survivor: the establishment of the therapeutic alliance. Our approach to this topic revolves around the alignment with preferential communication processes and personality-specific thematic belief systems.

In chapter 9, we introduce the notion of mitigating the acute posttrau-matic reaction through the use of the principles and practices of emergency mental health—in other words, crisis intervention. More specifically, we review the use of what may be the extant international standard in crisis intervention: Critical Incident Stress Management (CISM).

In chapter 10, interventions designed to achieve neurologic desensitiza-tion are reviewed. Both behavioral and psychopharmacological interventions are reviewed.

In chapter 11, we directly address the traumatic resolution. Using a personality-guided approach, we focus on the personality-grounded core explanatory, assumptive worldviews (*Weltanschauung*) that we believe are targets of the traumatic event and represent the phenomenological lesion within the posttraumatic disorders. We believe that trauma resolution is often best achieved through integrating the traumatic event into the most ego syntonic assumptive worldviews.

In chapter 12, we review the relationship between psychological trauma and permanent personality alteration in the form of the borderline personality disorder.

In summary, our therapeutic approach to PTSD involves:

1. A personality-guided approach to establishing the therapeutic alliance and creating the foundation for the reconstruction of a "safe" world (through the use of preferential communication processes and alignment with personality-specific beliefs);
2. Neurologic desensitization, wherein techniques are used to diminish the intensity of the pathognomonic ergotropic state of neurological hypersensitivity and increase perceptions of self-efficacy; and
3. Restoring personality-based assumptive worldviews and integrating the traumatic event.

7

A PERSONALITY-GUIDED APPROACH TO FORMING THE THERAPEUTIC ALLIANCE

There exists a virtual plethora of proposed psychotherapeutic techniques that offer the trauma patient relief from the torment and mental anguish that constitutes posttraumatic distress. The therapist who strives to offer the patient some mitigation of suffering would do well, however, to heed the admonition that, before using therapeutic techniques that directly target the posttraumatic distress syndrome, the therapist must work diligently to form a therapeutic alliance with the patient. The therapeutic alliance may be thought of as a constructive, working relationship wherein the therapist and the patient form a collaborative partnership, with the goal of that functional partnership mutually understood to be the mitigation, and potential elimination, of the syndrome of posttraumatic distress. It may well be that construction of the therapeutic alliance is the sine qua non of significant and lasting psychotherapeutic improvement. In this chapter, we address the personality-guided approach to forming the therapeutic alliance as a foundation for the treatment of posttraumatic distress.

THE IMPORTANCE OF THE THERAPEUTIC ALLIANCE

According to van der Hart, Brown, and van der Kolk (1989), the great psychiatrist Pierre Janet "was very much aware of the need to establish a special, safe patient–therapist relationship before attempting to deal with the traumatic memories" (p. 380).

According to Shea,

> From the first moment they see, hear, smell, and touch each other, the clinician and the patient begin the engagement process. In this complex interplay they reflect their sensory information onto the slippery screen of their memories. From these comparisons, both the clinician and the patient attempt to determine where each will fit into the other's life. (1998, p. 9)

Dryden elaborated:

> The first task for you as a counsellor is to greet your client and begin to establish a productive therapeutic alliance. . . . It is important that you show your client that you understand his concerns, demonstrate an unconditional acceptance of him as a person, and establish your credibility . . . that you take seriously the problems for which he is seeking help. (1999, pp. 80–81)

In his valuable text *Psychiatric Interviewing,* Shea (1998) stated that the first goal of the initial interview is establishing a therapeutic alliance. In *The Clinical Interview,* Othmer and Othmer (1994) stated that becoming an "ally" is a fundamental task that casts the therapist in the quest to build necessary rapport. Furthermore, according to Moursund (1993), establishing a healthy working relationship is the exclusive goal of the initial stage of psychotherapy. According to Wolberg (1988), this relationship is so vital to the overall success of the psychotherapeutic process that "all tasks must be subordinated to the objective of its achievement" (p. 493). Thus, we see a general consensus that the initial stage of any psychotherapeutic relationship must be characterized by efforts directed toward creating a constructive and collaborative working relationship between the therapist and the patient— in other words, a therapeutic alliance.

FOSTERING THE THERAPEUTIC ALLIANCE

Given the critical importance of the therapeutic alliance, the question naturally arises as to how the therapist may best foster such a constructive relationship. The therapeutic alliance is predicated and built solely on the establishment of a perceived sense of *safety* within the working relationship. The sense of safety is the therapeutic bedrock on which the therapeutic alliance, and ultimately the psychotherapeutic process, are founded.

Let us review our examination of Maslow's seminal work; it is relevant. Maslow formulated an often-cited hierarchy of needs. He stated,

> There are at least five sets of goals which we may call basic needs. These are briefly physiological, safety, love, esteem, and self-actualization. . . . These basic goals are related to each other, being arranged in a hierarchy of prepotency. This means that the most prepotent goal will monopolize consciousness and will tend of itself to organize the recruitment of the various capacities of the organism. (Maslow, 1943, p. 394)

The most fundamental of all psychological needs is the need for safety. Generally speaking, until lower order needs are satisfied, one cannot and will not progress up the hierarchy. Nor will one even attempt to attain higher order needs. Until the need for safety is satisfied, additional psychotherapeutic progress will be similarly stymied.

According to Maslow, if one's safety and protection are in question or directly challenged, the quest for safety becomes the dominating goal and "a strong determinant not only of [one's] current world outlook and philosophy but also of [one's] philosophy of the future . . . a man in this state, if it is extreme enough and chronic enough, may be characterized as living almost for safety alone" (Maslow, 1970, p. 39). This, then, is the fate of the individual with posttraumatic stress disorder (PTSD).

As Schiraldi (2000) noted, recovery from posttraumatic stress disorder is predicated on establishing a "safe" therapeutic environment. To be effective, "any therapy must first combat patients' demoralization and heighten their hopes of relief" (Frank & Frank, 1991, p. 33). More specifically, the superordinant goal in the psychotherapy of posttraumatic stress is the reestablishment within the patient of a belief in and a perceived sense of safety, first in the therapeutic relationship and next in oneself, working toward the goal of long-term functional independence.

Psychotherapeutically, the therapist must realize, and never lose sight of, the aforementioned goal of safety. Safety seems intimately interwoven with the conditions of interpersonal acceptance and trust. According to Brammer and MacDonald (1999), trust is a crucial element in the helping relationship. Patients "are willing generally to accept help from people they trust. For trust to develop, [patients] must have confidence in their helpers and must be able to believe what they say" (Brammer & MacDonald, 1999, p. 51). To facilitate the perceptions of trust and safety, the therapist must be willing to *adapt* to the patient's personal style (Moursund, 1993). Adaptation to the patient's style may be thought of as a form of personologic alignment—in other words, an interpersonal acknowledgment of, alignment with, and acceptance of foundational intrapersonal and interpersonal characteristics. In adapting to the patient's style, the therapist begins to engender a psychologically safe environment.

So far, we have argued that establishing a therapeutic alliance and creating a condition of psychological safety may be the sine qua non of the initial stage in the psychotherapy of posttraumatic distress. How, then, does the therapist go about establishing the condition of safety with an individual for whom the world is the antithesis of a safe environment? We have further argued that the perception of safety is facilitated through the process of personologic alignment, which leads to another query: How does the therapist foster the personologic alignment on which the therapeutic alliance and the psychotherapeutic process are ultimately based? We look to the science of rhetoric for insight into this process.

As Frank and Frank (1991) noted, "Both noble rhetoric and psychotherapy share the goal of enhancing the well-being of their targets" (p. 68). "The power of rhetoric raises the possibility that wider deliberate use of such procedures could enhance the overall effectiveness of psychotherapy" (Frank & Frank, 1991, p. 69). Thus, in many ways, the psychotherapeutic process resembles the process of rhetoric—in other words, the art of persuasion. So next we move to a brief discussion of the essential tenets of verbal persuasion.

The process of verbal persuasion has been studied for more than 2,000 years. The definitive work on this subject was written by the Greek philosopher Aristotle (*The Art of Rhetoric*, 1991).

Born in 384 b.c. in Stagira, a small town in northern Greece, Aristotle became a student of Plato and a teacher of Alexander the Great of Macedonia. With respect to the study and practice of rhetoric, the work of Aristotle not only defined the principles of verbal persuasion but elevated it to a noble art, if not a science.

Liberally interpreting Aristotle's *The Art of Rhetoric*, there exist three pillars, or processes, inherent in effective persuasion:

1. The establishment of the speaker's perceived credibility (trust, safety) in the mind of the listener (referred to as ethos);
2. The mobilization of emotions (sometimes broadly referred to as psyche) within the listener (the mobilization of emotions may also be thought of as increasing motivation within the listener); and
3. The use of logic (referred to as logos) to alter or direct the listener's behavior.

Initially, the most important of the three pillars of Aristotelian persuasion (ethos, psyche, and logos) is ethos. As noted, ethos may be thought of as the perceived credibility of the speaker. The credibility of the speaker is largely defined by the characteristics of the speaker's *trustworthiness* (sometimes operationalized as the speaker's reputation, experience, or expertise) and *safety* as perceived within the mind of the listener. We can extract from the work of Aristotle guidance on how to increase the ethos (perceived safety and trustworthiness) of the speaker (therapist), which is so important in the treatment of posttraumatic distress:

1. "Audience analysis"—in other words, the identification of relevant values, attitudes, and core beliefs held by the listener (patient), especially as they might be relevant to the current episode of posttraumatic distress; and
2. An initial alignment of oneself with the acknowledged importance, or fundamental essence, of those relevant values, attitudes, and core beliefs (relevant personologic qualities). In this context, alignment *does not* mean the use of deception or illegitimate endorsement; rather, alignment means finding some genuine common ground for agreement or mutual understanding. In the psychotherapeutic context, alignment means personologic alignment—in other words, acknowledging and adapting to the preexisting personologic inclinations and dispositions of the patient.

Once established, ethos may then serve as the springboard for enhancing motivation with the subsequent use of logos—in other words, the use of logic as a tool of persuasion. If the audience analysis reveals irrational or erroneous beliefs as being in evidence, then logic, as a tool of persuasion, might include the disputation of those relevant irrational or erroneous beliefs through the introduction of the principles of common sense, statistical probability, or the use of mutually understood "truths," scientific facts, laws, or observations to support one's argument. In some instances, alignment may need to be situational and may be defined as avoiding confrontation or contradiction if such will prove counterproductive to the healing process. For example, when challenged by the patient experiencing auditory hallucinations—"You do hear those voices don't you doctor?"—an aligning response might be, "Although I may not hear the voices, I certainly believe that they are real for you, and that's all that is important at this moment." Similarly, when faced with a patient possessing an impulsive, and most likely self-destructive, urge to quit her job, an aligning response could be, "Although quitting your job certainly seems like a viable option to you, the question is whether or not that is the best course of action for you at this time."

Although far more complex, perhaps a useful embodiment of these Aristotelian principles (especially ethos and logos) resides in William Shakespeare's *Julius Caesar* (Cunningham, 1970). In Act III, Scene 2, Julius Caesar has just been murdered by the stoic Brutus and his collaborators because they believed that Caesar had grown too ambitious. Enraged and desiring revenge, Caesar's closest friend, Marc Antony, wishes to claim Caesar's body and address the people of Rome.

Antony has correctly assessed his audience as (a) hostile to his point of view (that Brutus has just wrongly killed a great man and that Caesar's spirit is calling for revenge) and (b) favorably predisposed to Brutus's belief that Caesar was ambitious. To immediately accuse or confront Brutus, Cassius, and the others and to directly condemn their murderous actions would certainly have inflamed the people of Rome and led to Antony's murder as well. Therefore, Antony, in his speech that follows that of Brutus, having analyzed his audience, decides to initially *adapt* and *align* himself with the views of his audience through the verbal acknowledgment of, but not necessarily agreement with, those views. It will be recalled that Brutus murdered Caesar because he believed Caesar was too ambitious and aspired to be king. Brutus states,

> Romans, countrymen, and lovers! Hear me for my cause, and be silent, that you may hear: believe me for mine honor, and have respect to mine honor, that you may believe. . . . As Caesar loved me, I weep for him; as he was fortunate, I rejoice at it; as he was valiant, I honor him; but as he was ambitious, I slew him. (p. 115)

The persuasive challenge that faced Antony was a formidable one. Thus, rather than risk losing the interest, or evoking the disdain, of his audience of Romans through the use of direct refutation or confrontation, Antony chose to initially *adapt* through the acknowledgment of, but not necessarily the agreement with, their point of view (being ever so careful not to lie nor feign false kinship). Antony stated,

> Friends, Romans, countrymen, lend me your ears:
>   I come to bury Caesar, not to praise him.
>   . . . The noble Brutus
>   Hath told you Caesar was ambitious:
>   If it were so, it was a grievous fault,
>   And grievously hath Caesar answered it.
>   Here, under leave of Brutus and the rest . . .
>   Come I to speak in Caesar's funeral.
>   He was my friend, faithful and just to me:
>   But Brutus says he was ambitious;
>   And Brutus is an honorable man.
>   He hath brought many captives to Rome,
>   Whose ransoms did the general coffers fill:
>   Did this in Caesar seem ambitious?
>   When the poor have cried, Caesar hath wept:
>   Ambition should be made of sterner stuff:

Yet Brutus says he was ambitious;
And Brutus is an honorable man. . . .
I thrice presented him a kingly crown,
Which he did thrice refuse: Was this ambition?
Yet Brutus says he was ambitious,
And, sure, he is an honorable man. (pp. 119–121)

In the preceding, Antony initially aligns with the audience's belief that Brutus was an honorable man. He further acknowledges that *if* Caesar was ambitious, it was a grievous fault, deserving of grievous consequences. But Antony quickly intersperses logical evidence to contradict the claims that Caesar was ambitious. The most severe of contradictions was the fact that Caesar had three times refused the crown. Antony then asks how Caesar could possibly be an ambitious man. Later in the scene, Antony reads Caesar's will wherein he leaves his wealth to the citizens of Rome— hardly the act of an ambitious and selfish man. The citizens of Rome subsequently turn against Brutus, not because Antony directly confronted Brutus but rather because he wisely found a perceived common ground on which he and his audience could agree. Subsequently, he built a logical evidence-based argument that contained a foredrawn conclusion: Caesar was not ambitious, ergo Brutus must not be an honorable man.

LESSONS LEARNED FROM RHETORIC

The pedagogical imperative to be deduced from the preceding appears obvious. Had Antony failed to initially align with the listeners' belief system, his message would have had no credibility (ethos) and would have been summarily rejected. His logical arguments, no matter how otherwise compelling, would have been rejected because they would have fallen on "deaf ears." In this case without ethos, there could have been no logos.

How does the analysis of this Shakespearean soliloquy assist us in understanding the challenge presented by the psychotherapy of posttraumatic distress? Had Antony not established a *safe* communication environment (one in which he established his credibility by acknowledging that grievous acts should be dealt with in a grievous manner and by choosing not to directly confront the validity of Brutus's justifications for the murder of Caesar) the listeners were clearly more receptive to his subsequent logical message. Persons suffering from posttraumatic distress are living in an unsafe world. Their core beliefs, by definition, have been challenged, if not destroyed. Their concerns are not just real for them, they are imperatives. The failure to interpersonally align, the inclination to directly confront existing posttraumatic beliefs, risks adding further insult and injury. Failing to initially align creates a condition wherein the therapist risks becoming part of the problem rather than part of the solution. It is no small wonder that, in our experience, law enforcement and fire suppression professionals, airline pilots, nurses, physicians, and other groups of uniquely trained/educated professionals often tend to seek out members of their own profession with which to confide, rather than seek out mental health professionals. The issue of ethos is often perceived as low to begin with when dealing with those outside of one's "culture" ("How can you help me if you don't understand what I do and the culture within which it is done?"). The subsequent failure to personologically align may subsequently lead to a condition within psychotherapy wherein the patient is perceived as resistant for persisting in holding on to certain beliefs or worldviews, and the therapist is perceived as arrogant, unhelpful, ignorant, or argumentative.

PERSONOLOGIC PSYCHOTHERAPEUTIC ALIGNMENT

The most fundamental manner in which the therapist may align with the patient is on the personologic level. Personologic alignment may occur on the preferential communication process level or on the personality-specific thematic belief level.

Psychotraumatologist Pierre Janet (1919/1976) suggested that there may be two types of personalities from what we shall call a *preferential communication process* perspective: a cognitively oriented personality and an emotionally oriented personality. Similarly, personologist Theodore Millon (Millon & Davis, 1996) has suggested that all core personality styles may be divided into one of two process categories along what he refers to as the abstraction dimension: intellective reasoning (thinking) styles and affective resonance (emotional) styles.

The relevant therapeutic admonition would be to align with the personality-based preferential communication process: Initially use a cognitively oriented approach to the cognitively oriented patient and use an affectively oriented approach to the affectively oriented patient to create a safe psychotherapeutic environment, which in turn serves to construct the functional therapeutic alliance. Although rudimentary and seemingly simplistic, it may be that the brain simply cannot speak the language of the heart and similarly the heart may not speak the language of the brain. Thus, to increase the likelihood that the therapist will be understood in the initial stages of therapy, care should be taken to align along the preferential communication process dimension.

Millon's seminal work in the analysis of personality and personality disorders may be used to refine the personologic alignment of the therapist by illuminating the potential areas for personality-specific thematic alignment. In their text *Personality and Its Disorders*, Millon and Everly (1985) described eight basic, adaptive, and "normal" personality styles or patterns. They described each from a prototypic multidimensional perspective using prime exemplars projected on a standardized template of psychological and behavioral domains. Each of the eight personality styles is described along a standardized multidimensional template consisting of the following nine dimensions:

1. Behavioral appearance;
2. Interpersonal conduct;
3. Cognitive style;
4. Affective expression;
5. Self-image;
6. Preferential ego defense mechanism;
7. Sustaining reinforcement pattern;
8. Preferential communication process; and
9. Governing personality-specific thematic belief.

In chapter 8, we examine each of the eight basic personality styles using the nine prototypic dimensions and their prime exemplars.

KEY POINT SUMMARY

1. A two-factor conceptualization has guided our understanding of the phenomenology of PTSD, thus the same two-factor conceptualization will consequently serve as the overarching strategic formulation for the treatment of PTSD and related syndromes of posttraumatic distress. This strategic formulation will be the context within which the synergistic, personality-guided therapeutic approach to the treatment of PTSD will be structured.

2. Pierre Janet (1919/1976) appeared to advocate a two-pronged strategic approach to the treatment of psychological trauma subsequent to establishing therapeutic rapport: First, regulate the pathognomonically intense arousal, and second, assist the patient in making intellectual sense out of the traumatic experience. This approach is consistent with Everly's (1989, 1993a, 1993b, 1994, 1995) neurocognitive approach to the treatment of posttraumatic distress and is similarly consistent with Millon's (Millon et al., 1999) synergistic personality-guided therapy recommendations. Everly has advocated a two-factor strategic formulation wherein the therapist first uses methods for neurologic desensitization and second assists the patient to reintegrate a functional worldview.

3. As the noted physician Stuart Wolf once observed, "It is evident from the idiosyncratic nature of interpreting experience that to understand the impact of an event, the focus of inquiry must be the individual." This personologic focus must be initiated as the earliest aspect of the therapeutic process evolves in the formation of the therapeutic alliance. The direct therapeutic attendance to the traumatic event must come secondarily to the attendance to the therapeutic alliance.

4. The therapeutic alliance is a constructive, collaborative working relationship between the patient and the therapist. It is the sine qua non of psychotherapeutic improvement. The therapeutic alliance is based on a foundation of perceived interpersonal trust and safety.

5. Safety is the most fundamental of all psychological needs and if not satisfied can become the consuming focus of one's entire existence.

6. Trauma destroys the sense of safety and forces one to regress so as to focus one's attention on the attainment of the most rudimentary of needs—in other words, reestablishing safety from the psychological perspective.

7. The initial goal of psychotherapy is to establish the therapeutic alliance grounded in the patient's perception of trust and safety (referred to as ethos) within the therapist and the psychotherapeutic process. Ultimately, the long-term goal of therapy is the creation of a sense of intrapersonal trust, safety, and self-reliance within the patient.

8. In many ways, psychotherapy resembles the process of rhetoric (persuasion).

9. Aristotle's core pillars of persuasion are ethos (credibility, trust, safety), psyche (motivation, emotion), and logos (the use of logical appeals).

10. Achieving the initial goal within the psychotherapeutic process of interpersonal safety, and ultimately the construction of the therapeutic alliance, is best fostered through a process of adaptation, more specifically a process of personologic alignment with the patient.

11. Personologic alignment is achieved through alignment with the patient's preferential communication process—in other words, cognitive versus affective orientations and personality-specific thematic belief systems, as adapted from Millon. Sensitivity to these variables may not only facilitate the therapeutic alliance through the enhancement of ethos, but ego

dystonic declarations, confrontations, and unintentional rejection may be avoided.

12. In the final analysis, successful psychotherapy is likely to be built on a positive and constructive therapeutic alliance. The therapeutic alliance is greatly facilitated and functionally enhanced through personologic alignment as described within both the individual patient's preferential communication process and thematic belief system.

8

PERSONOLOGIC ALIGNMENT AND PERSONALITY-SPECIFIC BELIEFS

Chapter 7 introduced the reader to the concept of a personality-guided approach to forming the therapeutic alliance. The importance of the therapeutic alliance was discussed, along with the concept of considering the dynamics of the patient's preferential communication process as well as the personality-specific thematic belief systems (character style). In this chapter, we further explore personologic alignment within the personality-specific thematic belief systems. To do so, we must first explore a taxonomic framework for understanding personality. We extend the work of Everly and Millon (1985), thus creating a prototypic template of nine prime exemplars that may be used to describe, and otherwise distinguish, eight basic personality styles or patterns. We first describe the theoretical pillars on which Millon's system for personality classification is constructed. Finally, we offer clinical case examples that reflect the manifestations that personality factors may assume and the roles they may play in the phenomenology of posttraumatic distress.

A PERSONALITY CLASSIFICATION SYSTEM

Theodore Millon (1969, 1990; Everly & Millon, 1985; Millon & Davis, 1996) proposed an overall classification system for both "normal"

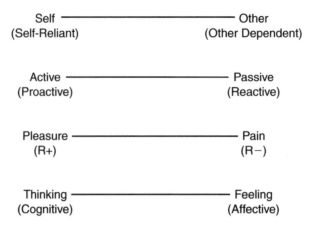

Figure 8.1. Four polarities of the theory.

and disordered variants of the human personality. In the present context, we shall be interested in the "normal" (functional and adaptive) variations to the expressed exclusion of personality disorders. Although, it should be noted that the personality matrix that we employ to examine normal personality styles can also be employed to examine personality disorders.

Millon proposed that the concept of reinforcement could be used to effectively examine variations in human personality and to identify prototypically distinct variations in personality. This assertion was made because of his belief that reinforcement patterns serve to undergird all variations of personality. Initially, Millon proposed that personality could be examined by virtue of three reinforcement polarities.

1. *Source of reinforcement*: Self (reliance on oneself for requisite reinforcement) versus others (reliance on others for reinforcement);
2. *Instrumental reinforcement patterns and processes*: Active (self-initiating and engaging) versus passive (pacific and reactive); and
3. *Type of reinforcement*: Positive reinforcement (R+)—in other words, the pursuit of pleasure—versus negative reinforcement (R−)—in other words, the avoidance of pain or suffering.

He later restructured the reinforcement model to include an evolutionary (survival) perspective and in doing so he added a fourth polarity (see Figure 8.1):

1. Source of reinforcement now viewed as the *priority for survival* from an evolutionary perspective: Self versus others;

EXHIBIT 8.1
A Reinforcement Matrix

Instrumental behavior pattern	Source of Reinforcement			
	Independent (self)	Dependent (others)	Ambivalent (confused)	Detached (neither self nor others)
Active (proactive)	1	3	5	7
Passive (reactive)	2	4	6	8

2. Instrumental reinforcement process becomes the preferred mode for pursuing survival from an evolutionary perspective: Active modification of the environment versus passive, reactive accommodation to the environment;
3. Type of reinforcement becomes the goal or aim of survival from an evolutionary perspective: Pursuit of pleasure (R+) versus avoidance of pain (R-); and
4. *Abstraction processes*: Intellective reasoning versus affective resonance.

Using initial polarities, it becomes possible to construct a classificatory reinforcement matrix that yields eight basic and prototypic personality styles. This matrix is demonstrated in Exhibit 8.1.

We begin with the horizontal axis that possesses four variations on the theme of sources of reinforcement:

- *Independent (Self-reliant)*: These individuals are inclined to be self-reliant. They are often power-seeking individuals who rely on themselves to secure pleasure and protection. They are most comfortable when they are in control and often gravitate to leadership positions. They tend to trust their own judgments or those of individuals they see as similar to themselves. These individuals are often thought of as being somewhat self-centered and lacking in empathy, however.
- *Dependent (Other-reliant)*: These individuals tend to be most comfortable seeking pleasure and protection from others. Interpersonal affection, affiliation, and support are essential for these persons. Often described as "social beings," interpersonal empathy and social sensitivity are often significant assets.
- *Ambivalent (Vacillating between Self-reliant and Other-reliant)*: These individuals characteristically vacillate between relying on themselves and relying on others. But rather than having

EXHIBIT 8.2
Normal Personality Patterns

Instrumental behavior pattern	Source of Reinforcement			
	Independent	Dependent	Ambivalent	Detached
Active (proactive)	Forceful personality	Sociable personality	Sensitive personality	Inhibited personality
Passive (reactive)	Confident personality	Cooperative personality	Respectful personality	Introversive personality

the best of both worlds by exhibiting adaptive vacillation depending on the demands of the situation, these individuals vacillate at the characterological level, sometimes leading to undue rigidity, on one hand, or negativism, on the other.

- *Detached* (Those who have difficulty finding a reliable source of reinforcement): These individuals seem unwilling or unable to achieve many pleasurable experiences.

Having described the horizontal axis within the personality classification matrix, let us now turn to the intersecting vertical axis. This axis consists of the two global instrumental behavioral patterns that may be used to seek reinforcement: active and passive.

- *Active Instrumental Patterns*: Individuals who pursue this instrumental pattern are usually proactive. They are often characterized by alertness, vigilance, persistence, and goal-directed behavior.
- *Passive Instrumental Patterns*: Passive and reactive, these individuals initiate few strategies on their own. Rather, they tend to wait for the opportunities others may provide. They display varying degrees of inertness, acquiescence, and unassertiveness.

The intersection of the horizontal and vertical axes yields a 4×2 matrix yielding eight personality styles. Exhibit 8.1 enumerated these styles; Exhibit 8.2 labels them. The two remaining descriptive polarities will be indicated as constituents of the prototypic templates listed later in the chapter.

Let us look at each of the eight theoretically pure personality prototypes, keeping in mind that, in reality, human beings tend to be a mixture of at least a primary and a secondary personality style. Each personality style, or pattern, will be described along nine prototypic descriptive dimensions using theoretically prime exemplars for each dimension. Finally, an actual clinical case example (replete with appropriate alterations to protect patient identities) is provided as a means of exemplifying characteristic points, or personality dynamics, that may be targets for personality-based thematic alignment in the construction of the therapeutic alliance. These dynamics may also prove useful in understanding therapeutic progress, or lack thereof.

To reflect back to the previous chapter, the nine descriptive and taxonomic personality dimensions are as follows:

1. Behavioral appearance (i.e., how the individual appears to others);
2. Interpersonal conduct (i.e., how the individual interacts with others);
3. Cognitive style (i.e., the characteristic nature of thought processes);
4. Affective expression (i.e., the characteristic nature of emotional expression);
5. Self-image (i.e., self-perception);
6. Preferential ego defense mechanism;
7. Sustaining reinforcement pattern;
8. Preferential communication process; and
9. Governing personality-specific thematic belief.

EIGHT BASIC PERSONALITY STYLES: DESCRIPTIONS AND CASES

Forceful–Aggressive (Controlling) Personality Style

The forceful–aggressive personality is characterized by:

1. An adventurous, risk-taking behavioral appearance;
2. Controlling, intimidating interpersonal conduct;
3. A subjective cognitive style;
4. Frequent angry affective expressions;
5. An assertive self-image;
6. Isolation as a defense mechanism;
7. Positive reinforcement (R+) appears to be the sustaining reinforcement mechanism wherein a forceful personality serves to secure preferential treatment, engender deference, and make available sources of pleasure that might not be

otherwise available. As a secondary note, it also protects against being taken for granted, subjugation, maltreatment, abuse, or manipulation;

8. An affective communication orientation; and
9. A general belief that power is an imperative, whereas the loss of power, the loss of self-determination may be catastrophic.

Case Study 1: Forceful–Aggressive

Randy, age 24, divorced with no children, was born the second of three boys and raised on a farm in northern Iowa. He recalled that his mother spoke of him as a strong willed and energetic baby, one who fought to have his way. His father struggled to keep the farm afloat and died when Randy was 15 years old. Randy described his father as a tough, dominant, disciplinarian who showed little warmth or affection. Before his father died, he would often come home drunk and physically abuse his brothers and his mother. Randy admitted that he hated his father but recognized that he served as a role model for his own toughness. His mother was utterly submissive to her husband and deferred all responsibilities to him.

Randy fought constantly with his two brothers and vividly recalls the day when he beat up his brother who was older by two years. Randy never relinquished the role as the dominant sibling from then on. Randy excelled at athletics, particularly football, and during his high school years was referred to as the "team enforcer." He hated to lose, and his aggressive locker room tirades after losses were legendary. He was encouraged to wrestle in high school, but his coaches felt that he lacked the discipline required to learn the finer techniques. For example, during his first attempt at wrestling, he repeatedly punched a practice opponent who successfully scored points on him. Instead, Randy began spending time in the weight room, and quickly added additional muscle to his already developed frame. Randy experimented with the use of steroids; however, he could not afford to continue taking them. By the end of his high school years, Randy was an imposing 6 foot 3 inches tall, weighed 245 pounds, and was an accomplished recreational weight-lifter.

Shortly after graduating from high school, Randy married his high school sweetheart. Their relationship had been tumultuous during their high school years—a combination of jealousy, infidelity, and intermittent mostly verbal aggression. Unfortunately, this pattern did not change once they were married. What finally did change after two years, however, was his wife's tolerance. After receiving numerous restraining orders, she ultimately filed for divorce and moved to an undisclosed location on the West Coast. Randy remained in Iowa and worked various semiskilled jobs before becoming a truck driver. He lived in a one-bedroom apartment and became a "regular" at a popular bar that had topless dancers and several pool tables.

Randy began playing pool with the same fervor and intimidation that he had on the football field and weight room. He was an affable winner, but periodically lost control after he lost, particularly if money was involved. Other regulars at the bar knew to stay away from Randy, particularly after his fourth beer and second shot of tequila. On one particularly crowded Friday evening, hours after receiving his paycheck, Randy was drinking a moderate amount and having good success at the pool table when he began playing pool against someone who clearly appeared out of his element. His new opponent was about 5′9″ and may have weighed 165 pounds. He was very "straight-laced," dressed in an oxford shirt and tie with a matching cardigan sweater. Randy, always vigilant of his surroundings, was instantly suspicious of the stranger. Randy won the first game; however, he lost the next two games. He realized that he was likely being hustled, and whispered to a friend that if he lost the next game for $50, he was going to "kick this guy's ass." Word quickly spread around the bar, and a crowd began to gather both inside and outside of the bar.

Randy was soundly beaten in next game of nine ball and was livid. He openly questioned not only his opponent's motives but also his obvious stupidity in choosing him to try and pull it on. Randy forced the stranger into the side parking lot, but no one predicted what happened next. Randy, with the encouragement of his entourage, charged the stranger, but was immediately struck to the ground by a well-executed kick to his right knee. The stranger, who was obviously skilled in the martial arts, proceeded to pummel and humiliate Randy, laughing at him as he administered the beating. The crowd was stunned, and simply watched as the stranger quickly made his way to his car and drove away.

Within days, Randy developed a constellation of symptomatology that would herald the subsequent development of posttraumatic stress disorder (PTSD). At the urging of friends, Randy reluctantly sought treatment for depression, intrusive images, and frequent nightmares wherein he continually saw his assailant standing over him laughing. By the third visit to his psychologist, Randy had become frustrated with the therapy process, noting that he had seen no real symptom improvement. The therapeutic process seemed more like a debate wherein the psychologist indicated to Randy that physical assault was likely to engender symptoms such as he was experiencing. Randy, however, rebutted that he had been "beaten up" before in his life by men much larger than this assailant and the experience left no lasting psychological discord as he was now experiencing. He also tried to explain to the psychologist that his "status" within his peer group had been irreparably harmed. The psychologist's approach had been to offer the revelation that there would always be more powerful, as well as less powerful, men and that he should feel comfortable with who he was without comparing himself to others. This approach proved ineffective.

Confident (Asserting) Personality Style

The confident personality is characterized by:

1. A poised, narcissistic, even arrogant behavioral appearance;
2. Unempathic interpersonal conduct;
3. An imaginative cognitive style;
4. A calm and serene affective disposition;
5. A confident self-image;
6. A rationalization defense;
7. Positive reinforcement (R+) as a sustaining reinforcement mechanism biased toward a somewhat entitled pursuit of pleasure;
8. A cognitive communication orientation; and
9. Egocentricism, a belief of personal superiority and a resultant sense of entitlement and privilege that are intertwined with the belief that "special" people deserve special recognition and special benefits in life.

Case Study 2: Confident (Asserting)

James, age 47, a pathologist who was married with one child, was born and raised as an only child in an affluent suburban area outside of Boston. He was born after his mother had suffered three miscarriages, so when James arrived, his parents doted on him. He never assumed any household or personal responsibilities. He attended selected private schools where he excelled in math and science. He had few friends his age, preferring instead to spend limited time with older children with similar academic interests or mostly taking time after school to work with his math and chemistry teachers. James entered and won the Northeast regional science competition for 13- to 15-year-olds when he was only 12. This title won James acclaim, including an interview by two of the local television news shows. James felt that he was well liked by his peers, although they may have thought him to be a "bit pompous and superior." In addition to his academic successes, James also was an accomplished pianist as well as highly touted tennis player. At his parents' country club, James won the double's title when he was 16; his partner was 24.

James received an academic scholarship to an Ivy League school, where he continued to excel academically. Despite encouragement from coaches, he opted not to play tennis but instead to focus on his studies. James assumed the role of a "loner" in college, preferring to spend his time with what he considered to be other "academically elite" students. James was accepted into a premier medical school where he worked hard excelling academically. He also developed a knack for applied research, and realized early in his clinical rotations at a community-based hospital that he would prefer limited patient contact. James acknowledged several factors that influenced this decision, including his discomfort working with "needy" patients. James decided, therefore, to specialize in pathology, because he also recognized that he had difficulty sharing his thoughts and feelings with others and "preferred the pleasure" of his own company to that of others.

Typical of his previous success, James was hired at a large metropolitan hospital in the northeast and within six years was the chief of pathology. He socialized infrequently, and admitted that most people probably viewed him as a "bit self-centered and entitled." A colleague fixed James up with his current wife, who described him as a talented and intelligent man who was a good provider but not very affectionate.

On a late fall afternoon, James was seated in first-class traveling back on an airline from a medical convention where he had given what he considered to be an important address. He willingly engaged in a conversation with the flight attendant who listened as James described his work. As James was dozing slightly to sleep, the attendant shook him urgently and requested his presence in the back of the plane where a passenger was apparently having a massive heart attack. James quickly went with the flight attendant and discovered an elderly man in considerable distress. Seated four rows ahead of the man was a 16-year veteran paramedic who has done hundreds of cardiac resuscitations. When it became apparent what was happening, the paramedic offered and then attempted to intervene; however, he was strongly rebuffed by James, who emphatically acknowledged his physician status. James had not, however, performed CPR on a patient since early in his residency and had not used the new portable defibrillators with which the plane had been equipped. Under the inordinate pressure of the setting with excessive commotion and concern, he was unable to activate the defibrillator or implement CPR improperly. As an apparent result of James' errors, the gentleman died before the plane could complete its emergency landing.

The paramedic publicly chastised James and blamed him for the passenger's death. The passengers and crew appeared to concur with the paramedic's assessment.

James diagnosed himself as suffering from PTSD six weeks after the incident. Although voluntarily seeking therapy, James proved to be a most challenging and resistant patient. James would routinely challenge his psychologist, resisting any psychotherapeutic interpretations that seemed inconsistent with his own self-perceptions. James would seize on any opportunity to "share" with his psychologist the "medical" perspective on the current topic. Therapy appeared to progress very slowly, if at all. Occasionally, James and his psychologist would engage in disagreements that frustrated the psychologist but seemed to invigorate James. James decided to terminate therapy during the session in which the psychologist offered to James the insight that "everyone makes mistakes."

Sociable (Outgoing) Personality Style

The sociable personality style is characterized by:

1. An animated, attention-seeking behavioral appearance;
2. Demonstrative, flirtatious, but often superficial interpersonal conduct;
3. A superficial cognitive style;
4. A dramatic, exaggerated affective expression;
5. A charming, sociable, and "desirable" self-image;
6. A dissociative ego defense;
7. Positive reinforcement (R+) as a sustaining reinforcement mechanism wherein interpersonal attention, affiliation, and "celebrity" yield a greater sense of self-worth;
8. An affective communication orientation; and
9. The belief that interpersonal affection, approval, affiliation, and support are essential to happiness and can be actively solicited; being unnoticed, unloved, or disdained are characterologically injurious.

Case Study 3: Sociable (Outgoing)

Diane, age 33, divorced but remarried with one child, was an attractive, spirited woman. Her father was a highly successful and wealthy business executive and considered Diane and her sister (four years older) as "display pieces," to be shown off to his friends and to help complete his "family life" but not necessarily to be "troubled with." Diane's mother was a charming but emotional woman who devoted considerable time to make her children "beautiful and talented." Diane and her sister excelled in tap and ballet from the age of 3, and both were frequently entered into child beauty pageants. Although he never attended the competitions, Diane's father expected to hear about the results as soon as they were completed. Diane also took voice lessons and developed an aptitude for baton twirling. Both daughters vied for their parents' approval, although Diane proved to be the more successful. However, despite her successes, she constantly had to "live up" to her parents' expectations to maintain let alone enhance her sense of self.

Diane was quite popular during her high school years; however, she was an average to below average student. She never had to search for a date and had many boyfriends. When she and her girlfriends went out together, Diane received considerable attention from boys and men. Diane was a cheerleader, sang with the high school band, and was the lead in several school plays. Despite her varied talents, Diane's sense of self was attached primarily to her appearance.

After graduating from high school, Diane attended the local community college, where she met and soon married a very handsome man two years her senior who was from a prominent local family. Despite the wealth and prominence, the relationship was essentially doomed from its inception. They had a daughter together but a divorce occurred several months after her birth.

Diane worked fanatically to regain her figure following the birth, and within a year of her divorce, she met and married a man in his early 40s. Her second husband, who like her first husband, was also wealthy and provided her with considerable attention and support. He also encouraged her to pursue her interests outside the home, which Diane did. Within two years of their marriage, she earned her real estate license, and with her husband's connections, she was soon selling million-dollar homes and properties. Diane enjoyed the attention that real estate sales provided. She also liked "dressing for success," mixing with an elite clientele, the country club life, and using her striking appearance to her advantage.

Her happiness changed suddenly one day during a preliminary walk through a property that was being built for clients of hers. As she made her way through the dimly lit basement, she slipped on some wooden debris and as she was falling the bridge of her nose was deeply cut with an exposed wire. Although her nose was not broken, the gash left Diane devastated. She refused to leave her home and began having intrusive images of the event. She avoided contact with her family and began to wear dark glasses. Months after the injury healed, she had cosmetic surgery done to minimize the residual scar. From all objective accounts, most would agree that the procedure was successful; in point of fact, there was no visible evidence that her nose had ever sustained an injury. For Diane, however, she remained devastated by the physical injury.

Diane sought psychotherapy for a constellation of depressive symptoms. Throughout the initial sessions a "reality-based" psychotherapeutic approach was initiated, but yielded no improvement. Platitudes offered by her family, such as "physical beauty is only skin-deep" routinely enraged Diane. In apparent frustration, Diane brought into her psychotherapy session a series of photographs that were taken of her face on her admission to the emergency department on the day of her accident.

Cooperative (Agreeing) Personality Style

The cooperative personality style is characterized by:

1. A docile behavioral appearance;
2. Compliant interpersonal conduct wherein conflict is avoided if possible;
3. An open, often naïve, cognitive style;
4. A warm, tender, and sensitive affective disposition;
5. A somewhat weak, or minimally competent, self-image;
6. Introjection as a preferred ego defense mechanism;
7. Negative reinforcement (R-) as a sustaining reinforcement mechanism wherein a cooperative personality serves to protect against abandonment, rejection, and interpersonal isolation;
8. An affective communication orientation; and
9. The belief that people are trustworthy, honest, and caring; that interpersonal support and affection are essential and can be "earned"; and that loneliness, rejection or abandonment may be devastating.

Case Study 4: Cooperative (Agreeing)

Mary, a 20-year-old single woman with no children, was born six weeks prematurely and raised as an only child in a small midwestern town. She had frequent illnesses as an infant, and her mother kept an excessively close watch over her. Her mother prevented Mary from engaging in undue exertions and limited her responsibilities at home. Mary remained pampered and overprotected throughout her childhood. She was treated in essence like a treasured family heirloom that could be broken at any time. Mary's mother insisted that Mary not be involved in physical activities, including physical education at school.

Mary was fairly small of stature and quite unassertive. Her academic and social life was also generally uneventful. Despite being kind-hearted and friendly, she had only one close friend at any time, and seemed quite content to let this person decide their social activities. Mary had little interest in dating, preferring instead to stay home on weekends reading books and assisting her mother in the kitchen. Following graduation from high school, Mary, with her mother's encouragement, went to work part-time in her aunt's local gift shop. Mary tolerated the job given that the shop was not too busy; however, she began complaining about having to take the bus to get to work. Her mother, who never learned how to drive and took public transportation when necessary, was understanding but felt that the responsibility of driving could only lead to trouble for Mary. Mary elicited the help of her aunt and her father, both of whom persuaded Mary's mother to let Mary earn her driver's license.

Mary successfully passed the driver's test, but was distraught over the perceived friction between her and her mother. Mary worked hard to make amends, and invited her mother to go for a ride with her in the family car she was sharing with her father. Her mother reluctantly agreed and the two ventured off for their inaugural ride together. Despite being visibly anxious, Mary concentrated on the road and felt that she was doing well. Her mother, who was also visibly anxious, made several comments to Mary about keeping her eyes on the road and not going too fast. Mary, not unexpectedly, was driving 5 miles below the speed limit and had her eyes fixated on the road. Mary's mother then began actively questioning Mary's desire and need to drive. As Mary, with tears in her eyes, quickly turned her head to respond to her mother, she experienced a tremendous collision to the passenger's side of the car. Mary experienced neck and back pain; her mother required hospitalization for a broken leg and a concussion. The cause of the accident was apparently the other driver's running of a stop sign.

Mary appeared to experience depressive symptoms within 48 hours postaccident. She willingly sought out psychotherapy, but her psychologist soon discovered that Mary's depressive symptoms more resembled a classic "grief" reaction and was resistant to the usual psychotherapeutic approaches.

Sensitive (Complaining) Personality Style

The sensitive personality style is characterized by:

1. An erratic, vacillating, behavioral pattern; superficial pleasantness interspersed with an often obstinate or manipulative behavioral appearance;
2. Outspoken, often contrary or passive–aggressive interpersonal conduct ("misery loves company");
3. A cynical, pessimistic cognitive style;
4. A negativistic affective disposition;
5. An image of self as disillusioned and discontented;
6. A preferred ego defense mechanism of displacement;
7. Negative reinforcement (R-) as a sustaining reinforcement mechanism wherein extreme sensitivity; overt complaining; obstinate, passive–aggressive, or manipulative behavior serves as means of exercising power and control, thus preventing a loss of power or control;
8. An affective communication orientation; and
9. The belief that life is a never-ending struggle for control at which others seem more successful, more appreciated, more

recognized; thus, few sacrifices are too great to retain power and express self-efficacy.

Case Study 5: Sensitive (Complaining)

Betty, age 41, married with two children, was born the eldest of two daughters in an upper-middle-class home. She described herself as an unwanted child, and indicated that her parents got married to make her birth "legitimate." Betty said that as long as she could remember, her parents bickered and argued. Betty's relatives said that her mother gave Betty considerable love and attention before her sister was born. Betty later assumed that this love and affection protected her and her mother from her father. Betty always felt antagonism from her father, later deducing that she must have represented for him the "cause" of his misery.

The bond that Betty shared with her mother was substantially reduced with her sister's birth. Her mother's attention was now focused on the new infant, and Betty felt abandoned and vulnerable. She attempted, sometimes desperately, over the next several years to please her mother, to distract her from her sister and recapture her affection and protection. This plan proved to be intermittently successful, a result in part to her mother becoming annoyed because Betty was too demanding. Her mother would display frequent outbursts of anger followed sometimes by feelings of guilt and affection. More common, however, were long periods of rejection and indifference.

Not surprisingly, Betty acknowledged at times hating her sister "with a vengeance," but mostly feared to express this hostility. Periodically, she might let her sister "have it," but often felt terrible after verbally or physically assaulting her following these incidents. Betty would become contrite, nurturant, and protective of her sister. This vacillating and ambivalent pattern served as the prototype for her relationships with most people.

Betty had her share of friends in school; however, she never felt like one of the "in crowd." She went to an all-women's college, where she experienced difficulties in social relationships. In particular, during her first two years at school she had four different roommates. Typically, Betty would initially become "very close" to her roommate; however, in usually less than a semester, she would become disillusioned. Betty would frequently begin noting faults with her friend and eventually became angry and even hostile (e.g., throwing clothes).

Betty, who was a business major in college, met her future husband, who attended a nearby college, during her senior year. She was inordinately jealous of his friends and overly concerned that he would find cause to leave her. She frequently threatened to end the relationship to avoid future hurt. Their marriage was fairly rocky, a result mostly to Betty's discontent. Her husband described her as emotionally labile, ranging from affectionate to demanding and intimidating.

Despite the demands of raising two children, Betty worked full-time as an assembly line worker performing repetitive physical tasks. After about one year, Betty developed carpal tunnel syndrome in her right wrist. Surgical intervention was prescribed and successfully performed. Betty went back to work and developed a similar condition in her left wrist. While off from work awaiting surgery, Betty discovered a memo at her human resources office that indicated that the company had been advised that there was a risk of inducing physical injuries, such as Betty's, through the assembly line activities. They had been further advised that the risk of carpal tunnel syndrome could be greatly reduced if each employee would wear protective wrist guards. The company chose to do nothing as the wrist guards were deemed to be too expensive. Any claims for physical injuries would simply be settled.

On discovery of this memo, Betty appeared to experience a relapse of recurrent pain in her right wrist. Psychologically, she became more argumentative and seemed to experience an agitated depression. Repeated visits to her surgeon yielded no effective relief from the reiterative pain cycle in her right wrist. When the surgeon suggested she see a psychiatrist, she sought an attorney and sued the surgeon for malpractice.

Subsequently, Betty did enroll in a pain management program, but seemed to derive no relief. During a counseling session, structured as part of the pain management program, Betty angrily declared that she felt betrayed by her employer and that she wanted them to "pay for what they did." She later indicated that she "would teach them a lesson."

Respectful (Conforming) Personality Style

The respectful personality style is characterized by:

1. A highly organized, conscientious, and detail-oriented behavioral appearance;
2. Polite and respectful interpersonal conduct;
3. A logical, somewhat rigid, and potentially obsessional cognitive style;
4. A reserved, restrained affective disposition;
5. A reliable, dutiful self-image;
6. Reaction formation as a preferential ego defense mechanism;
7. Negative reinforcement (R-) as a sustaining reinforcement mechanism wherein respectful, conforming behavior protects against inappropriate behavior, making mistakes, ambiguity, and loss of control;
8. A cognitive communication orientation; and
9. The belief that trustworthiness, reliability, self-responsibility, and predictability are personal essentials in life; that proper

behavior, respect for authority, attention to details, order, congruence, taking responsibility for one's actions, and understanding are necessary personal qualities; that ambiguity, illogic, and the loss of control are anxiogenic and potentially dangerous conditions.

Case Study 6: Respectful (Conforming)

Kyle, age 27, married with two children, was born and raised the second of two sons, younger than his brother by two years. His father was a highly respected police captain and his mother a high school teacher. Both were "efficient, orderly, and strict" parents. Home life was "extremely well planned," for example, "daily and weekly schedules of responsibility were posted." The family ate their meals at the same time every day, baths were coordinated, and bedtime was at 8:30 p.m. sharp. In essence, very little in the home was left for chance. Kyle and his brother also knew that their parents would be punitive if they failed to meet the noted expectations.

Kyle and his brother had their disagreements; however, Kyle resisted expressing hostility because his parents "would not tolerate emotions and angry feelings at home." Kyle's way of adapting to his environment was to become the "good boy." By being neat, orderly, and punctual, he realized that he was likely to receive preferential parental treatment. He consistently sought his parents' advice on practically all decisions, a practice that continued throughout his life.

Kyle, although not inherently gifted intellectually, worked hard in school and was known as a rather serious and overconscientious student. Two years after graduating from high school, Kyle took the tests to become a police officer or a fire fighter–paramedic. He was accepted into the academy of the latter, and eagerly pursued this career. He met and married a fellow paramedic, and they had two children, both boys, within three years of marriage. Kyle, like his father, assumed his responsibilities with unbridled dedication and worked hard to establish his own "house rules." At work, Kyle was noted to be a stickler for details and "did everything by the book." Even when his shift was slow and his peers were watching sports on television, Kyle would adhere to a self-imposed schedule that included reviewing procedural manuals and practicing treatment techniques. His coworkers soon dubbed him "extra-mile Kyle." Kyle accepted the good-natured kidding, but deep down knew that he was mortified at the thought of making a mistake.

Responding as a driver to a call regarding a possible heart attack on a Saturday afternoon, Kyle and his partner were traveling through a busy residential community. Paying close attention to his surroundings, Kyle suddenly heard children shouting for help from his driver's side. Although Kyle knew that he and his partner were likely two minutes from their assigned destination, he reflexively and instinctively turned his head sharply toward that call for help. In less than the second it took for Kyle to turn his head, he heard his partner shout for Kyle to brake; however, it was too late. The collision that ensued confirmed Kyle's worse fears; he had run over a pedestrian.

Kyle's world, as he knew it, abruptly came to an end. Posttraumatic symptomatology developed immediately and persisted so as to subsequently warrant a diagnosis of PTSD. At the urging of his wife, Kyle sought counseling to assist with the tension that had developed within the marriage. In addition, Kyle pursued individual psychotherapy with the intent of addressing the posttraumatic discord that was now affecting his career. Kyle complained of obsessional worries around making mistakes, being unsure of himself, being ashamed to be around other paramedics, and feeling "unworthy" to be a paramedic.

Inhibited (Hesitating) Personality Style

The inhibited personality style is characterized by:

1. A watchful, vigilant, and hesitant, behavioral appearance;
2. Shy, avoidant interpersonal conduct;
3. A worrisome cognitive style;
4. An uneasy, anxious affective disposition;
5. An image of self as lonely;
6. The use of fantasy as an ego defense mechanism;
7. Negative reinforcement (R–) as a sustaining reinforcement mechanism wherein vigilance, hesitancy, avoidance serves to protect against interpersonal rejection;
8. An affective communication orientation; and
9. The belief that interpersonal affiliation is desirable but that the pain of interpersonal rejection is so severe that social avoidance becomes justified.

Case Study 7: Inhibited (Hesitating)

William, a 29-year-old unmarried man, was born and raised the youngest of two children; he had a sister who was four years older. His mother was an anxious woman who frequently abused alcohol and isolated herself. His father abused alcohol regularly and was generally dominating and rejecting. His father died in a car accident when William was 15. The accident was apparently alcohol-related.

William was essentially a "loner" throughout school. He was not gifted athletically, and despite his attempts, often found himself picked last in gym class. William was, however, quite talented at video games and spent considerable time at a local arcade. He had little self-confidence when it came to affairs of the heart, but was attracted to several girls while in high school. Much to his surprise, one of these girls asked him to a school dance. Despite his reservations about going to a dance, William took advantage of the opportunity and actually enjoyed himself. He continued dating this young woman throughout much of high school; however, she broke up with him weeks before the senior prom. William was crushed, and stayed away from dating for the next several years. He considered himself to have little say and believed that most women would likely prefer to be with someone else.

After the next couple of years, William became involved in an on-line chat room for singles and began dating women sporadically that he met there. He spent considerable time daydreaming and fantasizing about these relationships. William continued to reside with his mother, noting that she "needed me"; therefore, he could not move out. William's sister had moved several hundred miles away and was recently divorced.

William worked for the past six years as a computer programmer for a large company. He was characterized by a supervisor as an efficient and quiet worker who rarely socialized with others. William would periodically go to watch the company-sponsored softball team, but he never signed up to play fearing others might make fun of him. He experienced considerable distress, however, when several new employees were assigned to his office section. Eventually, however, he found himself physically attracted to one of the new female employees.

Not long after the hiring, William, rather uncharacteristically, agreed to meet with a longtime coworker named Bob after work to discuss the ramifications of the personnel changes. William, who drank alcohol infrequently, consumed three beers and in a vulnerable moment about one hour into their discussion disclosed to Bob his amorous feelings for his new coworker. As soon as William heard himself utter the words, he tried to minimize his comments. Bob assured him that it was no big deal.

However, within a month of the infusion of new employees, a clique formed in William's office. William very much wanted to be a part of this "in-group," but his fear of rejection kept him from asserting himself. In a short period of time, he, along with one or two others, became the object of ridicule and taunting by members of the clique. To compound matters, Bob became part of clique, and disclosed to its members William's affections for the new coworker. The jokes and taunting escalated.

Introverted (Retiring) Personality Style

The introverted personality style is characterized by:

1. A passive behavioral appearance;
2. Unobtrusive interpersonal conduct;
3. A vague cognitive style;
4. Bland affective disposition;
5. A placid self-image;
6. Intellectualization as a preferred ego defense mechanism;
7. Negative reinforcement (R−) as a sustaining reinforcement mechanism wherein introversion and withdrawal serves to protect against overstimulation;
8. A cognitive communication orientation; and
9. The belief that solitude yields comfort.

Case Study 8: Introverted (Retiring)

John, a 31-year-old unmarried man, lived a rather isolated existence. His world consisted of working and home life. John was employed as a night watchman at a large automotive parts warehouse located in the outskirts of a large metropolitan area. He lived by himself. Interpersonal contacts were limited to those through work. Even there, he was a loner, eating by himself and confiding in no one. He would routinely decline offers for informal "get-togethers" or "arranged" dates with individuals from work. John's parents had passed away five years earlier. He had no siblings. John enjoyed the solitude of his work. The job had become fundamentally routine, requiring little innovative or extemporaneous thinking.

John's life changed dramatically as a result of a fire that ignited while he was working one evening. Apparently, an electrical short circuit ignited a fuel storage container with resultant pyrotechnic displays. Although never in actual physical danger himself, John was so affected by the initial ignition and the subsequent explosions that he was unable to place the emergency call to the fire department. Maintenance personnel did eventually make the emergency call. As the fire trucks and other emergency response vehicles arrived, John seemed to become even more anxious. He reported that the lights, sirens, and general upheaval left him overwhelmed and incapable of responding.

John suffered from the development of panic attacks almost immediately. He became even more reclusive and was unable to return to work. As part of the company's work retraining program, John was referred for counseling. The psychologist recognized the phobic phenomenology and instituted a program of systematic desensitization using a graduated in vivo exposure protocol. John began to "dread" going to the counseling. He reported that his symptoms had actually increased in severity over the 10 weeks of counseling.

THE ROLE OF PERSONALITY STYLE AND THERAPEUTIC ALLIANCE WHEN TREATING PTSD

We have reviewed the eight functional and adaptive personality styles adapted from Millon's theoretical formulation (Millon & Everly, 1985). These eight "normal" personality styles, or patterns, are presented in theoretically pure form using prime exemplars. It is understood that in actuality few if any individuals are pure prototypes. Rather, they will usually consist of a constellation of primary and secondary personality characteristics.

Reflecting on the clinical case studies, we see an emergence of personologic substrates manifesting themselves in various forms that have saliency in the overall clinical picture and its response to psychotherapy. But more important, we see illuminated the essential substrates on which the therapeutic alliance may be established and cultivated. Let us now review these cases.

In the case of Randy, the therapist failed to assess the influence of personality factors in Randy's presentation. The assumption was that physical assault, in and of itself, was the etiology of the posttraumatic distress. This perspective neglected the fact that previous assaults had failed to engender similar posttraumatic distress. The therapist failed to explore what made this assault unique. The psychologist's failure to recognize the characterological injury caused by the loss of social status and the fact that Randy's aggressive behaviors may no longer be an effective defense left Randy feeling defenseless and as if the psychologist did not fully understand his problem. Thus, Randy was not engaged in the therapeutic alliance. In fact, underscoring too early in the relationship the reality that there will always be more powerful men not only served to inhibit the formation of the therapeutic alliance but was actually anxiogenic. A more effective approach to working with a forceful–aggressive patient such as Randy is to initially align with his personality-based thematic belief in the value of strength and forceful behavior but to gradually show how useful lessons may be extracted from the incident that will make the patient "wiser" and perhaps even more socially and physically effective.

In the case of the physician, James, proclaiming the obvious, that everyone makes mistakes, neglected to focus on the narcissistic injury that James had endured. To underscore the error actually threatened additional narcissistic injury. To engage the person with the confident personality type in the therapeutic alliance, the psychologist must acknowledge the unique qualities of the individual patient early in the therapeutic process. Such a maneuver serves to reduce the counterproductive "one upsmanship" and enhances the therapist's credibility. Only through an acknowledgment of James's special self-perception will the therapist ever get the opportunity to address the more florid symptom presentation.

The case of Diane who presented with a sociable/outgoing personality style represented a unique challenge. The psychologist failed to understand that Diane, although the recipient of successful plastic surgery, felt vulnerable in the wake of her injury. The simple reality was that unless the psychologist at least initially aligned with the notion of the importance of physical beauty to the patient and society, a therapeutic alliance would be impossible to formulate. Certainly, over the course of therapy, the psychologist in working with a patient such as Diane would assist in modifying the characterological overreliance on physical beauty, but to have Diane receptive to any intervention the bond of common ground must be cultivated.

As we reflect on Mary, with her cooperative/agreeing style, we see that she was responding as if her mother had died in the car crash. The issues of who was at fault and Mary's guilt over wanting to learn to drive are initially secondary concerns to the formation of the therapeutic alliance. Mary's "grief" reaction is predicated on her dependence on her mother. Alignment must acknowledge the importance of her mother's role in her life and how frightening it must be to have almost lost her. In working with patients such as Mary, recognizing the personality-based dynamic allows the therapist to more directly and effectively address other issues relevant to the accident.

In the case of Betty, possessing the sensitive personality style, her disorder created a power struggle, initially between Betty and her employer and later between Betty and her surgeon. The therapeutic alliance could only be created with Betty by recognizing the importance of, and the manifest struggle for, power. More specifically, the perceived negligence of her employer was seen by Betty as a personal attack for which they had no right nor justification to initiate. The initial focus, to address the therapeutic alignment, would need to identify functional and more adaptive means that Betty may use to reestablish a sense of self-efficacy, self-determination, and a sense of fairness.

Kyle's respectful personality represented an added barrier to the resolution of his posttraumatic distress. Kyle responded to a call for help as his training and personality would seem to dictate. Yet, in doing so, another human being was injured. Kyle found himself in a double-bind situation. Initially, his psychologist attempted to introduce the notion that some of the blame might rest with the pedestrian. Kyle resisted this tact. Kyle's personality was one that embraced the notion of self-responsibility. The therapeutic alliance must begin at this point. A common mistake made by beginning therapists is to rush to try to make it better. Any such attempts, without first aligning with the needs and realities of the patient, will create a condition wherein the therapist becomes part of the problem rather than part of the solution. Therapy may then become a debate or series of confrontations rather than movement toward the resolution of distress.

William's history is indicative of a shy and avoidant personality style. Interpersonal rejection can be devastating to an individual such as William. The therapeutic alliance begins by acknowledging the pain of interpersonal rejection and the added suffering caused by the sense of betrayal engendered by Bob violating a confidential conversation. Social skills training subsequent to such an alignment might then be pursued.

Finally, the case of John underscores the exquisite sensitivity of the introverted individual. An unusually low threshold for stimulation makes this individual vulnerable to overstimulation and catastrophic decompensation in the face of high intensity stimulation. Clearly, alignment with this sensitivity would have prevented the iatrogenic exacerbation of John's symptoms through in vivo desensitization techniques.

The eight case studies are provided simply to sensitize the reader to the importance of constructing the therapeutic alliance on firm personologic tenets. Ideally, this serves to create an ego syntonic climate within which the often tumultuous process of psychotherapeutic change may be undertaken and better tolerated.

KEY POINT SUMMARY

1. Numerous authors have emphasized the importance of establishing the therapeutic alliance as a prerequisite to successful psychotherapy (Moursand, 1993; Othmer & Othmer, 1994; Shea, 1998; Strupp, 1980; Wolberg, 1988). This task becomes an imperative in the treatment of posttraumatic distress.
2. In chapters 7 and 8, we have attempted to demystify the construction of the therapeutic alliance through the introduction of the concept of personologic alignment—in other words, aligning with the patient on core characterological processes and beliefs.
3. We have introduced the importance of aligning within two domains: (a) preferential communication process orientations (cognitive versus affective) and (b) the personality-specific thematic beliefs.
4. To better understand the nature and importance of personality-specific themes to the client, we have introduced the reader to a taxonomic system for the classification of "normal" person-

ality styles, or patterns, based on the work of Theodore Millon (Millon & Everly, 1985).

5. Millon's theory of personality allows for the construction of a matrix for classifying and better understanding variants in normal personality functioning, which is based on the three polarities of human reinforcement: source of reinforcement, instrumental reinforcement process, and the type of reinforcement preferred (R+ or R−).

6. Expanding beyond the reinforcement matrix, we used a prototypic approach to personality description wherein we used nine domains to describe, in prototypic fashion using prime exemplars, eight discrete personality styles: Behavioral style; Interpersonal conduct; cognitive style; affective expression; self-image; preferential ego defense mechanism; sustaining reinforcement pattern; preferential communication process; and governing personality-specific thematic belief.

7. Finally, case examples were used to exemplify the nature and potential importance of personologic alignment in the construction of the therapeutic alliance.

9

MITIGATING POSTTRAUMATIC STRESS

The focus of this volume is on the treatment of posttraumatic stress disorders. Yet even within a book dedicated to treatment, it seems that some discussion of prevention, or mitigation, would be warranted. In the early 1960s, Gerald Caplan (1961, 1964) wrote extensively on the concept of prevention. Caplan (1964) discussed three levels of prevention:

1. Primary prevention—in other words, social and environmental engineering designed to reduce the incidence of traumatic stressors ("attenuation of hazardous circumstances," p. 68), as well as crisis intervention or emergency mental health, ("provision of services to foster healthy coping," p. 68) designed to mitigate distress and dysfunction;
2. Secondary prevention—in other words, early assessment and treatment; and
3. Tertiary prevention—in other words, rehabilitation subsequent to exposure to the traumatic stressor.

Rather than explore methods for the reduction of traumatic stressors, we explore the mitigation of acute posttraumatic symptomatology via the provision of crisis intervention services.

The mitigation of the presence, intensity, or chronicity of posttraumatic symptomatology has historically been achieved through psychological crisis intervention. Therefore, in this chapter, we review the nature and effectiveness of crisis intervention as a means of mitigating posttraumatic reactions.

On September 11, 2001, a terrorist attack was perpetrated on the people and government of the United States in a catastrophic manner. At 8:45 a.m. Eastern Standard Time, a hijacked American Airlines Flight 11 hit Tower 1 (north) of the World Trade Center in New York City. At 9:06 a.m. hijacked United Airlines Flight 175 hit Tower 2 (south) of the World Trade Center. At 10:00 a.m., the south tower collapsed, and at 10:29 a.m. the north tower collapsed. The death toll was estimated to approach 3,000 people.

While havoc was being wrought on New York City, another hijacked airplane, American Airlines Flight 77, struck the Pentagon in Washington, DC, at 9:40 a.m.

Finally, another hijacked airplane, United Airlines Flight 93 crashed in Shanksville, Pennsylvania, at 10:37 a.m. in what appeared to be an aborted terrorist attack that was to be directed to the Washington, DC, area as well.

One of the most obvious and immediate effects of these attacks on victims present and victims removed was to underscore the need for emergency mental health.

Because both authors of this volume participated in the emergency mental health efforts beginning within hours of the attacks and spanning over the subsequent weeks and months, first-hand perspectives were engendered. The need for emergency crisis intervention was evident for both primary civilian victims and for secondary emergency response personnel. As one walked through "ground zero," as the crash sites were called, cognitive disorientation, panic, depression, anger, and disbelief could all be seen to be present in primary and secondary victims alike.

Many mental health professionals responded to the terrorist acts; some were quite effective in their ability to mitigate acute distress, and some were not. It seemed that those who were the least effective possessed little or no crisis intervention training or experience or became overwhelmed with their own countertransference reactions as they themselves became victims. We believe that being well-grounded in an understanding of the core concepts and tactical foundations of crisis intervention is a useful tool to being an effective agent for the mitigation of posttraumatic distress. Therefore, we begin this chapter by providing an overview of basic principles relevant to emergency mental health.

CORE CONCEPTS

It may be suggested that rational discourse is predicated on the consistent use of terms. Similarly, the operationalization of terminology becomes corrupted with the imprecision of that terminology. Finally, it seems that effective clinical practice is guided by a reliable conceptual foundation; thus, we begin with a brief introduction to the terms and concepts on which this chapter is based.

Crisis

To understand the nature of crisis intervention, it is certainly helpful to understand the nature of a psychological crisis. A psychological crisis may be thought of as an acute response to an aversive or otherwise challenging event wherein:

1. Psychological homeostasis has been disrupted;
2. One's usual coping mechanisms have failed; and
3. There are signs or symptoms of distress, dysfunction, impairment (adapted from Caplan, 1961, 1964).

Critical Incident

The critical incident may be thought of as a stressor event that appears to cause, or be most associated with, a crisis response; an event that overwhelms a person's usual coping mechanisms (Everly & Mitchell, 1999). All traumas are critical incidents, but not all critical incidents reach the amplitude or intensity to be considered a traumatic event.

Crisis Intervention

Crisis intervention is an urgent and acute psychological support sometimes thought of as psychological first-aid. The hallmarks of crisis intervention (based on military psychiatry) have historically been *immediacy* (early intervention), *proximity* (intervention is often done within close physical proximity to the critical incident), *expectancy* (both the person in distress and interventionist have the expectation that the intervention will be acute and goal-directed), *simplicity* (relatively concrete, uncomplicated intervention strategies that avoid complex psychotherapy-oriented tactics), *innovation* (the intervention may need to be unique and flexible enough to meet the unique demands of the event), *pragmatism* (intervention is practical, problem-focused, and goal-directed), and *brevity* (the total duration of the intervention is short, typically consisting of one to three contacts).

The specific goals of crisis intervention are:

1. Acute stabilization of symptoms and signs of distress and dysfunction (to keep things from getting worse);

2. Facilitation of symptom reduction (intervene so as to reduce acute distress and dysfunction);

3. Restoration of acute, adaptive independent functioning (successful reduction of impairment); or

4. Facilitation of access to a higher, or more continuous, level of care, if needed (based on Caplan, 1961, 1964; Everly & Mitchell, 1999).

"Debriefing"

The term *debriefing* is used generically throughout the related literature to refer to virtually any form of early psychological intervention from crisis intervention with individuals, small group crisis intervention, and even counseling with medical patients. As a result considerable semantic confusion has emerged within both qualitative, as well as empirical, discussions.

Critical Incident Stress Debriefing (CISD)

The CISD refers to one specific model of small group psychological debriefing. The CISD model was developed by Dr. Jeffrey T. Mitchell (Mitchell, 1983; Mitchell & Everly, 2001). The CISD is a seven-phase, structured small-group (3–20) discussion, usually provided 1 to 14 days after the crisis (although in mass disasters it may be used three weeks or more postincident), and was designed to mitigate acute symptoms, assess the need for follow-up psychological services, and if possible provide a sense of postcrisis psychological closure (Mitchell & Everly, 2001). Psychological closure is generally thought to mean a facilitation of psychological and behavioral rebuilding in the wake of a crisis or trauma. The CISD usually takes 1 to 3 hours to complete. It is facilitated by the members of a CISD team, usually consisting of two to four specially trained crisis interventionists. Although originally developed for emergency services and disaster response personnel, the CISD may be used with primary victims of accidents, violence, disasters, the military, and even families and children of victims.

Critical Incident Stress Management (CISM)

Critical incident stress management (CISM) is a comprehensive, integrated multicomponent crisis intervention (emergency mental health) system (see Everly & Mitchell, 1999; Mitchell & Everly, 2001, for reviews). The CISM consists of an integrated array of crisis intervention services, including, but not limited to, preincident preparation, assessment and triage, psychological first aid with individuals, pastoral crisis intervention, crisis "town meetings," small group crisis intervention, family support services, and follow-up and referral for therapy.

PSYCHOLOGICAL TRIAGE

Effective crisis intervention must certainly be predicated on effective psychological triage. How do we ascertain who most needs assistance? How do we reduce the chances that we may inadvertently interfere with normal symptom manifestations and the natural recovery process? This is the essence of psychological triage.

The basic assumption governing intervention is that most "victims" will recover using their own natural recovery mechanisms. No formal psychological intervention will be required by most of those exposed to the traumatic stressor. However, to underestimate the severity of a victim's crisis state may lead to a career-threatening, marriage-threatening, or even life-threatening condition. But to overestimate the severity, to respond too aggressively, thereby interfering with natural recovery mechanisms, may also lead to adverse consequences as well.

Although there is no crystal ball that allows us to precisely predict who will most need subsequent assistance, there are both empirical and conceptual guidelines that may help in the process of triage in a psychological crisis.

Listed next are points to consider *before* responding to a crisis, trauma, or disaster:

1. Although virtually 100% of persons directly exposed to a traumatic event will experience some degree of distress, as noted earlier in this volume, somewhere between 9% and 35% of persons exposed may develop posttraumatic stress disorder (PTSD).
2. Not every person exposed to a traumatic, or critical, incident will need subsequent psychological support from the mental health community. The fact is that most individuals possess natural recovery mechanisms that will prove quite adequate in most times of catastrophe, whether personal or communal (Everly & Mitchell, 1999; NIMH, 2002).
3. Overly aggressive crisis intervention may interfere with the natural recovery mechanisms of those very individuals whom we seek to assist (Dyregrov, 1999; NIMH, 2002). Inappropriate intervention could also further jeopardize the well-being of the victim through engendering self-doubt or imposing an undesirable stigma. In situations that are not acutely life

threatening, the passage of time is usually helpful in deescalating a volatile situation and in eroding symptoms of distress.

Therefore, the following guidelines may be considered during the crisis intervention:

1. Crisis intervention services should be considered in the wake of a disaster, trauma, or critical incident, and crisis intervention services beyond general information sessions ("town meetings") should generally be implemented on an as-needed basis. The best predictors of PTSD appear to be the following peritraumatic (occurring during, or shortly after, a critical incident) reactions:
   a. Dissociation (estrangement from self; estrangement from environment);
   b. Intense depressive symptoms, "giving up";
   c. Psychogenic amnesia;
   d. Syncope, loss of consciousness;
   e. Dysfunctional symptoms of parasympathetic nervous system activity; and
   f. Malignant symptoms of sympathetic nervous system activity—for example, panic attacks and sustained elevated heart rate that does not attenuate even under nonthreatening environmental conditions (see Everly, 1999, for a review).
2. Other symptoms that generally require attention are:
   a. Expression of suicidal or homicidal inclinations;
   b. Evidence of self-medication;
   c. Expression of violent behavior or inclinations;
   d. Severe guilt reactions, including "survivor guilt";
   e. Expressions of helplessness and hopelessness;
   f. Vegetative depressive symptoms; and
   g. Brief psychotic reactions (see Everly, 1999, for a review).
3. Finally, the restoration of normal sleep patterns, cessation of dissociative symptoms, and the restoration of a normal startle response may be among the best indicators of "recovery" from a traumatic incident.

STATE-OF-THE-ART RECOMMENDATIONS

In the wake of the terrorism of September 11, 2001, new interest was focused on the field of early psychological intervention. A series of professional meetings were convened with the goal of generating guidelines for mitigating psychological distress subsequent to disasters and mass violence.

In August of 2002, the World Psychiatric Association meeting featured a plenary session by its president Juan Lopez-Ibor on the topic of disaster mental health. Lopez-Ibor (2002) asserted that certain principles of intervention were important. Among them, he noted the following:

1. Intervention should be as immediate as possible.
2. Mental health intervention should be integrated with physical health intervention.
3. Intervention should focus on entire populations, not just primary victims.
4. Assessment and triage are important elements.
5. Verbal intervention is important, debriefings, discussions, and social support both individually and in groups.
6. The stigma against seeking treatment should be reduced.
7. The provision of adequate information is important.
8. Sensitivity to situational and cultural diversity should be emphasized.
9. Preincident training is important.
10. Finally, the role of the mental health professional should be to integrate the social, biological, and systems response to disasters.

In September of 2002, the National Institute of Mental Health published its recommendations on mental health and mass violence (NIMH, 2002). Some of the key points are summarized next:

1. Early intervention will be defined as being within four weeks of the incident or mass disaster.
2. Expect normal recovery from the majority of those initially affected.
3. Mental health services should be integrated within the overall disaster response plan.
4. Receiving intervention should be voluntary.
5. Intervention itself should be structured within a hierarchy designed to meet basic needs first (survival, safety, shelter, physical health, food, psychological health, communications).
6. The key elements of early intervention were deemed to be preincident preparation, psychological first aid, needs assessment and monitoring, outreach and information dissemination, technical assistance, fostering resiliency and natural recovery mechanisms, triage, treatment (cognitive behavioral therapy was believed to show significant potential).

7. There should be a sensitivity to diversity (cultural, occupational) with intervention provided on an as-needed basis.
8. There is limited research on mass disaster mental health. Nevertheless, cognitive and behavioral interventions show promise. Stand-alone one-on-one recitals of incident-related facts without follow-up does not show evidence of reducing risk and may be disruptive to recovery mechanisms. A new nomenclature is needed—for example, the term "debriefing" is too generic and has lost functional utility.
9. Clinical research needs to be conducted.
10. Interventions should be based on defensible empiricism.
11. The providers of early psychological intervention can include mental health professionals, medical professionals, the clergy, school personnel, emergency responders, and community volunteers operating within a sanctioned system—for example, an incident command system. Specialized training is recommended.
12. No time table for postincident follow-up exists, however, it is expected that survivors without symptoms after two months will generally not require follow-up. On the other hand, follow-up should be offered to those with acute stress disorder or preexisting psychiatric problems, the bereaved, those requiring medical or surgical intervention, those at high risk because of intense or chronic exposure, and those who request follow-up. (See NIMH, 2002, for more discussion.)

In October of 2002, the Employee Assistance Professional Association released the results of its Disaster Preparedness Task Force (EAPA, 2002). The major recommendations from this organization, which serves the mental health needs of the business and industrial sectors, are listed next:

1. Disasters affect the workplace; as a result, the employee assistance professional can play a role in assisting the employee and the organization.
2. The employee assistance professional can assist the organization in developing a disaster response plan.
3. Critical incident and disaster response should be configured as a continuum of services consisting of preincident contingency planning, acute response, postincident response, follow-up, and response review/plan revision.
4. Preincident contingency planning should consist of risk assessment, policy development, management consultation marketing, supervisory training, disaster preparedness, critical incident stress management training, and collaboration.

5. Acute response intervention should consist of on-site response, coordination of response services, collaboration, logistical and technical support, and management consultation.

6. Postincident response should consist of psychological defusings, group critical incident stress debriefings, large group crisis management briefings (company "town meetings"), assessment and referral services, self-care for interventionists.

7. Follow-up services should consist of management briefings, disaster reviews, data collection and analysis, and training.

8. The response review and disaster plan revision should entail examining policies and procedures in light of lessons learned from the most recent incident. New disaster plans should be designed if necessary and new training should be implemented if needed. Research is encouraged.

In January of 2003, a group of nongovernmental volunteer organizations providing early psychological intervention services met in Washington, DC, to review and promote shared communications and practices. This meeting was facilitated by the Emotional and Spiritual Care Committee of the National Voluntary Organizations Active in Disaster (NVOAD). The primary voluntary provider organizations present were the American Red Cross, National Organization for Victims' Assistance, the Salvation Army, and the International Critical Incident Stress Foundation. Overall consensus was reached on the following points:

1. Early psychological intervention is valued.
2. Specialized training to provide such services is necessary.
3. Cooperation among service organizations is essential.
4. Early psychological intervention should be multi-component in nature to meet the needs of those affected.
5. Early psychological intervention should be considered but one point on an overall continuum of care. (NVOAD Emotional and Spiritual Care Committee, 2003)

In addition to the aforementioned practice review meetings, several review papers have addressed the issue of early psychological intervention.

Duggan (2002) reviewed "lessons learned" in the wake of the September 11th terrorist attacks regarding the provision of psychological support services to firefighters. He concluded, "The most effective methods for mitigating the effects of exposure to trauma and tragedy, those which will help keep our people healthy and in service, are those which use early intervention, are multi-modal and multi-component. That is, they use different 'active ingredients' in the treatment of critical incident stress, and these components are used at the appropriate time with the right target group" (p. 3).

Ritchie (2002) conducted a commissioned review on the management of critical incident stress in a military environment. After personal interviews and a comprehensive review of relevant literature, his recommendations included that there is value in providing "debriefings," that early psychological intervention should only be provided after more basic physiological needs have been met, that small group crisis intervention (i.e., critical incident stress debriefings; CISD) should only be provided in a small group format, that early psychological intervention should be provided within the context of a phase-sensitive multicomponent intervention system (critical incident stress management; CISM), and that early psychological intervention may promote unit cohesion and support in response to critical incidents in the military.

Finally, in what may be the most wide spectrum review of early psychological intervention (referred to therein as "psychological debriefing") to date, Arendt and Elkit (2001) analyzed 25 controlled (70 total) primary research investigations reaching the following conclusions:

1. The term *psychological debriefing* (PD) is reflective of an amalgam of psychological interventions. This heterogeneity has contributed to a controversy pertaining to clinical effectiveness. The exact meaning of the term needs to be clarified.
2. People are generally satisfied with psychological debriefing.
3. A preventive effect was discovered when PD was used with public safety groups.
4. Single-session PD used with individuals does not appear to exert a preventive effect.
5. PD should be used only in the originally prescribed group intervention format.
6. Effective group leadership and training are important elements in positive outcome associated with PD.
7. PD may be effective at reducing costs associated with trauma.
8. The exclusive use of the prevention of PTSD as an outcome variable in the assessment of the effectiveness of PD seems inappropriate.
9. PD may have value as a clinical screening tool.
10. When evaluating the effectiveness of PD, outcome criteria other than the prevention of PTSD should be tested.

It is clear that the state of the art recommendations or emergency mental health response in the wake of trauma and mass disaster emphasize the need for a phasic, integrated multicomponent crisis-intervention system. It would appear that to be most effective, the components of such a system should be used not only with tactical proficiency and skill but with strategic insight, so that the timing of the interventions is suited to the needs of the recipient population.

A MODEL OF "SYNERGISTIC" CRISIS INTERVENTION

As a good golfer would never play a round of golf with only one golf club, a good crisis interventionist would never attempt the complex task of intervention in a crisis or disaster with only one crisis intervention technology. This point has been underscored in the various recommendations mentioned previously. Rather, what appears to be indicated is an integrated multicomponent intervention system. It will be recalled from an earlier discussion that Millon has recommended just such an intervention system to be used within the context of psychotherapy. The embodiment of Millon's personality-guided therapy is synergistic psychotherapy—in other words, using a multitude of psychotherapeutic interventions in their most effective combinations at their most appropriate times (Millon & Davis, 2000). "The palette of methods and techniques available to the therapist must be commensurate with the idiographic heterogeneity of the patient for whom the methods and techniques are intended" (Millon et al., 1999, p. 145). Thus, synergistic psychotherapy is the application of multiple intervention techniques, either simultaneously (potentiated pairings) or serially (catalytic sequences) in such a tailored manner as to specifically address the essential phenomenological elements of the extant disorder and the unique personologic elements of the individual patient, in a combinatorial manner.

A review of long-standing institutional crisis intervention programs reveals that they tend to be integrated and multicomponential in nature, as consistent with Millon et al. (2000). Variations of the multicomponent model have been adopted by numerous and diverse organizations in a wide variety of workplace settings, including the Federal Aviation Administration (FAA), the U.S. Air Force (1997 Air Force Instruction 44153), the U.S. Coast Guard (1999 COMDTINST 1754.3), the U.S. Secret Service, the Federal Bureau of Investigation (FBI), the Bureau of Alcohol, Tobacco, and Firearms (ATF), the Airline Pilots' Association (ALPA), the Swedish National Police, the Association of Icelandic Rescue Teams, the Australian Navy, the Australian Army, and the Massachusetts Department of Mental Health selecting Flannery's (1998) Assaulted Staff Action Program (ASAP). In 1996, Occupational Safety and Health Administration (OSHA) document 3148-1996 recommended the implementation of comprehensive violence/crisis intervention programs in social service and health care settings. In 1998, OSHA 3153-1998 further recommended multicomponent crisis intervention programs for late-night retail stores. It should be noted that Flannery's ASAP CISM program was chosen as one of the 10 best programs for 1996 by the American Psychiatric Association.

Reflecting back on the "palette of methods and techniques available" to the crisis interventionist, various core competencies relevant to the practice of multicomponent crisis intervention would appear to emerge; they are (a) assessment and triage; (b) individual (1:1) crisis intervention; (c) small-group crisis intervention; (d) large-group crisis intervention; (e) strategic response planning (Everly, 2002).

RESEARCH FINDINGS

The issue of the clinical effectiveness of crisis intervention, as a means of mitigating acute symptoms of distress, first emerged in the clinical literature in the 1960s. Artiss (1963) reported that the psychotherapeutic elements of immediacy, proximity, and expectancy had been used successfully in military psychiatry to reduce psychiatric morbidity and increase return to combat rates for American soldiers. Solomon and Benbenishty (1986) confirmed with Israeli soldiers what Artiss had observed with the U.S. military. These authors concluded that early intervention, proximal intervention, and the role of expectation were each associated with positive outcome. Parad and Parad (1968) reviewed 1,656 social work cases and found crisis-oriented intervention to be effective in reducing florid psychiatric complaints and in improving patients' ability to cope with stress. Langsley, Machotka, and Flomenhaft (1971) followed 300 psychiatric patients randomly assigned to inpatient treatment or family crisis intervention groups. The crisis intervention group was found to be superior in reducing the need for subsequent hospital admissions at 6- and 18-month intervals. A similar finding was recorded by Decker and Stubblebine (1972) using a single group 2.5 year longitudinal design. Bunn and Clarke (1979), in a randomized investigation of crisis counseling, found support for the effectiveness of a crisis counseling session lasting about 20 minutes and applied within an emergent context with the relatives of seriously ill medical patients. Finally, it was Bordow and Porritt (1979) who initially demonstrated, through randomized experimental design, that multicomponent crisis intervention was superior to single-component crisis tactics. Empirical evidence such as this argues for the effectiveness of early intervention, crisis-based psychological support tactics, at the same time argues against the attribution of psychotherapeutic exclusivity to traditional individual or group psychotherapy. In fact, psychotherapy has historically been contraindicated in acute crisis situations (Debenham, Sargent, Hill, & Slater, 1941).

More recently, however, some concern over the effectiveness of psychological crisis intervention arose in the relevant literature with the publication of two Australian studies. McFarlane (1988) reported on the longitudinal course of posttraumatic morbidity in the wake of bush fires. One aspect of the study found that acute posttraumatic stress was predicted by avoidance of thinking about problems, property loss, and not attending undefined forms of psychological crisis intervention (referred to as "debriefings"). However, chronic variations of posttraumatic stress disorder were best predicted by a multivariate combination of premorbid, non–event-related factors, such as a family history of psychiatric disorders, concurrent avoidance and neuroticism, and a tendency not to confront conflicts. Finally, the cohort that developed delayed onset posttraumatic stress symptoms also found their symptoms predicted by a multivariate combination of preintervention and premorbid neuroticism scores, greater property loss, and also assumed participation in the undefined crisis intervention. Although these factors, when submitted to discriminant function analysis, only resulted in the correct identification of 53% of the delayed onset group and were clearly multivariate in nature, this study is often reported as evidence for concern over the use of crisis intervention.

The second of these studies to express concern over the use of crisis intervention was that of Kenardy et al. (1996). Kenardy's investigation purported to assess the effectiveness of crisis intervention ("stress debriefings") for 62 "debriefed helpers" compared to 133 who were apparently not debriefed subsequent to an earthquake in New Castle, Australia. This study is often cited as evidence for the ineffectiveness of debriefings, yet the authors stated, "we were not able to influence the availability or nature of the debriefing" (p. 39). They continued, "It was assumed that all subjects in this study who reported having been debriefed did in fact receive posttrauma debriefing. However, there was no standardization of debriefing services" (p. 47). These rather remarkable nonattributional epistemological revelations by the authors have failed to deter critics of crisis intervention and specifically debriefing, however the term may be used.

The work of Wessely, Rose, and Bisson (1998) and Rose, Bisson, and Wessely (2002), sometimes referred to as the Cochrane Review, and by Rose and Bisson (1998), represent empirical reviews that are held out to be methodologically robust because they use only investigations using randomization. They conclude that single-session one-on-one factual recitals of traumatic events with medical patients (debriefings) have shown no ability to reduce or prevent PTSD and may cause harm to some. *However, these authors noted that no generalizations can be made from these reviewed data sets regarding group psychological debriefings and no generalizations can be made regarding crisis intervention subsequent to mass disasters.*

To paraphrase the philosopher–psychologist William James, to disprove the assertion that all crows are black, one need only find one crow that is white! Therefore, it may be suggested that to disprove the assertion that *all* debriefing are ineffectual, one need only find one debriefing that is effective.

There exist several investigations that would appear to support the use of small-group crisis intervention (small-group debriefings). Robinson and Mitchell (1993, 1995) with emergency medical services personnel; Nurmi (1999) with rescue personnel in the wake of the sinking of the *Estonia*; Wee et al. (1999) with emergency medical technicians subsequent to the Los Angeles riots; Bohl (1991) with police; Bohl (1995) with fire personnel; Chemtob et al. (1997) with health care providers subsequent to Hurricane Iniki; and Jenkins (1996) with emergency medical personnel in the wake of a mass shooting all offer varying degrees of positive outcome data supportive of small-group crisis intervention debriefing. In each of the studies cited, emergency services or other health care personnel were the recipients of the crisis intervention. Each of these studies, however, may be criticized for their lack of randomized research participant assignment. However, five of the aforementioned studies possessed a static control condition, whereas one possessed a time-lagged control. These research designs are known to be vulnerable to selection, mortality, and maturation as threats to internal validity and the selection–intervention interaction threat to external validity (Campbell & Stanley, 1963). However, the results of a meta-analysis found cumulative evidence suggesting that the CISD is, indeed, associated with desired outcome (Everly & Boyle, 1999). Watchorn (2000) has shown that group debriefings may serve to prevent the development of PTSD. More specifically, Watchorn concluded that peritraumatic dissociation predicts long-term impairment, but for those who dissociated, subsequent debriefings were associated with less long-term impairment. Similarly, Deahl et al. (2000), in a randomized investigation of the CISD model of debriefing, found CISD effective in reducing alcoholism. This investigation was conducted with 106 British soldiers involved in a United Nations' peacekeeping mission. Soldiers were randomly assigned to a debriefing condition or a no-debriefing condition. In addition, all soldiers received an Operational Stress Training Package. At the six-month follow-up, the debriefed group evidenced a lower prevalence of alcohol abuse and lower scores on psychometrically assessed anxiety, depression, and PTSD symptoms.

It should be kept in mind that the interventions cited were not designed to be stand-alone interventions. Rather, as noted earlier, crisis intervention should be multifaceted. Crisis intervention should be a multicomponent endeavor, a fact that is often forgotten in actual practice. Richards (2001) has offered evidence in support of this assertion. Richards found that the CISM multicomponent system, when compared to the singular CISD tactic, was found to be even more effective in mitigating psychological distress. This finding has relevance to the suggestion that crisis intervention should be phasic and multicomponent in nature.

The effectiveness of integrated multicomponent CISM programs has now been suggested through qualitative analyses (Dyregrov, 1997, 1998, 1999; Everly, Flannery, & Mitchell, 2000; Everly & Mitchell, 1999; Miller, 1999; Mitchell & Everly, 1997), as well as through empirical investigations and even meta-analyses (Eid, Johnsen, & Weiseth, 2001; Everly, Flannery, Eyler, & Mitchell, 2001; Flannery, 1998; Flannery, Penk, & Corrigan, 1999; Flannery, Hanson, Penk, Flannery, & Gallagher, 1995; Flannery et al., 1998; Flannery, Everly, & Eyler, 2000; Western Management Consultants, 1996). Flannery's ASAP program is an exemplary CISM crisis intervention approach (Flannery, 1998, 1999a, 1999b, 1999c) used in hospitals, clinics, and schools.

The data supporting phasic, multicomponent crisis intervention systems is largely case study empiricism or based on quasi-experimental designs. Desired, randomized controlled trials in disaster research may be near to being impossible, and when possible, are often frought with bias (Jones & Wessely, in press).

KEY POINT SUMMARY

1. "Crisis intervention is a proven approach to helping in the pain of an emotional crisis" (Swanson & Carbon, 1989, p. 2520), yet more research is clearly needed. This is true in the practice of medicine, nursing, surgery, psychotherapy, and even crisis intervention. But it seems the most prudent approach to this issue lies in an examination of not only the intervention itself but in the issues with regard to the training qualifications of the interventionists, the timing of the intervention, and the suitability of the intervention for the recipient group or the nature of the adversity (e.g., acute situational adversity versus chronic illness, ongoing psychosocial discord, physical pain, physical scarring, protracted legal difficulties, a long-term rehabilitative process, etc.). Clearly, crisis intervention technologies are best directed toward acute situational adversity, well-circumscribed stressors, and acute adult-onset traumatic reactions (Dyregrov, 1997, 1998, 1999; Everly & Mitchell, 1999; Richards, 2001). Crisis intervention is not a substitute for psychotherapy and as such should not be held to the standards of psychotherapeutic outcome. Thus, including

crisis intervention in any review of "treatments" for PTSD (Foa, Keane, & Friedman, 2000) seems questionable.

2. As noted, crisis intervention is not a form of therapy per se, nor a substitute for treatment. Crisis interventions are designed to complement more traditional psychotherapeutic services. This is readily apparent if one understands that one of the expressed goals of crisis intervention is to assess the need for continued care.

3. Dyregrov (1998) has stated, "In my opinion the debate on debriefing is not only a scientific but also a political debate. It entails power and positions in the therapeutic world. As a technique . . . [debriefings] represented a threat to the psychiatric elite" (p. 7). Certainly, at the very least, the debriefing controversy is grounded in the semantics of what actually constitutes a debriefing and the applied role of the debriefing in the overall CISM context. We agree with George Engle that rational discourse is, indeed, grounded on the use of terminology in a consistent manner and the consistent operationalization of that same terminology.

4. The use of the term *debriefing* to mean individual counseling and individual early intervention with medical patients as is practiced in the United Kingdom has resulted in considerable confusion in the existing literature. These debriefing studies were conducted with medical patients using an individualized intervention format (Bisson, Jenkins, Alexander, & Bannister, 1997; Hobbs, Mayou, Harrison, & Worlock, 1996; Lee, Slade, & Lygo, 1996; Mayou, Ehlers, & Hobbs, 2000; Small, Lumley, Donahue, Potter, & Waldenstrom, 2000). Their contribution to our understanding of crisis intervention is that (a) crisis intervention is clearly not a substitute for psychotherapy but may be perceived as helpful nevertheless (Small et al., 2000); (b) crisis intervention may not always be suitable for patients in acute medical distress because it is not a substitute for analgesia, physical rehabilitation, psychological rehabilitation, reconstructive surgery, or financial counseling; and (c) crisis intervention should not be implemented as a stand-alone tactic outside of a multicomponent intervention system.

5. Critical Incident Stress Debriefing (CISD) represents an innovation in the field of emergency mental health because it represents the first widely standardized *group* crisis intervention model (Mitchell & Everly, 2001). There exist empirical investigations that generally support the notion that small group crisis intervention may be used as a means of mitigating psy-

chological distress (Arendt & Elklit, 2001; Bohl, 1991, 1995; Chemtob et al., 1997; Everly & Boyle, 1999, in a meta-analytical investigation; Jenkins, 1996; Nurmi, 1999; Wee et al., 1999), but more research is clearly needed, especially better controlled research.

6. Finally, current recommendations in the field of early psychological intervention emphasize the need for a phasic, integrated multicomponent intervention approach (Bordow & Porritt, 1979; EAPA, 2002; NIMH, 2002; Richards, 2001).

10

NEUROLOGIC DESENSITIZATION IN THE TREATMENT OF POSTTRAUMATIC STRESS

Although the primary focus of this book is on the influence and applicability of personality in the treatment of posttraumatic stress disorder (PTSD), the two-factor theory (as reviewed in chapter 2; also see Everly, 1993b, 1995) conceptualized PTSD as an integrative psychophysiological experience, even when the traumatic event causes no overt physical harm. Consistent with the neurological hypersensitivity aspect of this model, the *Diagnostic and Statistical Manual of Mental Disorders, 4th Edition* (DSM–IV; American Psychiatric Association, 1994) has acknowledged that a major category of symptoms in the diagnosis of PTSD is "persistent symptoms of increased arousal" (p. 424) that were not present before exposure to the trauma. This increased manifest arousal is considered to be a "neurologic hypersensitivity"—in other words, a lowered functional depolarization threshold or a status of heightened activation within the subcortical limbic system and its efferent pathways (Everly, 1990, 1993b, 1995). Gellhorn (1965) labeled this form of neurological hypersensitivity as "ergotropic tuning" that, in essence, describes a preferential pattern of autonomic nervous system (ANS) activity within the sympathetic nervous system (SNS). Post (1985, 1986) has suggested that extreme stress may activate limbic structures, resulting in a condition he referred to as *behavioral sensitization*, whereby the neurological tissues themselves could become hypersensitive following repeated exposure to psychosocially related stimuli. Post's theory relied heavily on the model known as "kindling" (Goddard & Douglas, 1960) in which intense or protracted stimulation of limbic structures may result in limbic hyperfunction, affective lability, and behavioral anomalies. Furthermore, Olney (1978) asserted that excessively intense stimulation of the central nervous system (CNS) mechanisms could become toxic at the level of neural substrates, a phenomenon known as *excitatory toxicity*. Finally, Everly (1990, 1993b, 1995) has argued that PTSD is a quintessential example of the "disorders of arousal" construction.

Collectively, these theories suggest that the pathogenic thread of neurological hypersensitivity and arousal may be a core, sustaining feature of PTSD (especially when PTSD reaches extremely severe proportions), which when combined with the personologic schemas covered in this volume may lead to potentially enduring, disruptive symptoms. Thus, it seems apparent, at least theoretically, that therapeutic interventions designed to *neurologically desensitize* (defined as any intervention that serves to lower manifest arousal) and reduce overall activity within the limbic circuitry will be a useful contributing, and sometimes essential, component in the treatment of PTSD. And indeed, the Expert Consensus Panels for PTSD (Frances, 1999) has recommended that relaxation training be considered as one aspect in the treatment of PTSD. Lex (1979) suggested that this neural desensitization entails a shift from ergotropic mechanisms to a trophotropic pattern that she described in the following way:

> heightened parasympathetic discharges, relaxed skeletal muscles, and synchronized cortical rhythm points to an interconnected "tripartite" hub—the limbic system, hypothalamus, and reticular formation of the paleocortex. (p. 135)

Herbert Benson's conceptualization of the "relaxation response," which in general entails reducing neuromuscular arousal, decreasing excitatory sympathetic nervous system responsivity, and ameliorating cognitive excitation, is an example of "antiarousal therapy" designed to mitigate the impact of excessive ergotropic tuning (Benson, 1975, 1996). Consistent with the formulations of Gellhorn and Weil, we believe that consistent repeated elicitation of the relaxation state will produce a carry-over effect wherein the lowered arousal state generalizes to become a lasting trait of lowered arousal and more normal neurological sensitivity.

Existing evidence suggests that there may be a myriad of strategies and techniques to elicit the relaxation response and achieve neurologic desensitization, and no one intervention appears to be superior to another, particularly with regard to the treatment of PTSD. The best intervention is, indeed, the intervention that the patient will practice on a consistent basis. This chapter provides an overview of some of the therapeutic interventions that engender the relaxation response and neurologic desensitization.

We are most interested in using behavioral tactics for neurologic desensitization because of their ability to engender:

1. An opposing therapeutic effect that serves to lower physiological arousal and reduce the intensity of the neurological hypersensitivity; and
2. A therapeutic increase in self-efficacy and self-control as a result of their ability to serve as a means of physiological self-regulation (Bandura, 1977, 1982, 1997).

In particular we review controlled breathing, neuromuscular relaxation, biofeedback, meditation, and hypnosis. Where available, specific applicability of empirical investigations in the treatment of PTSD is reviewed. Readers interested in more comprehensive coverage of these techniques, including sample protocols, are referred to Everly and Lating (2002). Finally, we briefly review the use of psychopharmacological agents as they represent agents for neurologic desensitization.

A WORD OF CAUTION

As noted throughout this volume, therapeutic and personologic alignment is a core feature of treatment success and should be established before specific relaxation techniques are introduced. Also, before implementing any of these relaxation techniques, it is important to help PTSD patients become aware of their body sensations and to assist them in learning to recognize and identify emotions (Rothschild, 2000). Moreover, we would be remiss if we did not mention that the elicitation of the relaxation response from any of the following techniques does include the possibility of undesirable side effects (Everly, 1989). Although rare (perhaps occurring in 3% of cases), side effects may include depersonalization, excessive trophotropic states, increased anxiety, headaches, and unexpected freeing of repressed ideation (Everly, 1989). We have also included in Appendix B a handout that may be used as a fast-acting behavioral technique for physiological self-regulation.

CONTROLLED BREATHING

Controlled breathing is one of the oldest and often considered the most effective acute intervention for the mitigation and treatment of excessive stress. Virtually all forms of breathing designed to elicit the relaxation response rely on mechanisms whereby diaphragmatic breathing, which is the deepest of all breaths, is engendered through the volitional initiation of skeletal muscle control. Deep diaphragmatic breathing is a virtual standard inclusion in textbooks that teach Yoga. During the diaphragmatic breath, the diaphragm (a thin, dome-shaped sheet of muscle that separates the chest cavity and the abdomen) flattens downward during inhalation. This causes the abdominal muscles to relax and rise and thus pushes the organs in the abdominal cavity forward, which creates a partial vacuum and allows air to descend into the lungs. Therefore, the major cause of deep inhalation is the movement of the diaphragm.

Mechanisms of Action

Although the specific mechanisms involved in stress reduction via breath control may differ depending on the technique used, a general therapeutic factor is thought to be the ability of the diaphragmatic breath to induce a temporary trophotropic state. Harvey (1978), for example, noted that "diaphragmatic breathing stimulates both the solar plexus and the right vagus nerve in a manner that enervates the parasympathetic nervous system and thus facilitating full relaxation" (p. 14). Exhalation is also thought to affect the relaxation response. In fact, simply breathing out may increase parasympathetic tone (Ballentine, 1976) and serve to slightly decrease neural firing in the amygdala and hippocampus (Frysinger & Harper, 1989). It is notable that during most types of diaphragmatic breathing expiration is protracted. Monks, for example, who are exceedingly proficient in the meditative art of zazen, have demonstrated an ability to increase the exhalation phase of their respiratory cycle to approximately 75% (an average person spends less than 60% of the time exhaling; Austin, 1998). Austin (1998) also noted that breathing techniques that induce prolonged exhalation may also increase the inhibitory tone of the vagus nerve and reduce respiratory drive in the brain stem.

Research

Controlled breathing has been used effectively in the treatment of patients following myocardial infarctions (van Dixhoorn, 1998), chest pain (Van Peski-Oosterbaan, Spinhoven, van Rood, Van der Does, & Bruschke, 1997), panic disorder (DiFilippo & Overholser, 1999), and hyperventilation (Han, Stegen, de Valck, & Clement, 1986; Holloway, 1994). In a seminal study of the benefits of respiratory control, McCaul, Solomon, and Holmes (1979) investigated the effects of breathing on 105 men waiting to receive shocks to the hand. Those participants taught how to regulate their breathing to only eight breaths per minute evidenced lower subjective arousal and decreased change in skin resistance and finger pulse volume compared to the control participants instructed to breath normally. Similarly, Everly (1979) demonstrated its ability to induce a lowered state of manifest arousal in less than 120 seconds. Foa (1997) has reported on the effectiveness of using controlled breathing, as part of stress inoculation training (SIT), in the treatment of chronic PTSD in women who had been the victims of rape, aggravated assault, or noncrime trauma. Given its ease of implementation and limited adverse effects (primarily the occurrence of hyperventilation), clinicians treating PTSD patients should consider controlled breathing as a highly suitable intervention. Moreover, controlled breathing as a form of physiological self-control provides a means to enhance one's perception of control (Bandura, 1977). Reestablishing a sense of self-control and self-efficacy is an essential aspect of the recovery from many psychological disorders (Bandura, 1997), especially panic disorder and PTSD.

NEUROMUSCULAR RELAXATION

The use of muscular relaxation to induce the relaxation response is most commonly attributed to Edmund Jacobson (1938, 1978). Jacobson initially recognized that a state of psychological relaxation could be induced by first relaxing the skeletal musculature. Jacobson's approach was to enlist a series of progressive muscular contractions and extensions to systematically activate major muscle groups. His system was referred to as "progressive relaxation." Subsequent writers altered Jacobson's elaborate protocols for tensing and relaxing major muscle groups to attain a state of relaxation. Everly (1989) recommended that a "passive" variant of progressive relaxation might be useful wherein the patient did not actually tense and relax muscles but simply used imagery focused on relaxing the skeletal musculature.

Mechanisms of Action

A convergence of literature in the area of stress-related manifestations refers repeatedly to the central role of the neuromuscular system (Benson, 1983; Everly, 1995; Gellhorn, 1958a, 1958b, 1964; Malmo 1975; Weil, 1974). Gellhorn, a preeminent figure in the field, demonstrated through a series of well-designed experiments that the nuclear origin of the sympathetic nervous system, the posterior hypothalamus, is dramatically affected by neuromuscular proprioceptive feedback from the skeletal musculature (1958a, 1958b, 1964).

Jacobson (1978) suggested that the core therapeutic actions of the neuromuscular–relaxation system reside in having the patient *learn* the difference between tension and relaxation. This learning is based on having the patient enhance his or her awareness of proprioceptive neuromuscular impulses that originate at the peripheral muscular levels and increase with striate muscle tension. According to Jacobson, these afferent proprioceptive impulses are major determinants of chronic diffuse anxiety and overall stressful sympathetic arousal. Once the patient learns adequate neuromuscular awareness, he or she may then effectively learn to reduce excessive muscle tension by consciously and progressively "letting go" or reducing the degree of contraction in the selected muscles. Jacobson referred to his system as progressive relaxation in part because the participant tenses (contracts) and then relaxes selected muscles and muscle groups in a predetermined manner to achieve the desired effect of relaxation.

Research

Neuromuscular relaxation, including Jacobson's progressive relaxation training, has demonstrated effectiveness for conditions such as vascular and muscle tension headaches (Blanchard et al., 1991), peptic ulcers (Thankachan & Mishra, 1996), hypertension (Argas, Taylor, Kraemer, Southam, & Schneider, 1987), and tinnitus (Jakes, Hallam, Rachman, & Hinchcliffe, 1986). Moreover, neuromuscular relaxation has been shown to decrease general arousal and engender the development of a calmer attitude (McGuigan, 1991).

The use of progressive muscle relaxation, used as part of a systematic desensitization regimen, demonstrated effectiveness in reducing symptoms of physiological reactivity, panic, and intrusion, in a man with a 10-year history of PTSD, and has been suggested as an alternative treatment to intensive exposure therapy for some chronic cases of PTSD (Frueh, de Arellano, & Turner, 1997). Applied muscle relaxation also demonstrated initial and 3-month follow-up effectiveness in a sample of 36 outpatients diagnosed with PTSD (Vaughan et al., 1994). Other studies have, however, found progressive relaxation training to be less effective than the use of exposure (Rothbaum, Meadows, Resick, & Foy, 2000) or self-exposure combined with cognitive restructuring (Echeburua, de Corral, Zubizarreta, & Sarasua, 1997), although integrative treatment models that incorporate muscle relaxation, along with interventions such as cognitive restructuring, concentration skills, role play, and exposure therapy have been proposed (Best & Ribbe, 1995; Hiley-Young, 1990). However, consistent with Bandura's (1977, 1982, 1997) notion of increasing self-efficacy through physiological self-regulation, we believe that neuromuscular relaxation training using whatever method the patient will reliably use can be an effective therapeutic tactic.

BIOFEEDBACK

The term *biofeedback* was reportedly coined at the inaugural meeting of the Biofeedback Research Society in 1969 as a shortened version of "biological feedback." Biofeedback may be conceptualized as a procedure in which data regarding an individual's biological activity are collected, processed, and relayed back to the person so he or she can modify that activity. An operant learning paradigm may then be inferred. The components of any given biofeedback strategy should include the following elements:

1. A means of detecting physiologic events (an electrode, a thermistor, etc.);
2. A means of amplifying the physiological signal;
3. A means of quantifying the physiologic event into meaningful data points;
4. Ideally, a means of recording and storing the acquired physiological data; and
5. A means of transducing the physiologic event signals into a useful feedback display (auditory tones, lights, numeric displays), thereby closing the "feedback loop."

There are several different types of biofeedback used to alleviate stress-related anomalies, including electromyographic (EMG), temperature, electroencephalographic (EEG), and electrodermal (EDR).

Mechanisms of Action

EMG biofeedback relies on an instrument (myograph) that is used to measure electrical impulses emitted from the efferent motor neurons innervating the skeletal musculature. Most commonly, noninvasive sensors are placed on the skin. One may place the sensors over virtually any striated muscle, although frontalis and trapezius muscles biofeedback have traditionally been used for low-arousal training because of their putative utility as a general index of arousal. The impulse is amplified and processed by the machine and produces numeric data, a display of lights, a meter deflection, a sound, or any combination of these. EMG data are measured in microvolts, which is one-millionth of a volt, and is used by participants to modify muscle tension.

The use of temperature biofeedback is based on the premise that peripheral skin temperature is a function of vasodilation and constriction. Thus, when the peripheral blood vessels are dilated, more blood is flowing through them, and the skin is warmer. By measuring the temperature in the extremities, it is possible to get an indication of the amount of constriction of the blood vessels. Vascular constriction and dilation are controlled by the sympathetic portion of the autonomic nervous system, thus the utility of using this variable as an index of arousal. Thermal biofeedback typically uses a heat-sensitive thermistor attached to the patient's finger that is then connected to an instrument that transforms the signal to either lights, sounds, or numbers that are displayed and used by the patient to acquire voluntary control over the skin temperature. The usual strategy involves teaching the patient to elevate skin temperature because such state increases are usually associated with episodic relaxation and a lowering of sympathetic nervous system tone.

EEG biofeedback is based on the premise that various brain wave patterns correlate with various states of consciousness and activity. Brain waves have been divided into four categories—alpha, beta, theta, and delta—depending on their predominant frequency (number of cycles per second) and amplitude (the number of neurons firing synchronously). Alpha waves, characterized by a frequency of 8 to 13 cycles per second and an amplitude of 20 to 100+ microvolts, are related to an awake relaxed state characterized by calmness and passive attention. Beta waves, which occur at a frequency of 14 or more cycles per second to as high as 80 cycles per second with low amplitude, are related to an awake attentive state or when one is aroused. Theta waves, which are characterized at 4 to 7 cycles per seconds and an amplitude of 20 microvolts or less, are considered part of the daydreaming state. Delta waves occur from .5 to less than 4 cycles per second and are associated with deep sleep. Thus, when one is resting, dominant EEG activity is in the alpha and theta range, whereas excitement shifts brain activity to the beta range. The most simplistic EEG paradigms usually involve having the patient attempt to generate alpha and theta activity from areas of the brain not usually known to generate such activity during the waking state.

Electrodermal biofeedback is a generic term that refers to the electrical characteristics of the skin. The galvanic skin response (GSR) is the oldest and most commonly used form. Generally, variation of the skin's electrical characteristics is a function of sympathetic neural activity, and more specifically, what is being measured is the conductance and resistance of sweat-gland activity. The most direct form of neurologic desensitization training involves teaching the patient to lower the directly measured electrical activity of the sympathetically innervated sweat glands. Reliability has historically been a challenge within this measurement domain.

Research

The various biofeedback modalities described have been shown to have applicability to a wide variety of stress-related clinical problems. These applications include, but are not necessarily limited to, vasoconstrictive syndromes (Green & Green, 1989; Thompson et al., 1999), bruxism (Biondi & Picardi, 1998), generalized arousal (Rubin, 1977), attention deficit hyperactivity disorder (Baumgaertel, 1999; Lubar, Swartwood, & O'Donnell, 1995), migraine headaches (McGrath, 1999), and urinary incontinence (Burgio & Goode, 1997; Butler, Maby, Montela, & Young, 1999; Johnson & Ouslander, 1999).

Biofeedback modalities have also been used specifically for PTSD, although the preponderance of the recent data appears to be assessment-, as compared to treatment-, related. However, we present the following areas of assessment with the recognition that developing objective psychophysiological indicators of PTSD has become increasingly relevant in determining treatment efficacy. Such measures may also have relevance for legal processes. For example, facial EMG reactivity (Carlson, Singelis, & Chemtob, 1997), eye-blink startle response (Grillon, Morgan, Southwick, Davis, & Charney, 1996), quantitative EEG parameters distinguishing PTSD patients from a control sample (Begic, Hotujac, & Jokic-Begic, 2001), EEG arousal during sleep (Woodward, Murburg, & Bliwise, 2000), and EMG, EDR, and heart rate (HR) responses to acoustic stimuli (Orr, Lasko, Metzger, & Pitman, 1997) are some of the recent assessment areas.

Although the treatment data using biofeedback is limited and somewhat equivocal (Silver, Brooks, & Obenchain, 1995), Carlson (1996) reported initial efficacy by using multisite EMG biofeedback (head, neck, upper back, and forearm) for 12 treatment sessions combined with home practice, in a sample of 19 Vietnam War combat veterans, 10 of whom were in the EMG relaxation group. Carlson (1996) noted the following advantages of combining relaxation with biofeedback: (a) its relative simplicity as compared to other therapy approaches with PTSD patients; (b) the ability to enhance patient motivation (i.e., their perception of control; (c) the use of physiological printouts and daily logs; and (d) the ability to objectify physiological change as a result of treatment.

MEDITATION

Meditation, in most Western cultures, refers to the act of thinking, planning, pondering, or reflecting. In the Eastern tradition, however, meditation is a growth-producing experience along more existential dimensions, where the overarching goal is one of attaining enlightenment. For the general purpose of this chapter, we consider meditation to be the autogenic practice of a variety of techniques that can induce the relaxation response by using a focal device. A focal device is a stimulus or something to focus awareness or dwell on. It may include mental repetition in the form of a word, phrase, or prayer (generally referred to as "mantra" meditation); physical repetition; visual concentration; or problem contemplation.

Mechanisms of Action

Although more than 60 years of scientific study have yet to determine the exact mechanisms of how meditation works, the role of the focal device is considered by many to allow the intuitive, nonegocentered mode of thought processing (thought to be activity from the brain's right neocortical hemisphere) to dominate consciousness instead of the more dominant ego-centered mode of processing (associated with the left hemisphere). However compelling, other researchers believe that it may be somewhat inaccurate to consider meditation as an exclusive right-hemisphere experience. Several researchers, using EEG in addition to other performance data, have suggested that the left to right hemispheric shift may occur in the beginning stages when one is learning meditation, but is unlikely to be as pronounced, or even occur at all, in experienced and well-trained meditators (Earle, 1981; Pagano, 1981). Although certainly noteworthy, because most people using meditation for relaxation purposes will likely be considered novices, the notion of a left to right hemispheric shift remains a viable explanation (Carrington, 1993). Other data suggest that meditation may produce other alterations in brain wave activity, including bursts in theta wave activity (Herbert & Lehmann, 1977), increased EEG coherence (Jevning, Wallace, & Beideback, 1992), and episodes of microawakening and microsleep (Austin, 1998), leading to a subjective experience of extraordinary awareness often referred to in the East as *nirvana* or *satori*. In its simplest form, meditation may simply be a restful stimulus to dwell on.

Research

Meditation has been used in a wide array of stress-related therapeutic applications (Sethi, 1989), including generalized arousal (Astin, 1997; Shapiro, Schwartz, & Bonner, 1998), anxiety disorders (Kabat-Zinn et al., 1992) and phobias (Bordeau, 1972). It has also been used effectively in the treatment of psoriasis (Kabat-Zinn et al., 1998), hypertension (Barnes, Schneider, Alexander, & Staggers, 1997), coronary artery disease (Buselli & Stewart, 1999), and chronic pain (Kabat-Zinn, Lipworth, & Burney, 1985). Regarding PTSD, case reports have purported the efficacy of meditation as part of a treatment protocol for chronic PTSD (Khouzam, 2001; Krippner & Colodzin, 1989). Moreover, in a study comparing the efficacy of a three-month transcendental meditation program versus three months of psychotherapy in a sample of 18 Vietnam veterans with PTSD symptomatology (10 of whom were in the transcendental meditation group and 8 of whom were in the psychotherapy group), Brooks and Scarano (1985) reported that the participants in the meditation treatment group had fewer symptoms of PTSD, reduced depression and anxiety, decreased alcohol consumption, and less family problems when compared to those in the psychotherapy group.

HYPNOSIS

According to Division 30 (Psychological Hypnosis) of the American Psychological Association, *hypnosis* is defined as "a procedure during which a health professional or researcher suggests that a client, patient, or subject experience changes in sensations, perceptions, thought, or behavior. The hypnotic context is generally established by an induction procedure" (Kirsch, 1994, p. 143). Hypnotic induction should be tailored to fit the individual; however, most inductions begin with the patient sitting comfortably while focusing on an identified target. The purpose of the induction, combined with deepening techniques, is to facilitate an experience of focused concentration with concurrent peripheral muscle relaxation along with increased suggestibility (Spiegel, 1994). Although there continues to be a lack of consensus regarding the mechanism of action related to the hypnotic process, Gruzelier (2000) has proposed that it entails an integrated, comprehensive system that incorporates the roles of cognition, neuropsychological dissociation, neurobiology, interpersonal, and environmental factors.

Mechanisms of Action

It is noteworthy that Division 30 has stated that hypnosis is not a type of therapy, like psychoanalysis or behavior therapy. Instead, it is used to facilitate psychotherapy. Thus, hypnosis is a technique that serves as an amplifier of or an extension to therapy. For example, Kirsch, Montgomery, and Sapirstein (1995), in a meta-analysis of studies using hypnosis as an adjunct to cognitive–behavioral therapy, reported a mean effect size of .87. Some of the clinical areas where hypnosis has been applied include phobic behavior (Morgan, 2001), obsessions (Taylor, 1985), obesity (Barabasz & Spiegel, 1989), functional infertility (Gravitz, 1995), enhancement of life (Dowd, 2000), and generalized stress management (Faymonville et al., 1997).

Research

As compared to the other relaxation techniques reviewed in this chapter, there is a clearly delineated history of the use of hypnosis for trauma-related symptoms. Pierre Janet, widely regarded as the first psychologist to formulate a systematic therapeutic approach to posttraumatic psychopathology, described more than 100 years ago the successful use of hypnotic techniques for the treatment of traumatic memories, life-threatening conditions, and enhanced relaxation (Cardeña, Maldonado, van der Hart, & Spiegel, 2000; van der Hart et al., 1995). Hypnosis was also used as a form of frontline psychotherapy and surgical anesthesia during World War I and World War II for symptoms of soldier's heart, shell shock, and combat fatigue (Gravitz & Page, 2002).

Cardeña et al. (2000) have suggested several specific ways in which hypnosis can be used in the treatment of PTSD. For example, they asserted that hypnosis may be used to help confront the memories associated with a traumatic event, facilitate the integration associated with a dissociative experience, provide different ways to conceptualize the trauma into more manageable images, address embarrassing or painful aspects or emotions, and enhance one's perception of control. The authors also provide, however, a cautionary note about the possibility of false memories occurring in highly hypnotizable individuals, and suggest that their occurrence may be a result of the types of questions asked or by general misperceptions about hypnosis (Brown, Scheflin, & Hammond, 1998; McConkey & Sheehan, 1995).

The recent efficacy of hypnosis on PTSD symptoms has been confined primarily to case studies following traumatic events such as industrial accidents (Jiranek, 2000), armed robberies (Ffrench, 2000), home burglaries (Lumsden, 1999), sexual assaults and rape (Desland, 1997; Manning, 1996), and the Holocaust (Somer, 1994). The lone randomized control study examining the efficacy of hypnotherapy compared it with psychodynamic psychotherapy and systematic desensitization on 112 participants with PTSD according to *DSM–III* criteria (Brom, Kleber, & Defares, 1989). Results revealed that for the 29 participants receiving an average of 14.4 sessions of hypnotherapy, there was a significant decrease in avoidance and intrusive symptoms.

Consistent with the formulations of Gellhorn and Weil, chronic repeated practice of techniques that induce a lowered state of arousal are thought to generalize to a chronic state of lowered arousal (Stoyva & Carlson, 1993). The value of the aforementioned behavioral interventions is not limited to their demonstrated ability to induce a relaxation response and thereby induce a state of neurological desensitization (the antithesis of the neurologically sensitized state of heightened arousal), but of equal importance is their ability to aid in physiological self-regulation and control, one of the four elements of self-efficacy (Bandura, 1977, 1997) and thus potentially useful in a direct contradiction of feelings of helplessness and loss of control that accompanies PTSD.

Psychotropic Medication

The Expert Consensus Panels for PTSD (Frances, 1999) have recommended the following guidelines for an overall treatment strategy for PTSD:

1. In older adolescents and nongeriatric adults with acute, mild PTSD (duration less than three months), psychotherapy should be initially administered. If no response, switch to another psychotherapeutic intervention or medication.
2. In older adolescents and nongeriatric adults with mild, chronic PTSD, psychotherapy or a combination of psychotherapy and medication should be initiated.
3. In adolescents and nongeriatric adults with more severe, acute, or chronic PTSD, psychotherapy or a combination of psychotherapy and medication should be used.

    Regarding the general selection of psychopharmacologic agents, the panel recommended:
    a. Starting with a selective serotonergic reuptake inhibitor (SSRI) for at least an 8-week trial. Sertraline (Zoloft) is the only medication currently approved for the treatment of PTSD;
    b. If no response, the panel recommended switching to antidepressants such as nefazodone (Serzone) or venlafaxine (Effexor XR).
    c. If a partial response is achieved, consideration should be given to adding a mood stabilizer such as divalproex (Depakote).

In the most severe cases of PTSD, it seems clear that a trial of psychotropic medication should be considered. If the underlying physiological substrates of PTSD reach convulsive and potentially self-sustaining proportions (kindling), medication may be the only intervention that can break the pathognomonic cycle.

In a review of psychopharmacology and PTSD, Platman (1999) has indicated that pharmacological agents may be selectively targeted toward specific aspects of the posttraumatic syndrome, if the physician deems such an approach warranted. The Expert Consensus Panels (Frances, 1999) have similarly noted that medications can be used to target especially problematic symptoms. An integration of these sources yields the following psychopharmacologic interventions for potential consideration:

1. *Learned helplessness:* clonidine, benzodiazepines, tricyclics, monamine oxidase inhibitors (MAOIs);

2. *Hyperstartle:* clonidine;
3. *Intrusive ideation:* MAOIs, selective serotonergic reuptake inhibitors (SSRIs) such as sertraline (Zoloft), paroxetine (Paxil), fluoxamine (Luvox), fluoxetine (Prozac), citalopram (Celexa);
4. *Panic:* alprazolam (Xanax), clonazepam (Klonopin);
5. *Depressed mood, numbing, avoidance:* SSRIs, nefazodone, venlafaxine;
6. *Impulsive rage:* lithium, carbamazepine;
7. *Sleep disturbance:* trazodone;
8. *Guilt or shame:* SSRIs, nefazodone (Serzone), venlafaxine (Effexor XR);
9. *Difficulty concentrating:* SSRIs, nefazodone, venlafaxine; and
10. *Flashbacks:* SSRIs, nefazodone, venlafaxine.

(Caution should be taken when benzodiazapines are used with patients with addictive potential. If psychotic symptoms emerge, consideration should be given to haloperidol [Haldol], olanzapine [Zyprexa], or other antipsychotic medications.)

KEY POINT SUMMARY

1. According to the *Diagnostic and Statistical Manual of Mental Disorders, 4th Edition* (American Psychiatric Association, 1994), a major category of symptoms in the diagnosis of PTSD involves increased physical arousal.
2. The arousal component of PTSD has been associated with hypersensitivity within the CNS, particularly the structures of the limbic system. Gellhorn (1965) labeled neurological hypersensitivity, particularly preferential responding of the sympathetic part of the ANS, as "ergotropic tuning."
3. Conversely, the relaxation response is engendered by reducing neuromuscular arousal, decreasing excitatory neurotransmitter responsivity, and decreasing cognitive excitation (Benson, 1975, 1996). The shift from a predominant ergotropic tuning response to a more active parasympathetic nervous system discharge has been described as movement toward a trophotropic pattern.
4. Thus, relaxation techniques designed to mitigate neurologically based hyperarousal should be a useful component of the overall treatment strategy for PTSD.

5. The Expert Consensus Panels for PTSD have recommended relaxation training as one aspect in the overall treatment plan for PTSD (Frances, 1999).

6. This chapter has provided a brief overview of the relaxation techniques of controlled breathing, neuromuscular relaxation, biofeedback, meditation, and hypnosis that have all been used successfully in treating a variety of anxiety-related disorders.

7. Controlled breathing, primarily diaphragmatic breathing, has been associated with inducing a temporary trophotropic state (Harvey, 1978), and given its relatively simplistic implementation, may also enhance a PTSD patient's perception of control or self-efficacy (Bandura, 1977).

8. Neuromuscular relaxation basically relies on learning the difference between tension and relaxation—or more technically, the awareness of the effect of proprioceptive impulses in the peripheral musculature. The overall results of data on the use of neuromuscular relaxation as part of a treatment protocol with PTSD patients have been equivocal; however, several studies have noted its efficacy (Best & Ribbe, 1995; Frueh, de Arellano, & Turner, 1997), especially as a means of lowering arousal (McGuigan, 1991).

9. Biofeedback may be considered a procedure that collects individual biological activity, processes it, and then relays it back to the person so he or she can modify that activity. The various types of biofeedback include EMG, temperature, EEG, and EDR. Although the primary use of biofeedback in relationship to PTSD has been in the area of assessment, there are data, albeit limited, that support its treatment efficacy (Carlson, 1996). More important, however, various forms of biofeedback have consistently been shown to be effective as means of lowering arousal—in other words, achieving neurological desensitization.

10. Meditation may generally be considered the autogenic practice of a variety of techniques that can induce the relaxation response by using a focal device. Although the exact mechanism of action remains elusive, suggested theories include a shift in the brain's hemispheric dominance from left to right as well as alterations in EEG activity. Case studies (Khouzam, 2001; Krippner & Colodzin, 1989) and a controlled investigation have noted the utility of using meditation with PTSD symptoms (Brooks & Scarano, 1985). Once again, however,

the utility of meditation in a treatment program for PTSD may be inferred from its demonstrated ability to lower arousal as has been repeatedly demonstrated (Astin, 1997; Kabat-Zinn et al., 1992).

11. Hypnosis is conceptualized as a procedure whereby a person may experience alterations in perceptions, thoughts, behaviors, or sensations following some form of induction process. It is noteworthy that hypnosis is not a form of therapy; instead, it is used to facilitate or enhance other forms of psychotherapy. Hypnosis has been used and documented in the treatment of trauma for more than a century, and Cardeña et al. (2000) have identified several specific ways in which hypnosis can be used to treat PTSD.

12. Finally, as the severity of PTSD increases, the neurologically sensitized nervous system is thought to play an increasingly important role in the perpetuation of the disorder, perhaps even reaching convulsive proportions. As a result, the use of psychotropic medications should be considered as a means of chemically inducing a neurological desensitization process in moderate to severe cases of PTSD or for other cases where in the clinical judgment of the physician such medication might prove valuable. SSRIs and anticonvulsant medications may prove particularly valuable in the treatment of PTSD and borderline personality disorder. Sertraline (Zoloft) is currently the only medication specifically approved for the treatment of PTSD, although one may anticipate other SSRIs being used.

11

FROM THE THERAPEUTIC ALLIANCE TO TRAUMA RESOLUTION: RESTORING ASSUMPTIVE WORLDVIEWS AND INTEGRATING THE TRAUMATIC EVENT

As explained earlier in this volume, human beings require, therefore they create, explanatory assumptive worldviews, or *Weltanshauung*, which provide order and meaning to the world. They provide safety through the provision of a set of rules, explanatory principles, and general behavior guidelines. In toto, these worldviews are imperatives. They serve to:

1. Set expectations for those things as yet unseen;
2. Provide meaning to the ambiguous;
3. Provide a sense of control over those things that may be otherwise uncontrollable; and
4. Provide an imperative sense of safety and protection against those things for which the individual possesses no other means of protection.

Let us briefly review what we believe are the core assumptive worldviews that were discussed in detail earlier in this volume:

1. The belief that the world is fair and just;
2. The belief that certain people, or types of people, can be trusted and relied on;
3. The need for safety (via understanding, prediction, or behavioral control);
4. The belief in oneself as a fundamentally competent and good person; and
5. The belief in an order and congruence to all things (e.g., faith, religion, science, etc.).

There exist numerous variations on these themes, but we believe that these represent the foundational and core assumptive worldviews most relevant to the study of posttraumatic stress disorder (PTSD).

Worldviews exert their greatest overall importance early in human psychosocial development largely because they may represent the child's primary defense system and overall source of protection (for, example the assumptive belief that mother and father will always be good to the child and will always protect the child). As the child ontogenetically progresses, assumptive beliefs become less rigid and more flexible in a healthful manner.

The traumatic event is any event that threatens, violates, or destroys an individual's assumptive worldview. The psychological goals of therapeutic intervention, therefore, become clear:

1. Restoring the assumptive worldviews (*Weltanschauung*); and
2. Integrating the traumatic event in such a way that the world is understandable, predictable and, ostensibly, safe through the synergistic use of personality-guided interventions.

In this chapter we review specific approaches for addressing the psychological hypersensitivity (the threatened or contradicted worldview) as depicted within our two-factor neuropersonologic formulation. In doing so, we draw on, and to some degree integrate, the contributions of Janet, (1919/1976), Bandura (1977, 1982, 1997), Janoff-Bulman (1992), Horowitz (1986), McCann and Pearlman (1990), Lerner (1980), Montado and Lerner (1998), Herman (1992), Taylor (1983), Millon (Millon et al. 1999), and Everly (1989, 1993a, 1993b, 1994, 1995).

PRINCIPLES OF RECOVERY AND RESTORATION

Before reviewing interventions specifically for the treatment of threatened or destroyed worldview formulations, let us briefly review the overall strategic plan once again. It will be recalled from the introduction to Part III that we advocate a strategic therapeutic approach to the treatment of PTSD wherein both phenomenological factors of the disorder are targeted.

Janet (1919/1976) appeared to advocate a two-pronged approach to the treatment of psychological trauma:

1. Regulation of intense arousal; and
2. Making intellectual sense out of the traumatic experience.

This approach is consistent with Everly's (1989, 1993a, 1993b, 1994, 1995) neurocognitive approach to the treatment of posttraumatic distress. Everly has advocated a two-factor strategic formulation wherein the therapist:

1. Employs methods for neurologic desensitization; and
2. Attempts to reintegrate a functional worldview.

Both Janet's approach and Everly's recommendations are consistent with Millon's (Millon et al., 1999) synergistic personality-guided therapy recommendations wherein the therapist, choosing from a variety of therapeutic tactics, selects those interventions that are best suited to the needs of the patient.

Thus, our overall therapeutic goals consist of:

1. Using a personality-guided approach to establishing the therapeutic alliance and creating the foundation for the reconstruction of a safe world (preferential process and thematic belief mechanisms);
2. Achieving neurologic desensitization, wherein techniques are used to diminish the intensity of the pathognomonic ergotropic state of neurological hypersensitivity and increase perceptions of self-efficacy; and
3. Restoring personality-based assumptive worldviews and integrating the traumatic event.

RESTORING ASSUMPTIVE WORLDVIEWS AND INTEGRATING THE TRAUMATIC EVENT: A BRIEF REVIEW

Taylor (1983), in the context of her studies on trauma and victimization, has written cogently on the ability of the human psyche to naturally recover from adversity. She noted, "These self-curing abilities are a formidable resource" (Taylor, 1983, p. 1161). Not only are they important social psychological characteristics to understand as part of crisis and victim phenomenology, but they are important dynamic healing forces that may prove of great value if harnessed or augmented by the therapist. But to be effectively harnessed or augmented, the therapist must first understand their nature. Taylor suggested three self-curing forces exist.

1. Gaining a sense of understanding with regard to the traumatic experience. Recovery is facilitated as the patient discovers reasonable and functional answers to these commonly asked questions:
   a. What caused this trauma to occur?
   b. What personal meaning does this event now have for the person in crisis?
2. Gaining a sense of mastery over the event and one's life in the wake of the crisis. Recovery is facilitated as the patient discovers reasonable and functional answers to these commonly asked questions:
   a. What can be done to control the traumatic event?
   b. How can the adverse reaction to the event be mitigated?
   c. How can the trauma be avoided in the future?
3. Gaining a sense of self-enhancement from the traumatic event. According to Taylor, self-enhancement is often achieved through a process of *comparison*. Taylor, Lichtman, and Wood (1984) have suggested that there are five commonly used comparative strategies:
   a. Comparing oneself with other crisis victims who experienced less fortunate outcomes (downward comparison).
   b. Focusing on one selective aspect of the crisis event, or outcome, that would allow the victim to seem advantaged.
   c. Creating hypothetical worst-case scenarios ("It could have been worse").
   d. Recognizing some beneficial outcome attributed to the crisis event.
   e. Recognizing that the rate of personal recovery is exceptional compared to others or that which would be expected.

JANOFF-BULMAN'S SHATTERED ASSUMPTIONS

Janoff-Bulman acknowledged that coping in the wake of trauma and victimization involves cognitive and emotional evaluative systems. She noted, "When coping is successful, both cognitive and emotional evaluate systems are 'satisfied'" (1992, p. 94). According to Janoff-Bulman (1995), "Coping with violent victimization involves coming to terms with the cognitive disorganization precipitated by the experience . . . from a cognitive perspective, the key to the victim's recovery process is the reestablishment of an integrated, organized set of basic assumptions or schemas" (p. 79). Focusing on the victim's assumptive world and relying on the individual interpretation of the victim allows a better understanding and appreciation of his or her response. Janoff-Bulman stated, "The survivor must rebuild shattered assumptions from prior viable assumptive worlds. Reexperiencing the event through unbidden thoughts and images is primarily in the service of this crucial cognitive reconstruction process" (1992, p. 106).

Janoff-Bulman presented three primary strategies used by survivors to help repair and rebuild their assumptions about the world:

1. The first involves appraisals based on comparisons with others where constructs such as "It could have been worse" and "I'm coping well" are used, not to reflect on others suffering as much as to allow the victim to feel better about her- or himself.
2. The second is an interpretation of one's personal role in the victimization that involves self-attributional strategies such as behavioral self-blame and characterological self-blame. Behavioral self-blame invokes the notion in the survivor that there is something that they could have done differently which in turn allows them a belief about control and a sense that the world can remain just if they do things differently. According to Janoff-Bulman (1992), "characterological self-blame is es-teem-related and corresponds to the more popular notions of self-blame associated with depression" (p. 125).
3. The third strategy focuses on ways to discover purpose or attempts by survivors to find or make meaning of the possible lessons learned from the experience.

In a seminal study by Janoff-Bulman and Wortman (1977), interviews were conducted at length with 29 survivors of paralyzing accidents ranging from auto accidents, industrial accidents, and random gunshots. Of the 29, 21 participants seemed to make sense of the occurrence by removing a sense of injustice of their fate. In fact, Janoff-Bulman and Wortman noted that 63% of the survivors used behavioral self-blame for at least part of the accident.

LERNER'S JUST WORLD

Lerner (1980) and Montada and Lerner (1998) proposed other tactics that may be used by people to help ameliorate or eliminate threats to the belief in a just world. Some of these tactics are predicated on the notion of acceptance of the "reality of injustice" and ways of dealing with it. For example, recognizing that agencies and resources exist that help victims and those less fortunate and appreciating that the taxes we pay to fund such agencies allow us to balance the potential risks and benefits of an emotional investment and personal involvement. Other tactics rely on more cognitive restructuring methods such as reinterpretation of the cause, outcome, or the character of the victim involved in the event. As demonstrated by a number of experimental outcomes (see Montada & Lerner, 1998, for a comprehensive review), these types of tactics have consistently resulted in a greater propensity to blame victims for their misfortune and a greater acceptance of general social inequalities. Reichle, Schneider, and Montada (1998) have recently demonstrated, with the use of cross-lag associations, that individuals who engaged in cognitive defenses associated with belief in a just world (i.e., blaming victims) at initial testing had higher ratings of belief in a just world at the time of later assessment. The implication of this finding is that condemning victims is not only a consequence of just world beliefs, but may actually function as a means of defending and even enhancing that belief.

Other strategies have also been used to preserve the belief in a just world (Lerner, 1980, 1998; Maes, 1998). One consists of constructing many different "meta"-worlds that take into account the variable statuses and social boundaries among people. If we believe that many different worlds exist, particularly one that includes the "world of victims," then we believe that the one most relevant to us must be just. According to Lerner (1980), this belief in disparate worlds allows us at times to provide little to help others. Another strategy is associated with certain religious doctrines in which consolation for present world injustices on earth may be remedied by a higher belief in an ultimate justice. This type of belief allows one to endure injustices without giving up the basic belief in a just world. According to Lerner (1998),

> The importance and prevalence of this belief in an omnipotent and omniscient justice restoring superhuman force watching over people's lives cannot be over-estimated. Highly sophisticated, mature people find it acceptable, and at times, necessary to seek this form of comfort when confronted with undeserved suffering. (p. 250)

Hafer and Olson (1998) investigated the role of individual differences in just world beliefs, as well as responses to personal negative outcomes. They concluded that "individuals who strongly believe in a just world typically perceive less unfairness in personal misfortune and experience less discontent than weak believers" (p. 84).

CONSTRUCTIVIST SELF-DEVELOPMENT THEORY

More than a decade ago, McCann and Pearlman (1990) formally introduced a new conceptual framework that has been used for assessing and treating traumatized individuals. The comprehensive heuristic model known as constructivist self-development theory (CSDT) consists of a blend of object relations, self-psychology, and social cognition theories and is grounded in the basic premises of psychoanalytical treatment. Thus, CSDT focuses on the interaction between the subjective response of the trauma by the survivor and its objective context, with an emphasis on the effects to the developing self. In a more recent review, Pearlman and Saakvitne (1995) stated, "CSDT understands the individual's adaptation to trauma as an interaction between his personality and personal history and the traumatic event(s) and its context, within the social and cultural contexts for the event and its aftermath" (p. 57). CSDT provides orderly assessment and practical treatment of the identified broad aspects of the self that are considered affected by trauma. One of these aspects is the survivor's frame of reference or worldview regarding beliefs and expectations about the self and others. McCann and Pearlman (1992) refer to this need as developing an individual meaningful frame of reference related to causality or personal attributions about the occurrence of events. Other aspects of CSDT include self capacities, ego resources, memory system, and psychological needs and related cognitive schemas. Included in this latter aspect are issues of safety, trust, esteem, intimacy, and control.

The stages of CSDT are as follows:

1. Assessment of personal history and the traumatic event;
2. Stabilization of acute symptoms of distress;
3. Strengthening of self-capacities;
4. Restoration of a balanced need structure;
5. Restoration of positive beliefs or schemas; and
6. Integration of the traumatic memories.

HOROWITZ'S COMPLETION TENDENCY

As noted previously, Janoff-Bulman (1992) has argued that discovering meaning following a traumatic event is a primary strategy in restoring and rebuilding assumptions about the world. Similarly, McCann and Pearlman (1992) have recognized the value of regulating self-esteem and other-esteem (and Herman emphasized the need for rebuilding a positive view of the self or restoration of a sense of personal worth as cornerstones of trauma recovery). Trauma pioneer Mardi Horowitz et al. (1993) explained repetitive intrusive ideas and feelings in the wake of a traumatic event as part of a completion tendency, or "an intrinsic cognitive motive to reduce the discrepancy between new information elicited by the life event, as retained in an active form of memory storage, and pre-existing inner models of meaning, or schemata" (Horowitz et al., 1993, p. 768). According to Horowitz, this personalized disequilibrium in appraised meaning is reduced through assimilation and accommodation that occurs in a trusting therapeutic relationship. Horowitz et al. (1993) conceptualized treatment of traumatized victims in the following way:

> With the establishment of a working alliance and the identification of a mutually agreed-upon focus, the patient can begin the process of working through the thoughts and feelings in terms of the focus. The process involves a reappraisal of the serious life event, the meanings associated with it, and its intersection with pre-existent features of personality. With the support and guidance of the therapist, the patient is helped to examine, in tolerable doses, aspects of the traumatic experience and its personal implications to the patient. The overall aim of this phase is to move the patient from either a rigidly overcontrolled orientation or undermodulated intrusive reactions to an affectively manageable exploration of the meanings the traumatic event has for the patient. (p. 771)

BANDURA'S SELF-EFFICACY

Bandura's concept of self-efficacy is especially useful in formulating a strategic approach to the treatment of posttraumatic distress. Enhancing self-efficacy is an essential and intrinsic process for the treatment of posttraumatic stress disorders because it not only enhances self-esteem but also contradicts the perception of helplessness while conveying the perception that the world is more controllable (i.e., safer).

Bandura (1977, 1982, 1997) has described four sources that affect the cognitive perception of self-efficacy:

1. *Performance:* "Enactive attainments provide the most influential source of efficacy information. . . . Successes raise efficacy appraisals, repeated failures lower them" (Bandura, 1982, pp. 26–27). Bandura has shown perceptions of self-efficacy to influence subsequent performance as well as autonomic nervous system activity. Though enactive attainment appears to be the single most powerful way of influencing perceptions of self-efficacy, it is important to note that attainment is in the eye of the beholder. Objective success shows no favorable impact on self-efficacy if the individual *perceives* that success as failure.

2. *Vicarious experience:* "Self-efficacy appraisals are also partly influenced by vicarious experiences. Seeing or visualizing similar others perform successfully can raise self-percepts of efficacy in observers that they too possess the capabilities to master comparable activities. . . . By the same token, observing others

to be of similar competence fail despite high efforts lowers observers' judgments of their own capabilities and undermines their efforts" (Bandura, 1982, p. 27). Such modeling of experience as described may be done in vivo, in vitro, or symbolically.

3. *Verbal persuasion:* Verbal persuasion includes such things as suggestion, education, and reinterpretation of exogenous, environmental, or interoceptive stimuli to improve perceptions of self-efficacy. Such cognitive alterations may be done by oneself or by another (e.g., a therapist). In the case of other-directed persuasion, the ethos of the therapist may certainly affect outcome.

4. *Physiological–affective arousal:* "People rely partly on their state of physiological arousal in judging their capabilities and vulnerability to stress. Because unusually high arousal usually debilitates performance, individuals are more likely to expect success when they are not beset by aversive arousal. . . . Fear reactions generate further fear through anticipatory self-arousal. . . . People can rouse themselves to elevated levels of distress that produce the very dysfunctions they fear. Treatments that eliminate emotional arousal . . . heighten perceived efficacy with corresponding improvements in performance" (Bandura, 1982, p. 28). Biofeedback and other techniques that induce the relaxation response are useful interventions within this domain, as discussed in chapter 10.

RESTORING ASSUMPTIVE WORLDVIEWS AND INTEGRATING THE TRAUMATIC EVENT: A STRATEGIC APPROACH

In interpreting Janet, van der Kolk, Brown, and van der Hart (1991) indicated, "Making intellectual sense out of a traumatic event leads to constructive coping and a subjective sense of calm and control" (p. 371). According to Maslow (1970), "Basic need gratification is primary in the dynamics of actual cure or improvement" (p. 68). In the terminology of this volume, the psychotherapy of posttraumatic stress entails assisting the patient in restoring the assumptive worldview constructions (*Weltanschauung*) and integrating the traumatic event in such a way that the Maslovian need for safety is again satisfied and the world is once again understandable and safe. To achieve this goal, we advocate the use of a synergistic, personality-guided therapeutic approach. We have taken the risk of oversimplification and have chosen to delineate this process in a series of therapeutic stages that follow.

Stage 1: Telling the "Trauma Story" and the Formation of the Therapeutic Alliance

Every traumatic incident involves a story that needs to be told and that needs to be heard. In a calm and accepting manner, the therapist encourages the patient to tell this story. The story will usually consist of four components. Although the story is not fully told until all components are described, the patient may simply not be able to fully describe all of the elements listed in the earliest stage of therapy. Nevertheless, the therapist should inquire about:

1. A description of the traumatic event;
2. A description of signs, symptoms, and any other personal reactions or changes in behavior that are a consequence of the traumatic event;
3. Any reactions or changes in behavior demonstrated by family members, friends, coworkers, or others that appear to be a direct, or indirect, consequence of the traumatic event; and
4. Any anticipated changes to the patient's personal life, career, or interpersonal relationships in the future as a result of the traumatic event.

The order of the four revelations in stage 1 are of less importance than is the need to allow the patient to tell the story in a supportive, accepting, and safe setting.

The benefits of this disclosure process are numerous:

1. It is believed that the cathartic process associated with traumatic disclosure is often intrinsically therapeutic (Pennebaker, 1999);
2. It provides the therapist with valuable information about the traumatic event(s);
3. It provides the therapist with valuable information about the individual; and
4. It allows for the facilitation of the therapeutic alliance, as described in chapters 7 and 8.

Therefore, it is usually within this stage and the next that both the personality-specific thematic beliefs and the preferential communication processes are revealed and are then subsequently aligned with during the course of the formation of the therapeutic alliance mentioned in chapters 7 and 8. The therapist should keep in mind that the goal of therapy is to reestablish a sense of safety, first in the therapeutic relationship and later in long-term independence.

Stage 2: Providing Information

Information is usually an anxiolytic. Many patients indicate that the worst part of being "ill" is not knowing what is wrong and not having a prognosis of some kind. This stage is designed to remedy this concern.

To the degree to which it seems appropriate, the therapist should provide hope, reassurance, and as much of a technical explanation of the patient's signs and symptoms as seems useful.

Robert J. Lifton (1988) noted the therapeutic utility of explaining the adaptive value of many symptoms that emerge in the wake of psychological trauma. Lifton, who has written extensively on victimization and survival, formulated numerous principles regarding psychological trauma. Listed next are selected principles that seem to have explanatory value to the patient in this stage of the therapeutic process and are, therefore, worthy of mention to most patients:

1. The concept of being a survivor: "Survival is an achievement" (Lifton, 1988, p. 8);
2. The role of human connectedness in survivors. Trauma engenders a discontinuity, a strain on interpersonal relationships, even family relationships. Recovery entails becoming reconnected;
3. The symptoms of dissociation represent a form of disconnectedness. Dissociation may be seen as a natural human response to extreme stress. The vulnerability for dissociation is present in all humans in varying degrees;
4. PTSD is a "normal adaptive process of reaction to an abnormal situation" (Lifton, 1988, p. 9);
5. Survivor guilt is a common posttraumatic reaction for the perception of having failed to halt the traumatic event or the failure to help others;
6. Depression, even psychic numbing, is an extreme form of dissociation and represents a discontinuity of the self;
7. The search for meaning is intimately involved in psychological trauma. According to Lifton (1988), "Without addressing this idea of meaning . . . we cannot understand post-traumatic stress disorder" (p. 10); and
8. Psychological traumatization and recovery involves issues of the transformation of the self.

We have found that explaining posttraumatic stress reactions in the context of a survival mechanism, albeit extreme and often maladaptive, is a useful normalization concept for many individuals. For example, we might say that if the person were cut, bleeding would be the expected consequence.

Similarly, psychological traumatization also brings with it an expectation of a symptomatic consequence manifest within the three symptom clusters reviewed in chapter 2. Each of the symptom clusters has survival value in response to the physically threatening reality of the traumatic event. For example,

1. Reexperiencing the event may be viewed as a means of searching for a remedy, a means of future prevention, or even merely a means of making sense out of the traumatic occurrence.
2. Heightened neurological arousal and exaggerated neural responsivity may be seen as an augmentation of one's protective "fight or flight" survival system.
3. Social withdrawal, avoidance, and numbing may be seen as energy-conservation mechanisms that also reduce the risk of subsequent exposure to traumatic events through behavioral and psychological withdrawal.

Stage 3: Neurological Desensitization and Stress Management

As soon as reasonably possible, the therapist should consider initiating efforts to neurologically desensitize the neural hypersensitivity that is a hallmark of PTSD. The more severe the PTSD, the more important direct efforts to desensitize become. Initially, we believe that behavioral techniques should be used, as described in chapter 10. Should these efforts prove of no avail, or should the severity of the neurological arousal be assessed as self-sustaining, then psychotropic medication should be considered, as described in chapter 10. Ultimately, we conceive of the patient with PTSD as suffering from a state of pathognomonic ergotropic tone. Efforts will usually need to be directed toward altering this neurological status in the trophotropic direction. As noted earlier, an added benefit of using behavioral techniques to induce the relaxation response (Benson, 1975) is the facilitation of an increase in self-efficacy through increased physiological self-regulation (Bandura, 1982).

In addition to the techniques used to engender the relaxation response as a means of facilitating neurological desensitization, we believe there is value in encouraging the patient to use other stress management techniques, anger management techniques, and related social skills programs as a means of fostering adaptive coping and increasing self-efficacy (see Girdano, Everly, & Dusek, 2001).

The work of Foa and her colleagues (see Foa et al., 2000) with cognitive behavioral therapy (CBT) should be mentioned at this point. Although the specific mechanisms of action are unclear, CBT appears to be the most well-researched and effective treatment for sexual assault victims at this point in time. There is reason to believe that the reexposure element of CBT exerts its therapeutic effect because of, or in combination with, some aspect of neurologic desensitization.

Stage 4: Identifying the Assumptive Worldview Most Challenged or Adversely Affected by the Traumatic Event

This stage in treatment is not necessarily a discrete stage per se but rather a process. It represents a process of discovery wherein the therapist carefully listens to the trauma story as told by the patient and attempts to identify the core assumptive worldview(s) most challenged or adversely impinged on by the traumatic event(s). Objective psychological tests are typically of little value. Rather, descriptive narratives, identification of recurrent dreams, recurrent flashbacks, or reiterative memories may be of greatest value. The use of projective tests such as the Rorshach, the Thematic Apperception Test (Murray, 1943), and specialized incomplete sentence stems may also be of value. As noted in chapter 5, there also exist worldview assessments that may be of value in this discovery process.

Stage 5: Restoring Functional Core Assumptive Worldviews

It may well be that the sine qua non of recovery from psychological traumatization is the restoration of adaptive functionality to the core assumptive worldviews. Certainly, we believe the greatest degree of recovery is achieved by doing so.

We believe that there are three primary strategies useful in restoring the functional utility of core assumptive worldviews (Everly, 1994, 1995):

1. Integrating the traumatic event into the patient's existing worldview in such a way that the patient comes to understand the event as actually consistent with the worldview (i.e., the event did not in actuality violate any core assumptive worldviews).

2. Allowing the traumatic event to be understood as an exception to an existing worldview (i.e., an "exception to the rule"), which despite its existence represents a low probability occurrence and does not serve to invalidate the overall utility, or functionality, of the general assumptive construction; thus, life as the patient knows it goes on.

3. Acknowledging the disconfirming, invalidating nature of the traumatic event on the assumptive worldview, thus necessitating the creation of a new worldview wherein the trauma more readily fits. The difficulty inherent in such a process is clearly

mitigated by assisting the patient to use the traumatic event to lead to a revelation of self-efficacy or to the revelation–creation of some greater good to self, family, or society that grows out of the traumatic experience.

Let us take a closer look at these interventions.

Integrating the traumatic event into the existing worldview requires the therapist to provide new information to the patient in the form of cognitive reinterpretations that have not been effectively considered to that point. We find there are at least two specific cognitive reinterpretations that may be useful:

1. Reinterpreting the traumatic event from one considered a personal failure to one considered a personal success (e.g., via considering some other relevant measure with which to determine success); and
2. Reinterpreting the role the patient specifically played in the etiology of the traumatic event (e.g., disputing or mitigating culpability, identifying mitigating circumstances previously ignored, or disputing overgeneralized self-blame).

Creating an "exception to the rule" condition involves less effort directed toward cognitive reinterpretation and more focus on cognitive flexibility. Within this intervention, the patient is encouraged to recall numerous rules by which he or she lives that nevertheless possess exceptions. The general acceptance of this phenomenon is then generalized to the assumptive worldview challenged or violated by the traumatic experience under consideration. Similarly, the low probability of recurrence is emphasized, while adding the notion of being better prepared to respond should the traumatic experience repeat itself.

Finally, replacing, or significantly modifying, an existing worldview on the basis of a traumatic violation once again requires cognitive reinterpretation. Several tactics may prove of value (also known as the "yes, but" strategy):

1. Reinterpreting the valence of the traumatic event from one considered catastrophic to one considered bad but possessing some positive, or redeeming, aspect to it. For example: (a) something of value can be learned from the event; (b) it could have been worse; (c) there is a "silver lining," etc.;
2. Reinterpreting the overall importance of the trauma—for example, reinterpreting the event as less important in the grand scheme of life, or less important as a determinant of happiness, than originally assumed;

3. Comparing oneself with other trauma victims who experienced less fortunate outcomes (downward comparison); and

4. Recognizing that the rate of personal recovery is exceptional compared to others or compared to that which would be expected.

A word of caution: This intervention may be met with resistance by the individual, if letting go of the original worldview creates a void in the personality schema or if it is perceived as being disloyal to someone or something that is important in the developmental processes of the individual (e.g., a parent, guardian, or some fostering institution).

Finally, the issue of termination of therapy is an important one. Termination is generally best accomplished when the patient has rediscovered a sense of safety within the therapeutic relationship and has been able to extend it beyond into the world outside of therapy. Such a sense of safety is achieved by integrating the traumatic event into the worldview constructions or helping the individual discover new mechanisms by which safety can be achieved.

SELECTED CASE EXAMPLES

In chapter 8, we introduced cases involving posttraumatic stress. Let us review those cases in light of the presented interventions.

Case 1: Randy

The reader will recall the case of 6'3" 245-lb. Randy who developed symptoms of posttraumatic distress subsequent to a bar fight in which he was beaten by a much smaller man. In the case of Randy, the therapist failed to assess the influence of personality factors in Randy's presentation. The assumption was that physical assault, in and of itself, was the etiology of the posttraumatic distress. This perspective neglected the fact that previous assaults had failed to engender similar posttraumatic distress. The therapist failed to explore what made this assault unique. The psychologist's failure to recognize the characterological injury caused by the loss of social status and the fact that Randy's aggressive behaviors may no longer be an effective defense left Randy feeling defenseless and as if the psychologist did not fully understand his problem. Thus, Randy was not engaged in the therapeutic alliance. In fact, by underscoring too early in the relationship the reality that there will always be more powerful men not only served to inhibit the formation of the therapeutic alliance but it was actually anxiogenic.

Randy was referred for continued psychotherapy, with a different psychologist when the psychologist Randy had initially seen felt he had failed to establish a constructive working relationship. Thus, the first approach with Randy was therapeutic alignment with the personality-based thematic belief of the value of strength.

Following this alignment, the second psychologist, having listened carefully to Randy's story, identified the violated assumptive worldview as that of self-efficacy and a subsequent violation of the presumption of safety.

The psychologist gently reminded Randy of two important facts: first, that he was chemically impaired on alcohol at the time of the assault, which reduced his usual physical competence; and second, that the martial arts training of his adversary was a unique advantage and that if it was truly important enough, Randy could become as skilled if not more so given his strength and size. These revelations rather quickly restored Randy's belief in himself and his ability to defend himself, if needed. Subsequent sessions were also targeted at the aggressive proclivities, which in this case were what jeopardized Randy in the first place.

Thus, the strategies that were most productive with Randy were integrating the traumatic event into the existing worldview (alcohol reduced his normal proficiency) and altering the incorrect notion that physical strength alone was sufficient protection (martial arts training does yield an advantage but one that Randy could also acquire if he deemed it essential).

Case 2: James

In the case of the physician, James, his lack of skill in emergency medicine contributed to the death of a person in a medical crisis. The therapist proclaiming the obvious, that everyone makes mistakes, neglected to focus on the narcissistic injury that James had endured. To underscore the error actually threatened further narcissistic injury. To engage the person with the confident personality type in the therapeutic alliance, the psychologist must usually acknowledge the unique qualities of the individual patient early in the therapeutic process. Such a maneuver serves to reduce the counterproductive one-upmanship and enhances the therapist's credibility. Only by acknowledging James's special self-perception will the therapist ever get the opportunity to address the more florid symptom presentation.

After having been referred for subsequent care, the therapist taking over the case chose to align by pointing out James's unique academic accomplishments and his position as a medical chief of service. The therapeutic tact that proved most successful was to integrate the traumatic event into the existing worldview that James was a competent physician—his competence was in pathology, not emergency medicine. A sense of self-efficacy was returned and the risk of similar trauma in the future was reduced by pointing out that he could have deferred to the paramedic, which was a valuable lesson learned, as well.

Case 3: Betty

In the case of Betty, possessing the sensitive personality style, her disorder created a power struggle, initially between Betty and her employer and later between Betty and her surgeon. The therapeutic alliance could only be created with Betty by recognizing the importance of, and the manifest struggle for, power. More specifically, the perceived negligence of her employer was seen by Betty as a personal attack for which they had no right or justification to initiate.

The violated worldview was revealed to be that of trust. Betty believed that her trust in her employer had been betrayed. The therapeutic tact initially taken was one of an exception to the rule. The memo from human resources clearly indicated a potential threat that was ignored by management. The exception to the rule strategy proved unsuccessful. Considering her normally pessimistic and doubting worldview, the psychologist chose to integrate this event as a confirmatory belief—one that she really did expect. Subsequent therapy focused on how she might retain self-efficacy and control in similar situations, should they arise in the future. The final aspect of therapy focused on letting go of responsibility for the things over which she had no potential control.

Case 4: Kyle

Kyle's respectful personality represented an added barrier to the resolution of his posttraumatic distress. It will be recalled that as an emergency rescue driver, Kyle took his eyes off of the road to respond to an apparent cry for help. In doing so, he hit a pedestrian. Kyle's belief in himself was subsequently destroyed.

In retrospect, Kyle responded to a call for help as his training and personality would seem to dictate. Yet, in doing so, another human being was injured. Kyle found himself in a double-bind situation. Initially, his psychologist attempted to introduce the notion that some of the blame might rest with the pedestrian. Kyle resisted this tact. Kyle's personality was one that embraces the notion of self-responsibility. The therapeutic alliance must begin there. A common mistake made by beginning therapists is to rush to try to make it better. Any such attempts, without first aligning with the needs and realities of the patient, will create a condition wherein the therapist becomes part of the problem rather than part of the solution. Therapy may then become a debate or series of confrontations rather than movement toward the resolution of distress.

Having aligned with Kyle on the importance of taking responsibility, the therapist asked Kyle to describe the outcome if he had not taken his eyes off of the road and had injured another pedestrian because of failing to respond as he had originally. This seeming double bind allowed Kyle to integrate the accident into his existing worldview by pointing out that tactically he made the right decision (he received no traffic violation).

Having addressed that issue, Kyle's revelation continued, but his distress lessened. An additional violated worldview was now revealed to be that of "doing things correctly" but still having a bad outcome. Therapy now used the exception to the rule strategy that subsequently proved effective with Kyle.

Case 5: John

Finally, the case of John, the night watchman at the automotive parts warehouse who was unable to call for help after an explosion and consequent fire, underscores the exquisite sensitivity of the introverted individual. An unusually low threshold for stimulation makes this individual vulnerable to overstimulation and catastrophic decompensation in the face of high-intensity stimulation. Clearly, alignment with this sensitivity would have prevented the iatrogenic exacerbation of John's symptoms through in vivo desensitization techniques.

The exception to the rule strategy ultimately proved most effective with John. John's belief in himself was threatened by his failure to perform his duties during the fire. By examining and aligning with John's sensitivity, it was subsequently possible for John to see himself as competent in other aspects of related work but to also realistically understand that he had limitations, as does every other human being, and that the possession of limitations does not equate to incompetence.

KEY POINT SUMMARY

1. We have advocated a personality-guided approach to the treatment of PTSD and related posttraumatic psychological disorders throughout this book. An amalgam of various philosophical and clinical orientations, the approach embraces the synergistic multicomponent approach to therapy advocated by Theodore Millon.
2. This approach entails a personality-guided approach to establishing the therapeutic alliance and creating the foundation for the reconstruction of a safe world (preferential process and personality-specific thematic belief mechanisms).
3. The approach includes neurological desensitization, wherein techniques are used to diminish the intensity of the pathognomonic ergotropic state of neurological hypersensitivity and increase perceptions of self-efficacy.

4. Finally, the approach includes restoring personality-based assumptive worldviews and integrating the traumatic event.
5. This approach is embodied in a five-stage process consisting of:
   a. Formulating the therapeutic alliance and allowing the patient to tell the "trauma story";
   b. Providing information about the nature of posttraumatic psychological reactions;
   c. Fostering neurologic desensitization and the use of other personal stress management techniques;
   d. Discovering the most salient worldview issues related to the present traumatic experience;
   e. Restoring functional, adaptive assumptive worldviews:
      i. Integrating the traumatic event into the patient's existing worldview in such a way that the patient comes to understand the event as actually consistent with the worldview (i.e., the event did not in actuality violate any core assumptive worldviews);
      ii. Allowing the traumatic event to be understood as an exception to an existing worldview (i.e., an "exception to the rule"), which despite its existence, represents a low probability occurrence and does not serve to invalidate the overall utility, or functionality, of the general assumptive construction; thus, life as the patient knows it goes on;
      iii. Acknowledging the disconfirming, invalidating nature of the traumatic event on the assumptive worldview, thus necessitating the creation of a new worldview wherein the trauma more readily fits. The difficulty inherent in such a process is clearly mitigated by assisting the patient to use the traumatic event to lead to a revelation of self-efficacy or to the revelation/creation of some greater good to self, family, or society that grows out of the traumatic experience.

12

PSYCHOLOGICAL TRAUMA AND THE BORDERLINE PERSONALITY

The premise on which this volume was created is that psychological trauma represents an attack on the core fabric of human personality. According to van der Hart et al. (1989), Pierre Janet believed that trauma arrested personality development in such a way that "the evolution of [people's] lives" has ceased. The natural corollary to that assertion is that as the severity of posttraumatic distress increases, so does the need for an understanding of personality dynamics and how specific elements of personality may be altered as a result of psychological traumatization. In essence, the dominion of the trauma may be so profound that it can change one's personality forever. This, of course, is recognized in the *ICD–10* (World Health Organization, 1990) and via the "associated features" section of the *DSM–IV* (American Psychiatric Association, 1994). But in this final chapter we take a more direct approach to this issue and explore a uniquely severe and possibly enduring manifestation of posttraumatic stress. We explore a form of posttraumatic manifestation that not only emerges as a result of an attack on the personality but a manifestation of posttraumatic stress that emerges not as a fragmented pathognomonic presentation but as a concretized personality disorder itself. We review the relationship between psychological trauma and the formally recognized borderline personality disorder (BPD). Is BPD an Axis II (personality disorders axis) manifestation of posttraumatic stress disorder (PTSD)?

197

OVERVIEW OF BORDERLINE PERSONALITY DISORDER

The construct of BPD has been actively investigated for several decades before its formal introduction as an identifiable diagnostic entity in the *DSM–III* (American Psychiatric Association, 1980). In 1938, psychoanalyst Adolf Stern first identified a group of extremely difficult patients to treat that neither fit into the "psychotic" nor "psychoneurotic" group. Stern's enumeration of the clinical symptoms of this borderline group portends many of the clinical features associated with the current *DSM–IV* (American Psychiatric Association, 1994) conceptualization. Stern, for example, addressed features such as inordinate hypersensitivity, negative therapeutic reactions including lability of affect and recurrent suicidal ideation or attempts, feelings of inferiority, and environmental sensitivity. Particularly relevant for the purpose of this chapter is Stern's recognition that,

> Actual cruelty, neglect and brutality by the parents of many years' duration are factors found in these patients. These factors operate more or less constantly over many years from earliest childhood. They are not single experiences. (1938, p. 470)

He further noted that "because of the above experiences this group never develops a sense of security acquired by being loved, which is the birthright of every child" (p. 470).

As currently defined by *DSM–IV*, the essential feature of BPD "is a pervasive pattern of instability of interpersonal relationships, self-image, and affects, and marked impulsivity that begins by early adulthood and is present in a variety of contexts" (American Psychiatric Association, 1994, p. 650). The erratic behavior of these individuals, which includes impulsive gambling, spending, sex, and binge eating, is typically described as unpredictable and certainly, at times, self-damaging. Overall, there are nine borderline criteria noted in *DSM–IV*, at least five of which are required for a diagnosis of BPD. Therefore, a myriad of symptom combinations are possible.

Within his comprehensive theory of personality and personality disorders, Theodore Millon (1969; Millon & Davis, 1996) views the BPD as a syndromal continuation of other personality disorders. BPD is perhaps best explained using Millon's four evolutionary polarities. The borderline patient is one who finds him- or herself in a condition of constant flux on each of the four polarities. Thus, the borderline patient vacillates between reliance on self and reliance on others. The borderline patient vacillates between being proactive and being reactive. The borderline patient vacillates between pursuing instrumental behaviors that are positively reinforcing (R+) versus negatively reinforcing (R-). Finally, the borderline patient vacillates between a reserved cognitive orientation verses an impulsive affective orientation.

Millon views the BPD as a severe personality disorder. It is likely that the more rapid the vacillation, the more severe the BPD.

Given the dynamism inherent from the polarities perspective, Millon (Millon et al., 1999) then described the borderline patient as:

1. Expressively spasmodic;
2. Interpersonally paradoxical;
3. Cognitively capricious;
4. Possessive of an uncertain self-image;
5. Using regression as the preferential ego defense mechanism; and
6. Affectively labile.

Millon's more dimensional description of the aspects of borderline personality, as compared to clearly delineated categories, provides additional support for the possible variability or different combinations of features associated with a diagnosis of BPD.

TRAUMA AND BORDERLINE PERSONALITY

The concept that early childhood traumas could evoke adult psychopathology is a core premise of the treatment discipline of psychoanalysis. This was clearly articulated earlier in Stern's account of the borderline group. Moreover, according to G. Davidson and Neale (1990),

> Initially, Freud postulated that traumatic childhood sexual experiences lay behind the neurotic problems of his patients. But by 1897 he came to realize that perverted acts against children would have to be far more prevalent than he was willing or able to assume. He then coupled his patients' reports of such trauma with his own supposition that the unconscious does not distinguish between fact and fantasy. (p. 36)

In proposing that his patients were reporting "fantasies" rather than actual events, Freud was able to retain the inherent tenets of his theory on neurotic anxiety. As accumulating data in the past 40 years have suggested, however, Freud's apparent lamenting about the actual prevalence of traumatic experiences such as sexual abuse and its impact on human functioning unfortunately may have been more accurate than he overtly accepted or admitted.

A century after Freud's initial speculations, a study by Zanarini and her colleagues (1997) reported that in a sample of 358 patients diagnosed with BPD, a staggering 91% acknowledged some form of abuse (e.g., emotional verbal, physical, sexual) and 92% acknowledged some form of neglect (e.g., physical, emotional, inconsistent treatment, failure to protect). More specifically, 61.5% reported a childhood history of physical or sexual abuse. Although the assured validity of retrospective self-report data is a methodological limitation of this study—and many other studies purporting a relationship between childhood sexual abuse and borderline personality disorder (Maughan & Rutter, 1997)—one cannot discount that when compared to the early writings of Freud, awareness of the occurrence and impact of early trauma is now acknowledged as an all too real phenomenon. What also appears evident from these data, and is certainly worth noting, is that the reported abuse seemed to invariably occur in a highly sensitized and emotionally charged environment typifying general disarray. It is clearly not difficult to imagine how one's personality development, including sense of self, intimacy, trust, body image, and impulsivity, may be adversely affected by these early traumatic events.

Although early conceptualizations regarding the underlying pathology of borderline personality generally focused on early attachment concepts such as separation (Akiskal, 1981; Soloff & Millward, 1983) and parental neglect (Frank & Paris, 1981; Walsh, 1977), it is Herman, Perry, and van der Kolk's (1989) study on a sample of 55 patients that is frequently cited as the first large-scale study examining the formative role of childhood trauma and borderline personality. The results of this seminal work revealed a strong association between reported childhood abuse and borderline personality. More specifically, for the 21 participants with borderline personality disorder, 81% reported a history of some form of trauma, 67% reported sexual abuse, 71% reported physical abuse, and 62% indicated that they had witnessed a trauma. An interesting feature of this study was that the Impact of Event Scale (IES; Horowitz, Wilner, & Alvarez, 1979) did not detect current symptoms of PTSD in these 21 BPD patients.

Several authors conclude, and we agree, that the incidence of childhood trauma alone does not provide a complete prescriptive etiology of BPD (Paris, 1997; Zanarini et al., 1998). In fact, according to Paris and Zweig-Frank (1997), there is no personality psychopathology in 80% of individuals with a history of childhood sexual abuse. Moreover, a meta-analysis of 21 studies from 1980 to 1995 with a total of 2,479 participants examining the association between childhood sexual abuse and BPD disorder revealed only a moderate pooled effect size ($r = .279$; Fossati, Madeddu, & Maffei, 1999). According to the results, other relevant mediator variables when considering the association between BPD and childhood sexual abuse include abuse by a nonrelative, genital fondling, penetration, number of perpetrators, and duration of abuse.

Although these data are noteworthy, the question of how many individuals diagnosed with BPD have a history of childhood trauma, including, but not limited to, sexual abuse is particularly salient for the treating clinician and consistent with the purpose of this applied clinical text. Data from the studies reviewed earlier provide numbers in excess of 80% and 90% for individuals with BPD reporting some form of childhood trauma, including abuse and neglect, and Goodman and Yehuda (2002) recently offered estimates that as many as 70% of individuals diagnosed with BPD have a history specifically related to childhood abuse. Thus, it seems possible that trauma in the form of neglect, abuse, and violence occurring at certain critical developmental times in temperamentally predisposed individuals may serve as a precursor in the development of BPD.

Continuing from a clinical perspective, van der Kolk, Hostetler, Herron, and Fister (1994) acknowledged that

> people who were traumatized when 3 years old may continue to process intense emotions in ways a 3-year-old child would. Individuals traumatized at a later stage of development would mobilize earlier developmental accomplishments to cope with the traumatizing situation, resulting in a different long-term adaptation. (p. 721)

Thus, it seems that borderline personality may evince itself differently in different subgroups based in part on environmental factors such as timing of the trauma and other parameters related to the individual and the situation. Goodman and Yehuda (2002) recently proposed that there are BPD subtypes that have the following specific core symptoms or clinical features that may be more directly affected by childhood trauma: impulsive aggression (suidical and parsuicidal actions), dissociation, identity disturbance, and affective instability. Therefore, it seems prudent for clinicians treating patients with BPD to assess for a history of trauma, including, but not limited to, childhood sexual abuse.

Borderline Personality Disorder and PTSD

More recent studies have investigated the concomitance between borderline personality and PTSD. Some researchers note that the conceptualization of borderline personality coincided with the increased empirical interest in PTSD, and further noted that both became official diagnostic entities in 1980, with the introduction of *DSM–III* (Fossati et al., 1999; Gunderson & Sabo, 1993). Others have suggested that PTSD and BPD have become predominantly women's diagnoses (Becker, 2000).

A major impetus for the concordance between PTSD and BPD is predicated on the work of Judith Herman (1992), who more than a decade ago introduced the concept of "complex PTSD." Within this construct, she described the psychological impact, emphasizing enduring personality changes and increased risk of repeated harm, in survivors of prolonged, repeated victimization. She also noted features such as chronic depression, substance abuse, dissociative symptoms, impulsivity, self-mutilation, and suicidality that are not part of the diagnostic criteria of PTSD. It is readily apparent from the contents of this chapter that many of these clinical features overlap with the Axis II diagnosis of borderline personality disorder. Herman's preliminary form of this complex PTSD syndrome, known as disorders of extreme stress not otherwise specified (DESNOS), was considered, yet not included, in the *DSM–IV*. What was clearly suggested, however, was that BPD be considered a trauma spectrum disorder, in which isolated or repeated traumatic childhood events served as the precursor to later coping and adaptation difficulties.

The *ICD–10* included, however, the separate diagnostic category of "Enduring Personality Change Following Catastrophic Experience" to address the difficulties that occur following extreme trauma. These characteristics include distrust, hostility, hypervigilance, alienation, and hopelessness (World Health Organization, 1990). In 1993, Gunderson and Sabo addressed the conceptual and phenomenological interface between PTSD and borderline personality disorder before the introduction of the *DSM–IV*. They noted, for example, the anger dyscontrol, emotional lability, dissociative processes, and suicidal thinking that are protypic of both diagnoses. More recently, Parson (1997) introduced the construct of Traumatic Stress Personality Disorder (TrSPD) as a synergistic composite condition combining the biological pathology (i.e., intrinsic neuronal dysfunction, increased sympathetic arousal, hypofunction of hypothalamic–pituitary–adrenocortical [HPA axis]) of PTSD with a personality disorder that collectively contributes to specific posttrauma adaptation. He then introduced broad, diverse assessment measures that combine projective, interview, and self-report tests to assess the construct (Parson, 1998), as well as the *intertheoretical therapy* model, which consists of an amalgam of accepted treatments including psychopharmacological, cognitive, behavioral, psychodynamic, and existential interventions. Parson's polythetic approach is consistent with Millon's synergistic psychotherapeutic recommendations.

With these theories serving as a framework, we now review some of the recent literature examining the connection between borderline personality disorder and PTSD. Using the Personality Disorder Examination (Loranger, Susman, Oldham, & Russakoff, 1988), a standardized diagnostic interview for *DSM–III–R* Axis II disorders, Southwick, Yehuda, and Giller (1993) assessed 34 male Vietnam War combat veterans with PTSD; 18 of the participants of the study were inpatients and 16 were outpatients. The results revealed that 76 percent of the 34 patients were diagnosed with BPD (83% of the inpatients and 69% of the outpatients).

In a study assessing 92 Vietnam veterans recruited from a Veteran's Administration PTSD clinic, 83 adult women with a history of childhood sexual abuse who were hospitalized and 57 outpatient women with a history of childhood sexual abuse who met criteria for PTSD, Shea, Zlotnick, and Weisberg (1999) investigated the personality features of these three different samples using the Personality Diagnostic Questionnaire–Revised (PDQ–R; Hyler & Reider, 1987). The PDQ–R is a 152-item, self-report, true–false inventory that assesses *DSM–III–R* personality disorders. Results revealed that 83% of the combat veterans, 52.6% of the sexual abuse outpatients, and 92% of the sexual abuse inpatients met PDQ–R criteria for borderline personality disorder, respectively.

Zanarini and her colleagues (1998), in a large-scale controlled study of male and female inpatients, 379 of whom (296 women and 83 men) met criteria for borderline personality disorder when given the Revised Diagnostic Interview for Borderlines (DIB–R; Zanarini, Gunderson, Frankenburg, & Chauncey, 1989), the Structured Clinical Interview for *DSM–III–R* (Spitzer, Williams, Gibbon, & First, 1990), and the Diagnostic Interview for *DSM–III–R* Personality Disorders (Zanarini, Frankenburg, Chauncey, & Gunderson, 1987), assessed Axis I comorbidity of borderline personality according to *DSM–III–R* criteria. Even when using the stringent alpha level of $p < 0.002$, 55.9% of the sample met criteria for PTSD according to the diagnostic measures. For the 296 women with borderline personality disorder, 60.8% met criteria for PTSD, and for the 83 men meeting criteria for borderline personality disorder, 34.9% met criteria for PTSD. As expected, however, having a diagnosis of PTSD does not necessarily serve as a precursor for the development of BPD. For example, Bollinger and colleagues (2000) reported the incidence of BPD in combat veterans to be as low as 5.7%.

In a study comparing the etiological and clinical characteristics of 45 women with PTSD and 26 women with PTSD and BPD, all of whom had a history of sexual abuse, Heffernan and Cloitre (2000) noted that age of abuse onset was earlier among the women with PTSD+BPD. Moreover, the data for this sample revealed that women who experienced severe verbal abuse by their mothers were six times more likely to have the additional BPD diagnosis and that problems with anger was the clinical measure most distinctly associated with PTSD+BPD. Also of note, the presence of BPD did not alter the symptom pattern of PTSD, which led the authors to conclude that "the two disorders are distinct and relatively independent symptom constellations" (p. 594).

In a recent study (Connor et al., 2002) examining health and psychosocial dysfunction in a community sample (1,541 respondents) in north central North Carolina, 150 individuals with posttraumatic stress symptoms (PTSS) were identified (i.e., had at least one posttraumatic symptom following a traumatic event). Within the 150 PTSS sample, the 15 who were also identified as having BPD were noted to have greater health status impairment as measured by self-ratings and also by data on psychotropic medication use and health services use. Moreover, the 15 individuals in the PTSS–BPD group evinced greater functional impairment on social, occupational, and early adverse life events (e.g., parental abuse, parental discord, poverty, and sexual assault).

With the recent interest in neurobiological conceptualizations of PTSD (see chapters 4 and 6), it is noteworthy that trauma-related morphological changes in the hippocampus and amygdala have recently been noted by Driessen and his colleagues (2000) in women with borderline personality disorder who were also assessed for early childhood traumatization. When compared to a healthy matched-control group, the 21 severely disturbed borderline patients were noted to have significantly smaller hippocampal volumes (15.7% left and 15.8% right) and amygdala volumes (7.9% left and 7.5% right). Of note, these differences occurred although there were no overall differences between the two groups in brain volume (the prosencephalon or the left and right temporal lobes). There were also significant correlations between scores on the Childhood Trauma Questionnaire (CTQ; Bernstein & Fink, 1998) and hippocampal volume. More specifically, the mean hippocampal volume was negatively correlated with CTQ total score ($r = -0.49$; $p < .001$) and mean period (duration) of traumatization ($r = -0.53$; $p < .001$), but only when the borderline personality patients and the control participants were analyzed together. Thus, the authors concluded that the proposal of trauma-induced hippocampal volume reductions in BPD participants was only partly supported. Other recent biological studies involving BPD and PTSD patients, including serotonergic responsivity (Rinne, Westenberg, den Boer, & van den Brink, 2000) and responses to the dexamethasone challenge test (Grossman et al., 2001), which measures cortisol suppression, have led Goodman and Yehuda (2002) to conclude that "PTSD and personality disorders, including BPD, are different from a neuroendocrine perspective and do not support the idea that PTSD and BPD are synonymous" (p. 343).

Treatment Considerations

A variety of conceptualizations and approaches to treatment have been attempted with borderline personality disorder. From the psychodynamic perspective, Otto Kernberg's (1985) object relations theory has been the most prominent. Object relations theory operates under the guiding premise that because of their "weak egos," individuals with BPD have particular difficulty tolerating the regressive probing of childhood conflicts that typifies psychoanalytical treatment. Thus, Kernberg's modified analytical treatment, which is much more directive than most analysis involves a targeted exploration of the primary defense mechanism of the borderline patient—namely "splitting" or dichotomizing. In essence, Kernberg assists borderline patients in using reality testing to better integrate the positive and negative aspects of a person into a whole as compared to separating aspects of an individual into black or white or all good or all bad.

Kroll (1993), in a text specifically designed to address treatment issues of PTSD–BPD patients, does not adhere strictly to a particular therapeutic modality. He offers, however, the conceptualization that

> the PTSD/borderline patient is ceaselessly enveloped and tormented by an ongoing, intrusive stream of consciousness consisting of memories, flashbacks, and internalized voices of condemnation that blend with self-critical denunciations, even as he/she tries to go about the daily business of life's routines. (pp. 102–103)

He then offered, and subsequently elaborated on, the following five general treatment strategies, which he acknowledged appear simplistic but may be rather daunting to accomplish:

1. Distinguish old patterns;
2. Assist the patient in becoming aware of how these patterns continue to function and their consequences;
3. If possible, to trace the old patterns back to childhood traumas (e.g., injuries, experiences, or responses) and to note the limitations of doing so;
4. For the therapist to recognize, and resist, the attempt of the patient to enact these old issues and to have the therapist become an unreasonable source of gratification; and
5. For the therapist to maintain a genuine presence in therapy while affirming the patient's "intrinsic value and permission for healthy growth" (p. 107).

Linehan's (1993, 1995) dialectical behavior therapy (DBT) is a form of cognitive–behavioral therapy that also includes empathic features of person-centered therapy and expressive psychodynamic psychotherapy, and was developed as a treatment of BPD, especially for chronically suicidal, severely out of control, or impulsive individuals. The dialectic perspective (1995) assumes the following three broad characteristics:

1. That individual parts of a system are related to a whole (i.e., behavior needs to be considered and understood in an environmental context);
2. That reality is essentially heterogeneous and requires ongoing synthesis to move patients toward a more balanced synthesis; and
3. That the individual and the environment are in a continual state of flux and therapy should help them become more accepting of ambiguity.

In essence, Linehan conceptualized emotional dysregulation as the fundamental problem of the borderline patient, with its etiology stemming from temperamental vulnerability and being raised in an invalidating environment.

Dialectical behavior therapy relies on four stages of treatment to address the motivational and capability deficits identified in borderline patients. The stages of treatment include pretreatment orientation, in which an overview of DBT is provided and an agreement to work together is made between the patient and the therapist. The first formal stage focuses on behavioral targets such as decreasing suicidal behaviors, actions that interfere or hinder therapeutic progression, behaviors that interfere with quality of life (e.g., substance abuse, high-risk sex, financial concerns), and addressing deficits in behavioral skills. After these target behaviors are stabilized, the second active stage of DBT focuses on the posttraumatic stress symptoms that Linehan purports are highly concomitant in the borderline patient. Consistent with the premise of this chapter, Linehan noted that "a target of treatment for most borderline patients will be the cognitive, emotional, and behavioral sequela of early trauma" (1995, p. 16). She implied that these traumas, including childhood experiences of neglect and loss, may be related to a current stressful presentation. Linehan further elaborates that,

> The treatment of post-traumatic stress involves having the patient accept the facts of the traumatic experience; reducing the stigmatization, self-invalidation, and self-blame associated with the trauma; reducing denial and intrusive stress responses; and synthesizing the "abuse dichotomy" (i.e., the tendency to oscillate back and forth between the belief that the abuser is all bad for abusing the patient and the belief that the patient is all bad because they were abused). (p. 16)

The final stage of DBT uses strategies to facilitate the patient's self-respect and to enhance and validate her or his sense of trust, self-care, and problem solving. Linehan described the functions of psychotherapy and the responsibilities of the therapist in the following ways:

> First, the therapist is responsible for helping the patient inhibit maladaptive, borderline behaviors and replace them with adaptive, skillful ones (especially skills learned in the other modes of treatment). Second, the therapist must identify and resolve motivational problems, including any social or environmental factors that are inhibiting the patient's use of effective skills or that are eliciting and reinforcing maladaptive behaviors. Third, the therapist serves as gatekeeper to other treatment modalities and also teaches the patient to manage and integrate disparate treatment modes the patient may receive. Finally, the therapist is the primary attachment person and crisis intervener, keeping the patient in therapy and alive until sufficient progress occurs. (pp. 10–11)

In a recent summary of published empirical results assessing the effectiveness of DBT, Scheel (2000) reported that DBT has been associated with decreased parasuicidal behavior and psychiatric hospitalizations, as well as with increased social adjustment and functioning, work performance, and retention in therapy.

Using Millon's synergistic personality-guided approach, treatment of the BPD consists of a combination of social skills training, cognitive therapy, behavioral techniques, and psychopharmacologic interventions. Strategically, the initial goal of therapy is to begin to stabilize the conflictual vacillating dynamism within each of the four polarities. This is, of course, predicated on establishing a solid therapeutic alliance with the patient. This process is likely to take a considerable amount of time and will be fraught with significant challenges, manipulations, and setbacks. However, once a trusting therapeutic alliance has been established (complete with appropriate boundary setting), significant progress will already have been made. Thus, affective and interpersonal stability are sought in preface to the reconstruction of a functional and adaptive sense of self. Anticonvulsant and selective serotonergic reuptake inhibiting medications have been used to assist in the stabilization process.

The therapy of BPD will, therefore, entail:

1. Establishing an appropriate and functional therapeutic alliance;
2. Extending the interpersonal lessons learned in establishing the therapeutic alliance to other interpersonal relationships;
3. Reducing the degree of affective vacillation;
4. Improving stress management and problem-solving skills; and
5. Reinforcing the development of a stronger, more self-reliant sense of self.

If BPD is indeed largely a result of neglect, abuse, or traumatization, as extant information would argue, then it seems clear that attendance to the dominion of the worldview would be not only appropriate but mandatory, lest we treat only the symptoms of this disorder. The previous chapter discussed three strategies for integrating or restoring worldviews. It seems evident that if the therapist chooses to attempt to go beyond the treatment of symptoms, then the BPD, perhaps more than any other posttraumatic disorder, calls for the establishment of a new worldview to replace the existing psychological malignancies. By definition, such a process would be lengthy and difficult. As Janet noted, trauma arrests personality development. Recovery, in its final and most profound manifestation, is a process of completing the personality development that was arrested by traumatic psychological injury.

KEY POINT SUMMARY

1. The purpose of this brief review was to examine the association between trauma, PTSD, and the occurrence of BPD. The chapter acknowledged the seminal work in the area of BPD by Adolf Stern followed by a review of Kernberg's object relations theory, Linehan's dialectical behavior theory, Kroll's text on PTSD/borderlines, and Millon's evolutionary construction.

2. We then explored the relationship between trauma and borderline personality followed by an overview of the concordance between PTSD and borderline personality disorder. These overall data do indeed suggest that personality may serve as a disease endpoint as the result of trauma. However, as conceptualized throughout this book, the development and expression of personality, in general, and BPD specifically, is dynamic and complex, which likely accounts for why there is not a perfect positive linear relationship between trauma, borderline personality, and PTSD.

3. Several authors conclude that the incidence of childhood sexual abuse alone does not provide a complete prescriptive etiology of borderline personality disorder, and others suggest that borderline personality may evince itself differently in different subgroups based in part on factors such as the timing and type of trauma.

4. The formation of borderline personality is a complex amalgam, most likely conforming to a diathesis stress model (Zanarini et al., 1998) and involving a mixture of genetics, biochemistry, neurology, temperament, and adverse environmental factors.

5. It is clear that BPD is related to psychological trauma. Given its heterogeneity, it would be far too simplistic an interpretation to claim that BPD is an Axis II variation of PTSD, but it seems clear that BPD is causally related to trauma, neglect, or abuse. To categorize adult-onset PTSD with what Herman has referred to as complex PTSD and borderline-like manifestations seems not only a taxonomic error but a phenomenological error as well. Finally, complex PTSD, borderline-like presentations, and the fully developed BPD seem to demand more complex synergistic psychotherapeutic approaches than are discussed in even this volume. The reader is referred to Linehan (1993, 1995), Kroll (1993), and Millon (Millon & Davis, 1996; Millon et al., 1999) for specific treatment recommendations.

APPENDIX A
PERSONALITY-GUIDED THERAPY OF POSTTRAUMATIC STRESS DISORDER: A SYNTHESIS

An amalgam of various philosophical and clinical orientations, this personality-guided approach to the treatment of posttraumatic distress and PTSD embraces the synergistic multicomponent approach to therapy advocated by Theodore Millon (1999). The key mechanisms described in this volume are outlined next and consist of the following:

I. TELLING THE TRAUMA STORY AND THE FORMATION OF THE THERAPEUTIC ALLIANCE

A personality-guided approach to establishing the therapeutic alliance is used with the goal of creating the foundation for the reconstruction of a safe world (using preferential process and personality-specific thematic belief mechanisms). Within this social microcosm, the patient is encouraged to tell the trauma story. The story usually consists of the following components:

A. A description of the traumatic event;

B. A description of signs, symptoms, and any other personal reactions or changes in behavior that are a consequence of the traumatic event,

C. Any reactions or changes in behavior demonstrated by family members, friends, coworkers, or others that appear to be a direct, or indirect, consequence of the traumatic event; and

D. Any anticipated changes to the patient's personal life, career, or interpersonal relationships in the future as a result of the traumatic event.

II. PROVIDING INFORMATION

The therapist provides information about the nature of posttraumatic reactions, in an effort to normalize and demedicalize, as much as reasonable, the reactions of the patient to the traumatic event. Posttraumatic stress may be explained in the context of survival.

III. FOSTERING NEUROLOGIC DESENSITIZATION

Fostering neurologic desensitization involves the use of the relaxation response, psychotropic medications, and the use of other personal stress management techniques designed to lower the functional irritability of the central nervous system and its effector systems. Any self-efficacy enhancing techniques are usually helpful (see Bandura, 1997). Enactive attainment, vicarious success, and physiological self-regulation techniques seem especially useful. Cognitive–behavioral techniques may also prove effective.

IV. DISCOVERING THE MOST SALIENT WORLDVIEW ISSUES AFFECTED BY THE TRAUMATIC EVENT

Through the use of exploratory dialogue and psychological testing, if applicable, the therapist attempts to discover the most salient worldview issues related to the present traumatic experience. These issues, according to the present construction, serve as the psychological foundations of the traumatic event and its subsequent response syndrome.

V. RESTORING FUNCTIONAL, ADAPTIVE ASSUMPTIVE WORLDVIEWS

Restoring functional, adaptive assumptive worldviews may be attempted via the following tactical interventions:

A. Integrating the traumatic event into the patient's existing worldview in such a way that the patient comes to understand the event as actually consistent with the worldview (i.e., the event did not in actuality violate any core assumptive worldviews);

1. Reinterpreting the traumatic event from one considered a personal failure, to one considered a personal success (e.g., via considering some other relevant measure with which to determine success);
2. Reinterpreting the role the patient specifically played in the etiology of the traumatic event (e.g., disputing culpability, identifying mitigating circumstances, or reducing overgeneralized self-blame).

B. Allowing the traumatic event to be understood as an exception to an existing worldview (i.e., an "exception to the rule"), which despite its existence represents a low probability occurrence and does not serve to invalidate the overall utility, or functionality, of the general assumptive construction; thus, life as the patient knows it goes on.

C. Acknowledging the disconfirming, invalidating nature of the traumatic event on the assumptive worldview, thus necessitating the creation of a new worldview wherein the trauma more readily fits. The difficulty inherent in such a process is clearly mitigated by assisting the patient to use the traumatic event to lead to a revelation of self-efficacy or to the revelation–creation of some greater good to self, family, or society that grows out of the traumatic experience (sometimes called the "yes, but" strategy).

1. Reinterpreting the valence of the traumatic event from one considered catastrophic to one considered bad, but possessing some positive, or redeeming, aspect to it. For example: (a) something of value can be learned from the event; (b) it could have been worse; (c) there is a "silver lining," etc.);
2. Reinterpreting the overall importance of the trauma. For example: reinterpreting the event as less important in the grand scheme of life or less important as a determinant of happiness than originally assumed);
3. Comparing oneself with other trauma victims who experienced less fortunate outcomes (downward comparison);
4. Recognition that the rate of personal recovery is exceptional compared to others, or compared to that which would be expected.

The process of termination is most easily achieved at the point at which the patient is capable of seeing the world as safe once again or the patient feels more realistically prepared to respond to its inherent risks.

APPENDIX B
A FAST-ACTING BEHAVIORAL
TECHNIQUE FOR PHYSIOLOGICAL
SELF-REGULATION

The most rapid way to control acute distress is through the voluntary control of respiratory mechanisms (Everly, 1989). The following technique uses the conscious manipulation of one's breathing patterns. This breathing technique has been shown to be effective in achieving acute reductions in blood pressure, muscle tension, and subjective reports of anxiety (Everly, 1979).

Patient Instructions:

STEP 1: Imagine a hollow bottle, or pouch, lying inside of your body directly beneath the surface of your navel.

STEP 2: As you inhale, taking a moderately deep breath (inhale for 2 to 3 seconds), imagine that the air you are inhaling goes directly to fill that internal pouch. As a result, you should feel your stomach rise as a result of the inhalation.

STEP 3: Once you have inhaled a moderately deep breath and without holding your breath, begin to exhale, to empty that imaginary pouch. As you exhale, say silently to yourself, "Relax." The exhalation should last 3 to 4 seconds.

STEP 4: Repeat steps 1–3.

STEP 5: Take five normal, but slower, breaths.

STEP 6: Repeat Steps 1–3 again. ·

STEP 7: Repeat Step 5 again.

If you feel dizzy or light-headed, inhale less deeply, or practice only one cycle. Never practice this technique without first obtaining clearance from your health care professional.

REFERENCES

Abramson, L. Y., Metalsky, G. I., & Alloy, L. B. (1989). Hopelessness depression. *Psychological Review*, 96, 358–372.

Adler, A. (1929). *The science of living*. New York: Greenberg.

Ainsworth, M. S. (1989). Attachments beyond infancy. *American Psychologist*, 44(4), 709–716.

Akiskal, H. S. (1981). Subaffective disorders, dysthymic, cyclothymic and biopolar II disorders in the borderline realm. *Psychiatric Clinics of North America*, 4, 25–46.

Albrecht, N. N., Talbert, S. F., Albrecht, J. W., Boudewyns, P. A., Hyer, L. A., et al. (1994). A comparison of MMPI and MMPI–2 in PTSD assessment. *Journal of Clinical Psychology*, 50(4), 578–585.

Al-Naser, F., & Everly, G. S., Jr. (1999). Prevalence of posttraumatic stress disorder among Kuwaiti firefighters. *International Journal of Emergency Mental Health*, 1, 99–101.

Al-Naser, F., Everly, G., & Al-Khulaif, I. (2001). Overcoming the effects of disasters. *International Journal of Emergency Mental Health*, 3, 11–13.

American Psychiatric Association. (1952). *Diagnostic and statistical manual of mental disorders*. Washington, DC: American Psychiatric Association.

American Psychiatric Association. (1968). *Diagnostic and statistical manual of mental disorders* (2nd ed.). Washington, DC: Author.

American Psychiatric Association. (1980). *Diagnostic and statistical manual of mental disorders* (3rd ed.). Washington, DC: Author.

American Psychiatric Association. (1987). *Diagnostic and statistical manual of mental disorders* (3rd ed., rev). Washington, DC: Author.

AmericanPsychiatric Association. (1994). *Diagnostic and statistical manual of mental disorders* (4th ed.). Washington DC: Author.

Amir, N., McNally, R. J., Riemann, B. C., & Clements, C. (1996). Implicit memory bias for threat in panic disorder: Application of the "white noise" paradigm. *Behaviour Research and Therapy*, 34, 157–162.

Amir, N., McNally, R. J., & Wiegartz, P. S. (1996). Implicit memory bias for threat in posttraumatic stress disorder. *Cognitive Therapy and Research*, 20(6), 625–635.

Arendt, M., & Elklit, A. (2001). Effectiveness of psychological debriefing. *Acta Psychiatrica Scandinavica*, 104, 423–437.

Argas, W. S., Taylor, C. B., Kraemer, H. C., Southam, M. A., & Schneider, J. A. (1987). Relaxation training for essential hypertension at the worksite: II. The poorly controlled hypertensive. *Psychosomatic Medicine*, 49, 264–273.

Aristotle. (1991). *The art of rhetoric*. New York: Penguin.

Armstrong, J., & Loewenstein, R. J., (1990). Characteristics of patients with multiple personality and dissociative disorders on psychological testing. *Journal of Nervous and Mental Disease*, 178, 448–454.

Artiss, K. (1963). Human behavior under stress: From combat to social psychiatry. *Military Medicine, 128,* 1011–1015.

Astin, J. A. (1997). Stress reduction through mindfulness meditation: Effects on psychological symptomatology, sense of control, and spiritual experiences. *Psychotherapy & Psychosomatics, 66*(2), 97–106.

Austin, J. H. (1998). *Zen and the brain: Toward an understanding of meditation and consciousness.* Cambridge, MA: MIT Press.

Ballentine, R. (1976). *Science of breath.* Glenview, IL: Himalayan International Institute.

Bandura, A. (1977). Self-efficacy: Toward a unifying theory of behavior change. *Psychological Review, 84,* 191–215.

Bandura, A. (1982). The self and mechanisms of agency. In J. Suls (Ed.), *Psychological perspectives on the self* (pp. 3–39). Hillsdale, NJ: Erlbaum.

Bandura, A. (1997). *Self-efficacy: The exercise of control.* New York: Freeman.

Barabasz, M., & Spiegel, D. (1989). Hypnotizability and weight loss in obese subjects. *International Journal of Eating Disorders, 8,* 335–341.

Barnes, V., Schneider, R., Alexander, C., & Staggers, F. (1997). Stress, stress reduction, and hypertension in African Americans: An update and review. *Journal of the National Medical Association, 7,* 464–476.

Baumgaertel, A. (1999). Alternative and controversial treatments for attention-deficit/hyperactivity disorder. *Pediatric Clinics of North America, 46*(5), 977–992.

Beaton, R., Murphy, S., & Corneil, W. (1996, Sept.). *Prevalence of posttraumatic stress disorder symptomatology in professional urban fire fighters in two countries.* Paper presented to the International Congress of Occupational Health, Stockholm, Sweden.

Beck, A., & Freeman, A. (1990). *Cognitive therapy of personality disorders.* New York: Guilford Press.

Beck, A. T., & Steer, R. A. (1987). *Beck Depression Inventory.* San Antonio, TX: Psychological Corporation.

Becker, D. (2000). When she was bad: Borderline personality disorder in a posttraumatic age. *American Journal of Orthopsychiatry, 70*(4), 422–432.

Beckham, J. C., Crawford, A. L., & Feldman, M. E. (1998). Trail Making Test performance in Vietnam combat veterans with and without posttraumatic stress disorder. *Journal of Traumatic Stress, 11*(4), 811–819.

Begic, D., Hotujac, L., & Jokic-Begic, N. (2001). *International Journal of Psychophysiology, 40*(2), 167–172.

Benson, H. (1975). *The relaxation response.* New York: Morrow.

Benson, H. (1983). The relaxation response: Its subjective and objective historical precedents and physiology. *Trends in Neuroscience, 6,* 281–284.

Benson, H. (1996). *Timeless healing: The power and biology of belief.* New York: Scribner.

Benton, A. L. (1974). *Revised Visual Retention Test* (4th ed.). New York: Psychological Corporation.

Benton, A. L., Hamsher, K. deS., Varney, N. R., & Spreen, O. (1983). *Contributions to neuropsychological assessment.* New York: Oxford University Press.

Bernard, C. (1945). *Introduction to the study of experimental medicine.* Paris: Flammarian. (Original published 1865).

Bernstein, D. P., & Fink, L. (1998). *Childhood Trauma Questionnaire: A retrospective self-report (CTQ).* San Antonio, TX: Psychological Corporation.

Bersoff, S. (1970). Rorschach correlates of traumatic neurosis of war. *Journal of Projective Techniques and Personality Assessment, 34*(3), 194–200.

Best, C. L., & Ribbe, D. P. (1995). Accidental injury: Approaches to assessment and treatment. In J. R. Freedy & S. E. Hobfoll (Eds.), *Traumatic stress: From theory to practice* (pp. 315–337). New York: Plenum Press.

Bielski, R., & Friedel, R. (1976). Prediction of tricyclic antidepressant response. *Archives of General Psychiatry, 33,* 1479–1489.

Biondi, M., & Picardi, A. (1998). Temporomandibular joint pain-dysfunction syndrome and bruxism: Etipatholgenesis and treatment from a psychosomatic integrative viewpoint. In G. A. Fava & H. Freyberger (Eds.), *Handbook of psychosomatic medicine* (pp. 469–490). Madison, CT: International Universities Press.

Bisson, J. I., Jenkins, P., Alexander, J., & Bannister, C. (1997). Randomized controlled trial of psychological debriefings for victims of acute burn trauma. *British Journal of Psychiatry, 171,* 78–81.

Bisson, J. I., McFarlane, A., & Rose, S. (2000). Psychological debriefing. In E. Foa, A. McFarlane, & M. Friedman (Eds.), *Effective treatments for PTSD* (pp. 39–59). New York: Guilford Press.

Black, I., Adler, J., Dreyfus, C., Friedman, W., Laganuna, E., et al. (1987). Biochemtistry of information storage in the nervous system. *Science, 236,* 1263–1268.

Blake, D. D., Weathers, F. W., Nagy, L. M., Kaloupek, D. G., Gusman, F. D., et al. (1995). The development of a clinician-administered PTSD scale. *Journal of Traumatic Stress, 8,* 75–90.

Blake, D. D., Weathers, F. W., Nagy, L. M., Kaloupek, D. G., Klauminzer, G., et al. (1990). A clinician rating scale for assessing current and lifetime PTSD: The CAPS-1. *Behavior Therapist, 13,* 187–188.

Blanchard, E. B., & Buckley, T. C. (1999). Psychophysiological assessment of posttraumatic stress disorder. In P. A. Saigh & J. D. Bremner (Eds.), *Posttraumatic stress disorder: A comprehensive text* (pp. 248–266). Needham Heights, MA: Allyn & Bacon.

Blanchard, E. B., Hickling, E. J., Taylor, A. E., Loos, W. R., & Gerardi, R. J. (1994). The psychophysiology of motor vehicle accident related posttraumatic stress disorder. *Behavior Therapy, 25,* 453–467.

Blanchard, E. B., Kolb, L. C., Gerardi, R. J., Ryan, P., & Pallmeyer, T. P. (1986). Cardiac response to relevant stimuli as an adjunctive tool for diagnosing posttraumatic stress disorder in Vietnam veterans. *Behavior Therapy, 17*, 592–606.

Blanchard, E. B., Kolb, L. C., Pallmeyer, T. P., & Gerardi, R. J. (1982). A psychophysiologcal study of post-traumatic stress disorder in Vietnam veterans. *Psychiatric Quarterly, 54*, 220–229.

Blanchard, E. B., Nicholson, N. L., Taylor, A. E., Steffeck, B. D., Radnitz, C. L., et al. (1991). The role of regular home practice in the relaxation treatment of tension headache. *Journal of Consulting and Clinical Psychology, 59*, 467–470.

Blomhoff, S., Reinvang, I., & Malt, U. F. (1998). Event-related potentials to stimuli with emotional impact in posttraumatic stress patients. *Biological Psychiatry, 44*(10), 1045–1053.

Bohl, N. (1991). The effectiveness of brief psychological interventions in police officers after critical incidents. In J. T. Reese, J. Horn, & C. Dunning (Eds.), *Critical incidents in policing* (rev.; pp. 31–38). Washington, DC: U.S. Department of Justice.

Bohl, N. (1995). Measuring the effectiveness of CISD. *Fire Engineering,* 125–126.

Bollinger, A. R., Riggs, D. S., Blake, D. D., & Ruzek, J. I. (2000). Prevalence of personality disorders among combat veterans with posttraumatic stress disorder. *Journal of Traumatic Stress, 13*(2), 255–270.

Bordeau, L. (1972). Transcendental meditation and yoga as reciprocal inhibitors. *Journal of Behavior Therapy and Experimental Psychiatry, 3*, 97–98.

Bordow, S., & Porritt, D. (1979). An experimental evaluation of crisis intervention. *Social Science and Medicine, 13*, 251–256.

Bornstein, R. (1998). Reconceptualizing personality disorder diagnosis in the DSM–V. *Clinical Psychology, 5*, 333–343.

Bowlby, J. (1969). *Attachment and loss, Vol. I: Attachment.* New York: Basic Books.

Brammer, L., & MacDonald, G. (1999). *The helping relationship* (7th ed.). Boston: Allyn & Bacon.

Bremner, J. D. (1999). Does stress damage the brain? *Biological Psychiatry, 45*, 797–805.

Bremner, J. D., Innis, R. B., Chin, K., Staib, L. H., Salomon, R. M., et al. (1997). Positron Emission Tomography measurement of cerebral metabolic correlates of yohimbine administration in posttraumatic stress disorder. *Archives of General Psychiatry, 54*, 246–256.

Bremner, J. D., Randall, P., Scott, T. M., Bronen, R. A, Seibyl, J. P., et al. (1995). MRI-based measurement of hippocampal volume in combat-related posttraumatic stress disorder. *American Journal of Psychiatry, 152*, 973–981.

Bremner, J. D., Randall, P. R., Vermetten, E., Staib, L., Bronen, R. A., et al. (1997). MRI-based measurement of hippocampal volume in posttraumatic stress disorder related to childhood physical and sexual abuse: A preliminary report. *Biological Psychiatry, 41*, 23–32.

Bremner, J. D., Scott, T. M., Delaney, R. C., Southwick, S. M., Mason, J. W., et al. (1993). Deficits in short-term memory in posttraumatic stress disorder. *American Journal of Psychiatry, 150*(7), 1015–1019.

Breslau, N., Chilcoat, H. D., Kessler, R. C., & Davis, G. C. (1999). Previous exposure to trauma and PTSD effects of subsequent trauma: Results from the Detroit Area Trauma Survey of Trauma. *American Journal of Psychiatry, 156*, 902–907.

Breslau, N., Kessler, R., Chilcoat, H., Schultz, L., Davis, G., et al. (1998). Trauma and posttraumatic stress disorder in the community. *Archives of General Psychiatry, 55*, 626–633.

Briere, J. (1997). Psychological assessment of child abuse effects in adults. In J. P. Wilson & T. M. Keane (Eds.), *Assessing psychological trauma and PTSD* (pp. 43–68). New York: Guilford Press.

British Psychological Society. (1990). *Psychological aspects of disaster*. Leicester, UK: British Psychological Society.

Brom, D., Kleber, R. J., & Defares, P. B. (1989). Brief psychotherapy for posttraumatic stress disorder. *Journal of Consulting and Clinical Psychology, 57*, 607–612.

Brooks, J. S., & Scarano, T. (1985). Transcendental meditation in the treatment of post-Vietnam adjustment. *Journal of Counseling & Development, 64*(3), 212–215.

Brown, D., Scheflin, A., & Hammond, C. (1998). *Memory, trauma treatment, and the law*. New York: Norton.

Bryer, J. B., Nelson, B. A., Miller, J. B., & Krol, P. A. (1987). Childhood sexual and physical abuse as factors in adult psychiatric illness. *American Journal of Psychiatry, 144*, 1426–1430.

Bunn, T., & Clarke, A. (1979). Crisis intervention. *British Journal of Medical Psychology, 52*, 191–195.

Burgio, K. L., & Goode, P. S. (1997). Behavioral interventions for incontinence in ambulatory geriatric patients. *American Journal of the Medical Sciences, 314*(4), 257–261.

Buschke, H. (1973). Selective reminding for analysis of memory and learning. *Journal of Verbal Learning and Verbal Behavior, 12*, 543–550.

Buselli, E. F., & Stuart, E. M. (1999). Influences of psychosocial factors and biopsychosocial interventions on outcomes after myocardial infarction. *Journal of Cardiovascular Nursing, 13*(3), 60–72.

Butcher, J. N., Dahlstrom, W. G., Graham, J. R., Tellegen, A., & Kaemmer, B. (1989). *Minnesota Multiphasic Personality Inventory (MMPI–2). Manual for administration and scoring*. Minneapolis: University of Minnesota Press.

Butler, R. N., Maby, J. I., Montela, J. M., & Young, G. P. (1999). Urinary incontinence: Primary care therapies for the older woman. *Geriatrics, 54*(11), 31–34, 39–40, 43–44.

Cain, D. P. (1992). Kindling and the amygdala. In J. P. Aggleton (Ed.), *The amygdala* (pp. 539–560). New York: Wiley-Liss.

Campbell, D. T., & Stanley, J. C. (1963). *Experimental and quasi-experimental designs for research*. Chicago: Rand McNally.

Campfield, K., & Hills, A., 2001. Effect of timing of Critical Incident Stress Debriefing on posttraumatic symptoms. *Journal of Traumatic Stress, 14,* 327–340.

Cannon, W. B. (1929). *Bodily changes in pain, fear, hunger, and rage*. New York: Norton.

Cannon, W. (1932). *The wisdom of the body*. New York: Norton.

Caplan, G. (1961). *An approach to community mental health*. New York: Grune & Stratton.

Caplan, G. (1964). *Principles of preventive psychiatry*. New York: Basic Books.

Cardeña, E., Maldonado, J., van der Hart, O., & Spiegel, D. (2000). Hypnosis. In E. B. Foa, T. M. Keane, & M. J. Friedman (Eds.), *Effective treatments for PTSD* (pp. 247–279). New York: Guilford Press.

Carlson, J. G. (1996). Behavioral interventions for posttraumatic stress disorder. In C. D. Spielberger, I. G. Sarason, J. J. T. Brebner, E. Greenglass, P. Laungani, et al. (Eds.), *Stress and emotion: Anxiety, anger, and curiosity* (Vol. 16; pp. 269–303). New York: Taylor & Francis.

Carlson, J. G., Singelis, T. M., & Chemtob, C. M. (1997). Facial EMG responses to combat-related visual stimuli in veterans with and without posttraumatic stress disorder. *Applied Psychophysiology & Biofeedback, 22*(4), 247–259.

Carmil, D., & Breznitz, S. (1991). Personal trauma and world view—Are extremely stressful experiences related to political attitudes, religious beliefs, and future orientation? *Journal of Traumatic Stress, 4*(3), 393–405.

Carrington, P. (1993). Modern forms of meditation. In P. Lehrer & R. Woolfolk (Eds.), *Principles and practice of stress management* (pp. 139–168). New York: Guilford Press.

Catherall, D. R. (1989). Differentiating intervention strategies for primary and secondary trauma in post-traumatic stress disorder: The example of Vietnam veterans. *Journal of Traumatic Stress, 2*(3), 289–304.

Catherall, D. R. (1998). Treating traumatized families. In C. R. Figley (Ed.), *Burnout in families: The systematic cost of caring* (pp. 187–215). Boca Raton, FL: CRC Press.

Charles, G., Hansenne, M., Ansseau, M., Pitchot, W., Machowski, R., et al. (1995). P300 in posttraumatic stress disorder. *Neuropsychobiology, 32*(2), 72–74.

Chemtob, C. M., Tomas, S., Law, W., & Cremniter, D. (1997). Postdisaster psychosocial intervention. *American Journal of Psychiatry, 154,* 415–417.

Cohen, S., Evans, G., Stokols, D., & Krantz, D. (Eds.). (1980). *Behavior, health and environmental stress*. New York: Plenum Press.

Connor, K. M., Davidson, J. R. T., Hughes, D. C., Swartz, M. S., Blazer, D. G., et al. (2002). The impact of borderline personality disorder on post-traumatic stress in the community: A study of health status, health utilization, and functioning. *Comprehensive Psychiatry, 43*(1), 41–48.

Copeland, M. E., & Harris, M. (2000). *Healing the trauma of abuse: A women's workbook*. Oakland, CA: New Harbinger.

Costello, C. G. (1995). The advantages of focusing on the personality characteristics of the personality disordered. In C. Costello (Ed.), *Personality characteristics of the personality disordered* (pp. 1–23). New York: Wiley.

Courtois, C. A. (2000). The aftermath of child sexual abuse: The treatment of complex posttraumatic stress reactions. In L. Szuchman & F. Muscarella (Eds.), *Psychological perspectives on human sexuality* (pp. 549–572). New York: John Wiley & Sons.

Cunningham, H. (1970). *Julius Caesar*. New York: Amcso.

Dalton, J. E., Pederson, S. L., & Ryan, J. J. (1989). Effects of posttraumatic stress disorder on neuropsychological test performances. *International Journal of Clinical Neuropsychology, 11*(3), 121–124.

Darves-Bornoz, J. M., Lepine, J. P., Choquet, M., Berger, C., Degiovanni, A., et al. (1998). Predictive factors of chronic post-traumatic stress disorder in rape victims. *European Psychiatry, 13*(6), 281–287.

Davidson, G. E., & Neale, J. M. (1990). *Abnormal psychology* (5th ed.). New York: John Wiley & Sons.

Davidson, J. R. T. (1996). *Davidson Trauma Scale* [Manual]. Ontario, Canada: Multi-Health Systems.

Davidson, J. R. T., Hughes, D., & Blazer, D. (1991). Post-traumatic stress disorder in the community: An epidemiological study. *Psychological Medicine, 21,* 713–721.

Davidson, J. R. T., Kudler, H. S., & Smith. (1990). *The Structured Interview for PTSD (SI–PTSD)*. Unpublished manuscript, Department of Psychiatry, Duke University, Durham, NC.

Davidson, J. R. T., Malik, M. A., & Travers, J. (1997). Structured interview for PTSD (SIP): Psychometric validation for *DSM–IV* criteria. *Depression and Anxiety, 5*(3), 127–129.

Davidson, J. R. T., Smith, R. D., & Kudler, H. S. (1989). Validity and reliability of the *DSM–III* criteria for post-traumatic stress disorder: Experience with a structured interview. *Journal of Nervous and Mental Disease, 177,* 336–341.

Deadwyler, S., Gribkoff, V., Cotman, D., & Lynch, G. (1976). Long-lasting chances in the spontaneous activity of hippocampal neurons following stimulation of the entorhinal cortex. *Brain Research Bulletin,* 1–7.

Deahl, M., Srinivasan, M., Jones, N., Thomas, J., Neblett, C., et al. (2000). Preventing psychological trauma in soldiers. The role of operational stress training and psychological debriefing. *British Journal of Medical Psychology, 73,* 77–85.

Debenham, G., Sargent, W., Hill, D., & Slater, E. (1941). Treatment of war neurosis. *Lancet, 240,* 107–109.

Decker, L. R. (1993). The role of trauma in spiritual development. *Journal of Humanistic Psychology, 33*(4) 33–46.

Decker, J., & Stubblebine, J (1972). Crisis intervention and prevention of psychiatric disability: A follow-up. *American Journal of Psychiatry, 129,* 725–729.

Delanoy, R., Tucci, D., & Gold, P. (1983). Amphetamine effects on LTP in dendate granule cells. *Pharmacology, Biochemistry, and Behavior, 18,* 137–139.

Delis, D. C., Freeland, J., Kramer, J. H., & Kaplan, E., & Ober, B. A. (1987). *California Verbal Learning Test: Adult version manual*. San Antonio, TX: Psychological Corporation.

Derogatis, L. R. (1983). *SCL–90–R administration, scoring, and procedures manual II for the revised version* (2nd ed.). Towson, MD: Clinical Psychometrics Research.

Desland, M. (1997). Post-traumatic stress disorder. *Australian Journal of Clinical & Experimental Hypnosis, 25*(1), 61–73.

DiFilippo, J. M., & Overholser, J. C. (1999). Cognitive–behavioral treatment of panic disorder: Confronting situational precipitants. *Journal of Contemporary Psychotherapy, 29*(2), 99–113.

Doane, B. (1986). Clinical psychiatry and the physiodynamics of the limbic system. In B. Doane & K. Livingston (Eds.), *The limbic system* (pp. 285–315). New York: Raven Press.

Dobbs, D., & Wilson, W. P. (1960). Observations on persistence of war neurosis. *Diseases of the Nervous System, 21*, 686–691.

Dowd, E. T. (2000). *Cognitive hypnotherapy*. Northvale, NJ: Jason Aronson.

Driessen, M., Herrmann, J., Stahl, K., Zwaan, M., Meier, et al. (2000). Magnetic resonance imaging volumes of the hippocampus and the amygdala in women with borderline personality disorder and early traumatization. *Archives of General Psychiatry, 57*, 1115–1122.

Dryden, W. (1999). *Rational emotive behavioural counseling* (2nd ed.) London: Sage.

Duggan, H. (2002). CISM at the World Trade Center: Lessons learned from Sept 11. ICHIEFS On-line Resource September 1.

Dyregrov, A. (1997). The process of psychological debriefing. *Journal of Traumatic Stress, 10*, 589–604.

Dyregrov, A. (1998). Psychological debriefing: An effective method? *Traumatologye, 4*, (2), n.p.

Dyregrov, A. (1999). Helpful and hurtful aspects of psychological debriefing groups. *International Journal of Emergency Mental Health, 1*, 175–181.

Dyregrov, A., & Mitchell, J. (1992). Work with traumatized children—Psychological effects and coping strategies. *Journal of Traumatic Stress, 5*(1), 5–17.

Earle, J. B. (1981). Cerebral laterality and meditation: A review of the literature. *Journal of Transpersonal Psychology, 13*, 155–173.

Echeburua, E., de Corral, P., Zubizarreta, I., & Sarasua, B. (1997). Psychological treatment of chronic posttraumatic stress disorder in victims of sexual aggression. *Behavior Modification, 21*(4), 433–456.

Eid, J., Johnsen, B., & Weisaeth, L. (2001). The effects of group psychological debriefing on acute stress reactions following a traffic accident. *International Journal of Emergency Mental Health, 3*, 145–154.

Emery, G., & Lesher, E. (1982). Treatment of depression in older adults: Personality considerations. *Psychotherapy Research and Practice, 19*, 500–505.

Employee Assistance Professionals' Association (EAPA). (2002, November). *Report of the Disaster Preparedness Task Force*. Boston: Author.

Epstein, S., Lipson, A., Holstein, C., & Hub, E. (1992). Irrational reactions to negative outcomes: Evidence for two conceptual systems. *Journal of Personality and Social Psychology, 62*, 328–339.

Everly, G. S., Jr. (1979). A psychophysiological technique for the rapid onset of a trophotropic state. *IRCS Journal of Medical Science, 7*, 423.

Everly, G. S., Jr. (1987). Principle of personologic primacy and personologic psycho-therapy: A rationale for personality-based approaches to psychotherapy. In C. Green (Ed.), *Proceedings of the Conference on the Millon Inventories* (pp. 3–7). Minnetonka, MN: NCS.

Everly, G. S., Jr. (1989). *A clinical guide to the treatment of the human stress response*. New York: Plenum Press.

Everly, G. S., Jr. (1990). Post-traumatic stress disorder as a disorder of arousal. *Psychology and Health, 4*, 135–145.

Everly, G. S., Jr. (1993a). Neurophysiological considerations in the treatment of PTSD: A neurocognitive perspective. In J. Wilson & B. Raphael (Eds.), *International handbook of traumatic stress syndromes* (pp. 795–801). New York: Plenum Press.

Everly, G. S., Jr. (1993b). Psychotraumatology: A two-factor formulation of posttrau-matic stress. *Integrative Physiological and Behavioral Science, 28*, 270–278.

Everly, G. S., Jr. (1994). Brief psychotherapy for posttraumatic stress disorder: The role of Weltanschaaung. *Stress Medicine, 10*, 191–196.

Everly, G. S., Jr. (1995). An integrative two-factor model of post-traumatic stress. In G. S. Everly, Jr., & J. Lating (Eds.), *Psychotraumatology: Key papers and core concepts in Post-traumatic stress* (pp. 27–48). New York: Plenum Press.

Everly, G. S., Jr. (1999). Toward a model of psychological triage. *International Journal of Emergency Mental Health, 1*, 151–154.

Everly, G. S., Jr. (2000a). Five principles of crisis intervention: Reducing the risk of premature crisis intervention. *International Journal of Emergency Mental Health, 2*, 1–4.

Everly, G. S., Jr. (2000b). Crisis management briefings (CMB): Large group crisis intervention in response to terrorism, disasters, and violence. *International Journal of Emergency Mental Health, 2*, 53–57.

Everly, G. S., Jr. (2000c). Pastoral crisis intervention: Toward a definition. *International Journal of Emergency Mental Health, 2*, 69–71.

Everly, G. S., Jr. (2000d). The role of pastoral crisis intervention in disasters, terrorism, violence, and other community crises. *International Journal of Emergency Mental Health, 2*, 139–142.

Everly, G. S., Jr. (2002). Thoughts on training guidelines in emergency mental health and crisis intervention. *International Journal of Emergency Mental Health, 4*, 138–140.

Everly G. S., Jr., & Benson, H. (1989). Disorders of arousal and the relaxation response. *International Journal of Psychosomatics, 36*, 15–22.

Everly, G. S., Jr., & Boyle, S. (1999). Critical Incident Stress Debriefing (CISD): A meta-analysis. *International Journal of Emergency Mental Health, 1,* 165–168.

Everly, G. S., Jr., Flannery, R. B., Jr., & Eyler, V. (2002). Critical Incident Stress Management (CISM): A statistical review of the literature. *Psychiatric Quarterly, 73,* 171–182.

Everly, G. S., Jr., Flannery, R. B., Jr., Eyler, V., & Mitchell, J. T. (2001). Sufficiency analysis of an integrated multicomponent approach to crisis intervention: Critical Incident Stress Management. *Advances in Mind–Body Medicine, 17,* 174–183.

Everly, G. S., Jr., Flannery, R. B., & Mitchell, J. (2000). Critical Incident Stress Management: A review of literature. *Aggression and Violent Behavior: A Review Journal, 5,* 23–40.

Everly, G. S., Jr. & Horton, A. M., Jr. (1989). Neuropsychology of post-traumatic stress disorder: A pilot study. *Perceptual and Motor Skills, 68,* 807–810.

Everly, G. S., Jr., & Lating, J. M. (1995). *Psychotraumatology: Key papers and core concepts in post-traumatic stress.* New York: Plenum Press.

Everly, G. S., Jr., & Lating, J. M. (2002). *A clinical guide to the treatment of the human stress response* (2nd ed.). New York: Kluwer/Plenum Press.

Everly, Jr., G. S., Jr., & Mitchell, J. T. (1999). *Critical Incident Stress Management (CISM). A new era and standard of care in crisis intervention* (3rd ed.). Ellicott City, MD: Chevron.

Everly, G. S., Jr., & Mitchell, J. T. (2001). America under attack: The "10 Commandments" of responding to mass terrorist attacks. *International Journal of Emergency Mental Health, 3,* 133–135.

Everly, G. S., Jr., & Piacentini, A. (1999, March). *The effects of CISD on trauma symptoms: A meta-analysis.* Paper presented to the APA-NIOSH Work, Stress and Health '99: Organization of Work in a Global Economy conference, Baltimore.

Falsetti, S. A., Resnick, H. S., Resick, P. A., & Kilpatrick, D. G. (1993). The Modified PTSD Symptom Scale: A brief self-report measure of posttraumatic stress disorder. *Behavior Therapist, 16,* 161–162.

Falsetti, S. A., Resick, P. A., Resnick, H. S., & Kilpatrick, D. G. (1997). Modified PTSD Symptom Scale: Self-report version (MPSS–SR). In E. B. Carlson (Ed.), *Trauma assessments* (pp. 220–221). New York: Guilford Press.

Faymonville, M. E., Mambourg, P. H., Joris, J., Vrijens, B., Fissette, J., et al. (1997). Psychological approaches during conscious sedation: Hypnosis versus stress reducing strategies: A prospective randomized study. *Pain, 73,* 361–367.

Ffrench, C. (2000). The meaning of trauma: Hypnosis and PTSD. *Australian Journal of Clinical & Experimental Hypnosis, 28*(2), 199–199.

Fifkova, E., & Van Harreveld, A. (1977). Long lasting morphological changes in dendritic spines and dentate granule cells following stimulation of the entorhinal cortex area. *Journal of Neurocytology, 6,* 211–230.

Figley, C. R. (Ed.). (1995). *Compassion fatigue: Coping with secondary stress disorder in those who treat the traumatized.* New York: Brunner/Mazel.

Flannery, R. B., Jr. (1998). *The Assaulted Staff Action Program.* Ellicott City, MD: Chevron.

Flannery, R. B., Jr., (1999a). Treating family survivors of mass casualties: A CISM family crisis intervention approach. *International Journal of Emergency Mental Health, 1,* 243–250.

Flannery, R. B., Jr. (1999b). Critical Incident Stress Management (CISM); The assaultive psychiatric patient. *International Journal of Emergency Mental Health, 1,* 169–174.

Flannery, R. B., Jr. (1999c). Critical Incident Stress Management and the Assaulted Staff Action Program. *International Journal of Emergency Mental Health, 1,* 103–108.

Flannery, R. B., Jr., Anderson, E., Marks, L., & Uzoma, L. (2000). The Assaulted Staff Action Program (ASAP) and declines in rates of assaults: Mixed replicated findings. *Psychiatric Quarterly, 71,* 165–175.

Flannery, R. B., Jr., Everly, G. S., Jr., & Eyler, V. (2000). The Assaulted Staff Action Program (ASAP) and declines in assaults: A meta-analysis. *International Journal of Emergency Mental Health, 2,* 143–146.

Flannery, R. B., Jr., Hanson, M., Penk, W., Flannery, G., & Gallagher, C. (1995). The Assaulted Staff Action Program: An approach to coping with the aftermath of violence in the workplace. In L. Murphy, J. Hurrell, S. Sauter, & G. Keita (Eds.), *Job stress interventions* (pp. 199–212). Washington, DC: American Psychological Association.

Flannery, R. B., Jr., Hanson, M., Penk, W., Goldfinger, S., Pastva, G., et al. (1998). *Psychiatric Services, 49,* 241–243.

Flannery, R. B., Jr., Penk, W., & Corrigan, M. (1999). The Assaulted Staff Action Program (ASAP) and declines in the prevalence of assaults: A community-based replication. *International Journal of Emergency Mental Health, 1,* 19–22.

Fletcher, K. E. (1996). Psychometric review of World View Survey. In B. H. Stamm (Ed.), *Measurement of stress, trauma, and adaptation* (pp. 443–444). Lutherville, MD: Sidran Press.

Foa, E. B. (1995). *Posttraumatic Stress Diagnostic Scale (PDS) manual.* Minneapolis, MN: National Computer System.

Foa, E. B. (1997). Trauma and women: Course, predictors, and treatment. *Journal of Clinical Psychiatry, 58*(9), 25–28.

Foa, E. B., Cashman, L., Jaycox, L., & Perry, K. (1997). The validation of a self-report measure of posttraumatic stress disorder: The Posttraumatic Diagnostic Scale. *Psychological Assessment, 9*(4), 445–451.

Foa, E. B., Keane, T. M., & Friedman, M. J. 2000. Effective treatments for PTSD: *Practice guidelines from the International Society for Traumatic Stress Studies.* New York: Guilford Press.

Foa, E. B., & Tolin, D. F. (2000). Comparison of the PTSD Symptom Scale-Interview version and the Clinician-Administered PTSD Scale. *Journal of Traumatic Stress, 13*(2), 181–191.

Foa, E. B., Riggs, D. S., Dancu, C. V., & Rothbaum, B. O. (1993). Reliability and validity of a brief instrument for assessing posttraumatic stress disorder. *Journal of Traumatic Stress, 6*, 459–473.

Forbes, D., Creamer, M., Nicholas, A., Elliott, P., McHugh, T., et al. (2002). The MMPI–2 as a predictor of symptom change following treatment for posttraumatic stress disorder. *Journal of Personality Assessment, 79*(2), 321–336.

Fossati, A., Madeddu, F., & Maffei, C. (1999). Borderline personality disorder and childhood sexual abuse: A meta-analytic study. *Journal of Personality Disorders, 13*(3), 268–280.

Frances, A. (1999). Treatment of posttraumatic stress disorder. *Journal of Clinical Psychiatry, 60*, entire supplement 16.

Frances, A., & Hale, R. (1984). Determining how a depressed woman's personality affects the choice of treatment. *Hospital and Community Psychiatry, 35*, 883–884, 954.

Frank, G. (1992). On the use of the Rorschach in the study of PTSD. *Journal of Personality Assessment, 59*(3), 641–643.

Frank. L. R. (2001). *Quotationary.* New York: Random House.

Frank, H., & Paris, J. (1981). Recollections of family experience in borderline patients. *Archives of General Psychiatry, 38*, 1031–1034.

Frank, J. D., & Frank, J. B. (1991). *Persuasion & healing* (3rd ed.). Baltimore: Johns Hopkins University Press.

Frankl, V. (1959). *Man's search for meaning.* Boston: Beacon.

Friedman, M. J., Charney, D. S., & Deutch, A. Y. (1995). *Neurobiological and clinical consequences of stress: From normal adaptation to post-traumatic stress disorder.* Philadelphia: Lippincott-Raven.

Frueh, C. B., de Arellano, M. A., & Turner, S. M. (1997). Systematic desensitization as an alternative exposure strategy for PTSD. *American Journal of Psychiatry, 154*(2), 287–288.

Frysinger, R., & Harper, R. (1989). Cardiac and respiratory correlations with unit discharge in human amygdala and hippocampus. *Electroencephalography and Clinical Neurophysiology, 72*, 463–470.

Gaston, L., Brunet, A., Koszycki, D., & Bradwejn, J. (1998). MMPI scales for diagnosing acute and chronic PTSD in civilians. *Journal of Traumatic Stress, 11*(2), 355–365.

Gellhorn, E. (1957). *Imbalance and the hypothalamus.* Minneapolis: University of Minnesota Press.

Gellhorn, E. (1958a). The physiological basis of neuromuscular relaxation. *Archives of Internal Medicine, 102*, 392–399.

Gellhorn, E. (1958b). The influence of curare on hypothalamic excitability and the electroencephalogram. *Electroencephalography and Clinical Neurophysiology, 10*, 697–703.

Gellhorn, E. (1964). Motion and emotion. *Psychological Review, 71,* 457–472.

Gellhorn, E. (1965). The neurophysiological basis of anxiety. *Perspectives in Biology and Medicine, 8,* 488–515.

Gellhorn, E. (1967). *Principles of autonomic-somatic integrations.* Minneapolis: University of Minnesota Press.

Gellhorn, E. (1968). Central nervous system tuning and its implications for neuropsychiatry. *Journal of Nervous and Mental Disease, 147,* 148–162.

Gellhorn, E., & Kiely, W. (1972). Mystical states of consciousness. *Journal of Nervous and Mental Disease, 154,* 399–405.

Gellhorn, E., & Loofbourrow, G. (1963). *Emotions and emotional disorders.* New York: Harper & Row.

Girdano, D., Everly, G. S., Jr., & Dusek, D. (2001). *Controlling stress and tension: A holistic approach* (6th ed.): Boston: Allyn Bacon.

Gittelman-Klein R., & Klein, D. (1969). Premorbid asocial adjustment and prognosis in schizophrenia. *Journal of Psychiatric Research, 7,* 35–53.

Glenn, D. M., Beckham, J. C., Sampson, W. S., Feldman, M. E., Hertzberg, M. A., et al. (2002). MMPI–2 profiles of Gulf and Vietnam combat veterans with chronic posttraumatic stress disorder. *Journal of Clinical Psychology, 58*(4), 371–381.

Gloor, P. (1986). Role of the human limbic system in perception, memory, and affect. In B. Doane & K. Livingston (Eds.), *The limbic system* (pp. 159–169). New York: Raven Press.

Goddard, G., & Douglas, R. (1976). Does the engrain of kindling model the engram of normal long-term memory? In J. Wads (Ed.), *Kindling* (pp. 1–18). New York: Raven Press.

Goddard, G., McIntyre, D., & Leech, C. (1969). A permanent change in brain function resulting from daily electrical stimulation. *Experimental Neurology, 25,* 295–330.

Golden, C. J. (1976). Identification of brain disorders by the Stroop Color and Word Test. *Journal of Clinical Psychology, 32,* 621–626.

Golden, C. J. (1978). *Stroop Color and Word Test.* Chicago: Stoelting.

Golier, J., & Yehuda, R. (2002). Neuropsychological processes in post-traumatic stress disorder. *Psychiatric Clinics of North America, 25,* 295–315.

Goodman, M., & Yehuda, R. (2002). The relationship between psychological trauma and borderline personality disorder. *Psychiatric Annals, 36*(2), 337–345.

Gravitz, M. A. (1995). Hypnosis in the treatment of functional infertility. *American Journal of Clinical Hypnosis, 38,* 22–26.

Gravitz, M. A., & Page, R. A. (2002). Hypnosis in the management of stress reactions. In G. S. Everly, Jr., & J. M. Lating (Eds.), *A clinical guide to the treatment of the human stress response* (pp. 241–252). New York: Plenum Press.

Gray, J. (1982). *The neuropsychology of anxiety.* New York: Oxford University Press.

Gray, J. (1985). Issues in the neuropsychology of anxiety. In A. Tuma & J. Maser (Eds.), *Anxiety and anxiety disorders* (pp. 5–26). Hillsdale, NJ: Erlbaum.

Green, E., & Green, A. (1989). General and specific applications of thermal biofeedback. In J. Basmajian (Ed.), *Biofeedback* (3rd ed.; pp. 209–221). Baltimore: Williams & Wilkins.

Griffin, M. G., Resick, P. A., & Mechanic, M. B. (1994, Nov.). *Psychophysiological & nonverbal assessment of peritraumatic dissociation in rape victims.* Paper presented at the 10th Annual Meeting of the International Society for Traumatic Stress Studies, Chicago, IL.

Grillon, C., Morgan, C. A., Southwick, S. M., Davis, M., & Charney, D. S. (1996). Baseline startle amplitutde and prepulse inhibition in Vietnam veterans with posttraumatic stress disorder. *Psychiatry Research, 64*(3), 169–178.

Gronwall, D. (1977). Paced auditory serial addition task: A measure of recovery from concussion. *Perceptual and Motor Skills, 44,* 367–373.

Grossman, R., Yehuda, R., Santamaria, N., Schmeidler, J., Silverman, J., et al. (2001). Hypothalamic–pituitary–adrenal axis activity in personality disordered subjects: Associations with psychological trauma, depression and comorbid posttraumatic stress disorder. *Biological Psychiatry, 49,* 59.

Gruzelier, J. H. (2000). Redefining hypnosis: Theory, methods, and integration. *Contemporary Hypnosis, 17,* 51–70.

Gunderson, J. G., & Sabo, A. N. (1993). The phenomenological and conceptual interface between borderline personality disorder and PTSD. *American Journal of Psychiatry, 150*(1), 19–27.

Gurvits, T. V., Gilbertson, M. W., Lasko, N. B., Tarhan, A. S., Simeon, D., et al. (2000). Neurologic soft signs in chronic posttraumatic stress disorder. *Archives of General Psychiatry, 57,* 181–186.

Hafer, C. L., & Olson, J. M. (1998). Individual differences in the belief in a just world and responses to personal misfortune. In L. Montada & M. J. Lerner (Eds.), *Responses to victimization and belief in a just world* (pp. 65–86). New York: Plenum Press.

Hall, C., & Lindzey, G. (1957). *Theories of personality.* New York: Wiley.

Hammarberg, M. (1992). Penn Inventory for posttraumatic stress disorder: Psychometric properties. *Psychological Assessment: A Journal of Consulting and Clinical Psychology, 4*(1), 67–76.

Hammarberg, M. (1996). Psychometric review of the Penn Inventory for Post Traumatic Stress Disorder. In B. H. Stamm (Ed.), *Measurement of stress, trauma, and adaptation* (pp. 231–232). Lutherville, MD: Sidran Press.

Hammarberg, M., & Silver, S. (1994). Outcome of treatment for posttraumatic stress disorder in a primary care unit serving Vietnam veterans. *Journal of Traumatic Stress, 7*(2), 1–22.

Han, J. N., Stegen, K., de Valck, C., & Clement, J. (1996). Influence of breathing therapy on complaints, anxiety and breathing patterns in patients with hyperventilation syndrome and anxiety disorders. *Journal of Psychosomatic Research, 41*(5), 481–493.

Harvey, J. (1978). Diaphragmatic breathing: A practical technique for breath control. *Behavior Therapist, 1,* 13–14.

Hathaway, S. R., & McKinley, J. C. (1951). *Minnesota Multiphasic Personality Inventory: Manual for administration and scoring.* New York: Psychological Corporation.

Hays, J. R. (1995). Trailmaking test norms for psychiatric patients. *Perceptual & Major Skills, 80*(1), 187–194.

Hedges, L. E. (2000). *Terrifying transferences: Aftershocks of childhood trauma.* Northvale, NJ: Jason Aroson.

Heffernan, K., & Cloitre, M. (2000). A comparision of postraumatic stress disorder with and without borderline personality disorder among women with a history of childhood sexual abuse: Etiological and clinical characteristics. *Journal of Nervous and Mental Disease, 188*(9), 589–595.

Henry, J. P., & Stephens, P. (1977). *Stress, health, and the social environment.* New York: Springer.

Herbert, R., & Lehmann, D. (1977). Theta bursts: An EEG pattern in normal subjects practicing the transcendental meditation technique. *Electroencephalography and Clinical Neurophysiology, 42,* 245–252.

Herman, J. L. (1992a). *Trauma and recovery.* New York: Basic Books.

Herman, J. L. (1992b). Complex PTSD: A syndrome in survivors of prolonged and repeated trauma. *Journal of Traumatic Stress, 5,* 377–391.

Herman, J. L., Perry, J. C., & van der Kolk, B. A. (1989). Childhood trauma in borderline personality disorder. *American Journal of Psychiatry, 146*(4), 490–495.

Hiebert-Murphy, D., & Woytkiw, L. (2000). A model for working with women dealing with child sexual abuse and addictions: The Laurel Centre, Winnipeg, Manitoba, Canada. *Journal of Substance Abuse Treatment, 18*(4), 387–394.

Hiley-Young, B. (1990). Facilitating cognitive–emotional congruence in anxiety disorders during self-determined cognitive change: An integrative model. *Journal of Cognitive Psychotherapy, 4*(2), 225–236.

Hiroto, D.S. (1974). Locus of control and learned helplessness. *Journal of Experimental Psychology, 102*(2), 187–193.

Hobbs, M., Mayou, R., Harrison, B., & Worlock, P. (1996). A randomized controlled trial of psychological debriefing for victims of road traffic accidents. *British Medical Journal, 313,* 1438–1439.

Holloway, E. A. (1994). The role of the physiotherapist in the treatment of hyperventilation. In B. H. Timmons & R. Ley (Eds.), *Behavioral and psychological approaches to breathing disorders* (pp. 157–175). New York: Plenum Press.

Holmes, R. (1985). *Acts of war.* New York: Free Press.

Homer. (1999). *The Iliad* (Trans. W. H. D. Rouse). New York: Signet.

Horowitz, M. (1986). *Stress response syndromes.* London: Jason Aronson.

Horowitz, M., Field, N. P., & Classen C. C. (1993). Stress response syndromes and their treatment. In L. Goldberger & S. Breznitz (Eds.), *Handbook of stress: Theoretical and clinical aspects* (2nd ed.; pp. 757–773). New York: Free Press.

Horowitz, M. J., Wilner, N., & Alvarez, W. (1979). Impact of Event Scale: A measure of subjective stress. *Psychosomatic Medicine, 41*, 209–218.

Horton, A. M. (1995). Neuropsychology of PTSD: Problems, prospects, and promises. In G. S. Everly, Jr., & J. Lating (Eds.), *Psychotraumatology: Key papers and core concepts in post-traumatic stress* (pp. 147–156). New York: Plenum Press.

Huber, M. (2001). Activation of thalama cortical system in post-traumatic flashbacks. A PET Study. *Traumatology, 7*, 131–141.

Hyler, S. E., & Reider, R. O. (1987). *Personality Diagnostic Questionnaire–Revised (PDQ–R)*. New York: New York State Psychiatric Institute.

Jacobson, E. (1938). *Progressive relaxation*. Chicago: University of Chicago Press.

Jacobson, E. (1978). *You must relax*. New York: McGraw-Hill.

Jaffe, D. (1985). Self-renewal: Personal transformation following extreme trauma. *Journal of Humanistic Psychology, 25*(4), 99–124.

Jakes, S. C., Hallam, R. S., Rachman, S., & Hinchcliffe, R. (1986). The effects of reassurance, relaxation training and distraction on chronic tinnitus sufferers. *Behavioral Research and Therapy, 24*, 497–507.

Janet, P. (1976). *Principles of psychotherapy*. New York: Arno. (Original work published 1919).

Janoff-Bulman, R. (1992). *Shattered assumptions: Towards a new psychology of trauma*. New York: Free Press.

Janoff-Bulman, R. (1995). Victims of violence. In G. S. Everly & J. Lating (Eds.), *Psychotraumatology: Key papers and core concepts in post-traumatic stress* (pp. 73–86). New York: Plenum Press.

Janoff-Bulman, R. (1996). Psychometric review of World Assumption Scale. In B. H. Stamm (Ed.), *Measurement of stress, trauma, and adaptation* (pp. 440–441). Lutherville, MD: Sidran Press.

Janoff-Bulman, R., & Wortman, C. B. (1977). Attributions of blame and coping in the "real world": Severe accident victims react to their lot. *Journal of Personality and Social Psychology, 35*, 351–363.

Jenkins, M. A., Langlais, P. J., Delis, D., & Cohen, R. A. (2000). Attentional dysfunction associated with posttraumatic stress disorder among rape survivors. *Clinical Neuropsychologist, 14*(1), 7–12.

Jenkins, S. R. (1996). Social support and debriefing efficacy among emergency medical workers after a mass shooting incident. *Journal of Social Behavior and Personality, 11*, 477–492.

Jevning, R., Wallace, R. K., & Beidebach, M. (1992). The physiology of meditation: A review. A wakeful hypometabolic integrated response. *Neuroscience and Biobehavioral Reviews, 16*, 415–424.

Jiranek, D. (2000). Use of hypnosis in pain management and post-traumatic stress disorder. *Australian Journal of Clinical & Experimental Hypnosis, 28*(2), 176–187.

Johnson, T. M., & Ouslander, J. G. (1999). Urinary incontinence in the older man. *Medical Clinics of North America, 83*(5), 1247–1266.

Jones, E., & Wessely, S. (in press). Forward psychiatry in the military. *Journal of Traumatic Stress*.

Jones , J. C., & Barlow, D. H. (1990). The etiology of post-traumatic stress disorder. *Annual Psychology Review, 10*, 299–328.

Joy, R. (1985). The effects of neurotoxicants on kindling and kindled seizures. *Fundamental and Applied Toxicology, 5*, 41–65.

Kabat-Zinn, J., Lipworth, L., & Burney, R. (1985). The clinical use of mindfulness mediation for the self-regulation of chronic pain. *Journal of Behavioral Medicine, 8*(2), 163–190.

Kabat-Zinn, J., Massion, A. O., Kristeller, J., Peterson, L. G., Fletcher, K. E., et al. (1992). Effectiveness of a meditation based stress reduction program in the treatment of anxiety disorders. *American Journal of Psychiatry, 149*, 936–943.

Kabat-Zinn, J., Wheeler, E., Light, T., Skillings, A., Scharf, M. J., et al. (1998). Influence of a mindfulness meditation-based stress reduction intervention on rates of skin clearing in patients with moderate to severe psoriasis undergoing phototherapy (UVB) and photochemotherapy (PUVA). *Psychosomatic Medicine, 60*(5), 625–632.

Kardiner, A. (1941). The traumatic neuroses of war. *Psychosomatic Medicine Monographs, 11*–111.

Kayser, A., Robinson, D., Nies, A., & Howard, D. (1985). Response to phenelzine among depressed patients with features of hysteroid dysphoria. *American Journal of Psychiatry, 142*(4), 486–488.

Keane, T. M., Caddell, J. M., & Taylor, K. L. (1988). Mississippi Scale for combat-related posttraumatic stress disorder: Three studies in reliability and validity. *Journal of Consulting and Clinical Psychology, 56*, 85–90.

Keane, T. M., & Kaloupek, D. G. (1997). Comorbid psychiatric disorders in PTSD: Implications for research. In R. Yehuda & A. McFarlane (Eds.), *Psychobiology of posttraumatic stress disorder* (pp. 24–34). New York: Annals of the New York Academy of Sciences.

Keane, T. M., & Kaloupek, D. G. (2002). Diagnosis, assessment, and monitoring outcomes in PTSD. In R. Yehuda (Ed.), *Treating trauma survivors with PTSD* (pp. 21– 42). Washington, DC: American Psychiatric Association.

Keane, T. M., Kolb, L. C., Kaloupek, D. G., Orr, S. P., Blanchard, E. B., et al. (1998). Utility of psychophysiological measurement in the diagnosis of posttraumatic stress disorder: Results from a department of veterans affairs cooperative study. *Journal of Consulting and Clinical Psychology, 66*(6), 914–923.

Keane, T. M., Malloy, P. F., & Fairbank, J. A. (1984). Empirical development of an MMPI subscale for the assessment of combat-related posttraumatic stress disorder. *Journal of Consulting and Clinical Psychology, 52*, 888–891.

Kenardy, J. (2000). The current status of psychological debriefing. *British Medical Journal, 321*, 1032–1033.

Kenardy, J. A., Webster, R. A., Lewin, T. J., Carr, V. J., Hazell, P. L., et al. (1996). Stress debriefing and patterns of recovery following a natural disaster. *Journal of Traumatic Stress, 9*, 37 –49.

Kernberg, O. (1985). *Borderline conditions and pathological narcissism*. Northvale, NJ: Jason Aronson.

Khouzam, H. R. (2001). Religious meditation and its effect on posttraumatic stress disorder in a Korean War veteran. *Clinical Gerontologist, 22*(3–4), 125–131.

Kimble, M., Kaloupek, D., Kaufman, M., & Deldin, P. (2000). Stimulus novelty differentially affects attentional allocation in PTSD. *Biological Psychiatry, 47*(10), 880–890.

Kiritz, S., & Moos, R. (1974). Physiological effects of social environments. *Psychosomatic Medicine, 36*, 96–114.

Kirsch, I. (1994). Defining hypnosis for the public. *Contemporary Hypnosis, 11*, 142–143.

Kirsch, I., Montgomery, G., & Sapirstein, G. (1995). Hypnosis as an adjunct to cognitive behavioral psychotherapy: A meta-analysis. *Journal of Consulting and Clinical Psychology, 63*, 214–220.

Klerman, G. D., Weissman, M., Rounsaville, B., & Chevron, E. (1984). *Interpersonal psychotherapy of depression*. New York: Basic Books.

Knight, J. A. (1997). Neuropsychological assessment in posttraumatic stress disorder. In J. P. Wilson & T. M. Keane (Eds.), *Assessing psychological trauma and PTSD* (pp. 448–492). New York: Plenum Press.

Kolb, L. C. (1987). A neuropsychological hypothesis explaining post-traumatic stress disorder. *American Journal of Psychiatry, 114*, 989–995.

Koretsky, M. B., & Peck, A. H. (1990). Validation and cross-validation of the PTSD subscale of the MMPI with civilian trauma victims. *Journal of Clinical Psychology, 45*, 72–76.

Krikorian, R., & Layton, B. S. (1998). Implicit memory in posttraumatic stress disorder with amnesia for the traumatic event. *Journal of Neuropsychiatry & Clinical Neurosciences, 10*(3), 359–362.

Krippner, S., & Colodzin, B. (1989). Multi-cultural methods of treating Vietnam veterans with post-traumatic stress disorder. *International Journal of Psychosomatics, 36*(1–4), 79–85.

Kroll, J. (1993). *PTSD/borderlines in therapy*. New York: W. W. Norton.

Kulka, R. A., Schlenger, W. E., Fairbank, J. A., Hough, R. L., Jordan, B. K., et al. (1988). *The National Vietnam Veterans Readjustment Study (NVVRS): Description, current status, and initial PTSD prevelance estimates*. Washington, DC: Veteran's Administration.

Kulka, R. A., Schlenger, W. E., Fairbank, J. A., Hough, R. L., Jordan, B. K., et al. (1990). *Trauma and the Vietnam war generation: Report of the findings from the national Vietnam veterans readjustment study*. New York: Brunner/Mazel.

Kulka, R. A., Schlenger, W. E., Fairbank, J. A., Hough, R. L., Jordan, B. K., et al. (1991). Assessment of posttraumatic stress disorder in the community: Prospects and pitfalls from recent studies of Vietnam veterans. *Psychological Assessment, 3*(4), 547–560.

Langsley, D., Machotka, P., & Flomenhaft, K. (1971). Avoiding mental health admission: A follow-up. *American Journal of Psychiatry, 127*, 1391–1394.

Lazarus, R. S. (1966). *Psychological stress and the coping process.* New York: McGraw-Hill.

Lazarus, R. S., & Folkman, S. (1984). *Stress, appraisal, and coping.* New York: Springer.

LeDoux, J. E. (1992). Emotion and the amygdala. In J. P. Aggleton (Ed.), *The amygdale* (pp. 339–352). New York: Wiley-Liss.

Lee, C., Slade, P., & Lygo, V. (1996). The influence of psychological debriefing on emotional adaptation in women following early miscarriage. *British Journal of Psychiatry, 69*, 47–58.

Lee, K., Schottler, F., Oliver, M., & Lynch, G. (1980). Brief bursts of high-frequency stimulation produce two types of structural change in rat hippocampus. *Journal of Neurophysiology, 44*, 247–258.

Lerner, M. J. (1980). *The belief in a just world: A fundamental delusion.* New York: Plenum Press.

Lerner, M. J. (1998). The two forms of belief in a just world; Some thoughts on why and how people care about justice. In L. Montada & M. J. Lerner (Eds.), *Responses to victimization and belief in a just world* (pp. 247–269). New York: Plenum Press.

Levi, L. (1972). Psychosocial stimuli, psychophysiological reactions and disease. *Acta Medica Scandinavica* (suppl. 528).

Levin, P., & Reis, B. (1997). The use of the Rorschach in assessing trauma. In J. Wilson, & T. Keane (Eds.), *Assessing psychological trauma and PTSD* (pp. 529–543). New York: Guilford Press.

Lex, B. W. (1979). The neurobiology of ritual trance. In E. G. d'Aguili, C. D. Lauflin, & J. MacManis (Eds.), *The sprectrum of ritual* (pp. 117–151). New York: Columbia University Press.

Lezak, M. D. (1983). *Neuropsychological assessment* (2nd ed.). New York: Oxford University Press.

Lifton, R. J. (1988). Understanding the traumatized self: Imagery, symbolization, and transformation. In J. P. Wilson, Z. Harel, & B. Kahana (Eds.), *Human adaptation to extreme stress: From the Holocaust to Vietnam* (pp. 7–31). New York: Plenum Press.

Linehan, M. (1993). *Cognitive–behavioral treatment of borderline personality disorder.* New York: Guilford Press.

Linehan, M. (1995). *Treating borderline personality disorder: The dialectical approach (program manual).* New York: Guilford Press.

Litz, B. T., Penk, W. E., Walsh, S., Hyer, L., Blake, D. D., et al. (1991). Similarities and differences between MMPI and MMPI–2 applications to the assessment of post-traumatic stress disorder. *Journal of Personality Assessment, 57*, 238–254.

Loong, J. W. K. (1988). *The Continuous Performance Test.* San Luis Obispo, CA: Wang Neuropsychological Laboratory.

Lopez-Ibor, J. (2002). Psychopathology of disasters. *Medscape Psychiatry & Mental Health, 2*(2).

Loranger, A. W., Susman, V. L., Oldham, J. M., & Russakoff, M. (1988). *The Personality Disorder Examination (PDE) manual.* Yonkers, New York: DV Communications.

Lubar, J. F., Swartwood, M. O., Swartwood, J. N., & O'Donnell, P. H. (1995). Evaluation of the effectiveness of EEG neurofeedback training for ADHD in a clinical setting as measured by changes in T. O. V. A. scores, behavioral ratings, and WISC–R performance. *Biofeedback and Self-Regulation, 20*(1), 83–99.

Lumsden, A. (1999). Treatment of PTSD utilising CBT and hypnotherapy. *Australian Journal of Clinical & Experimental Hypnosis, 27*(2), 15–157.

Lyons, J. A., Gerardi, R. J., Wolfe, J., & Keane, T. M. (1988). Multidimensional assessment of combat-related PTSD: Phenomenological, psychometric, and psychophysiological considerations. *Journal of Traumatic Stress, 1,* 373–394.

Lyons, J. A., & Keane, T. M. (1992). Keane PTSD scale: MMPI and MMPI–2 update. *Journal of Traumatic Stress, 5,* 111–117.

Lyons, J. A., & Wheeler-Cox, T. (1999). MMPI, MMPI–2, and PTSD: Overview of scores, scales, and profiles. *Journal of Traumatic Stress, 12*(1), 175–183.

Ma, L., & Smith, K. (1986). Individual and social correlates of the just world belief: A study of Taiwan college students. *Psychological Reports, 57,* 35–38.

Macklin, M. L., Metzger, L. J., Litz, B. T., McNally, R. J., Lasko, N. B., et al. (1998). Lower precombat intelligence is a risk factor for posttraumatic stress disorder. *Journal of Consulting and Clinical Psychology, 66*(2), 323–326.

MacLean, P. D. (1949). Psychosomatic disease and the "visceral brain." *Psychosomatic Medicine, 11,* 338–353.

MacLean, P. D. (1975). On the evolution of three mentalities. *Man–Environment System, 5,* 213–224.

Maes, J. (1998). Eight stages in the development of research on the construct of belief in a just world? In L. Montada & M. J. Lerner (Eds.), *Responses to victimization and belief in a just world* (pp. 163–185). New York: Plenum Press.

Maier, M. H. (1993). *Military aptitude testing: The past fifty years* (DMDC Technical Report No. 93–007). Monterey, CA: Defense Manpower Data Center Personnel Testing Division.

Malloy, P. F., Fairbank, J. A., & Keane, T. M. (1983). Validation of a multimethod assessment of post-traumatic stress disorder in Vietnam veterans. *Journal of Consulting and Clinical Psychology, 51,* 488–494.

Malmo, R. B. (1975). *On emotions, needs, and our archaic brain.* New York: Holt, Rinehart, & Winston.

Manning, C. (1996). Treatment of trauma associated with childhood sexual assault. *Australian Journal of Clinical and Experimental Hypnosis, 24,* 36–45.

Maslow, A. (1943). A theory of human motivation. *Psychological Review, 50,* 394–395.

Maslow, A. H. (1968). *Toward a psychology of being.* Princeton, NJ: Van Nostrand.

Maslow, A. H. (1970). *Motivation and personality* (2nd ed.). New York: Harper & Row.

Mason, J. B. (1972). Organization of psychoendocrine mechanisms: A review and reconsideration of research. In N. Greenfield & R. Sternbach (Eds.), *Handbook of psychophysiology* (pp. 3–76). New York: Holt, Rinehart & Winston.

Mason, J. W. (1968a). A review of psychendocrine research on the sympathetic-adrenal medullary system. *Psychosomatic Medicine, 30,* 631–653.

Mason, J. W. (1968b). Organization of psychoendocrine mechanisms. *Psychosomatic Medicine, 30* (Entire Part 2).

Mason, J. W. (1968c). A review of psychoendocrine research on the pituitary-adrenal cortical system. *Psychosomatic Medicine, 30,* 576–607.

Mason, J. W., Wang, S., Yehuda, R., Bremner, J., Riney, S., et al. (1995). Some approaches to the study of clinical implications of thyroid alterations in post-traumatic stress disorder. In M. J. Friedman, D. Charney, & A. Deutch (Eds.), *Neurobiological and clinical consequences of stress* (pp. 367–380). Philadelphia: Lippincott-Raven.

Maughan, B., & Rutter, M. (1997). Retrospective reporting of childhood adversity: Issues in assessing long-term recall. *Journal of Personality Disorders, 11*(1), 19–33.

Mayou, R. A., Ehlers, A., & Hobbs, M. (2000). Psychological debriefing for road traffic accident victims: Three-year follow-up of a randomised controlled trial. *British Journal of Psychiatry, 176,* 589–593.

McCann, L., & Pearlman, L. A. (1990a). *Psychological trauma and the adult survivor; Theory, therapy and transformation.* New York: Brunner/Mazel.

McCann, L., & Pearlman, L. A. (1990b). Vicarious traumatization: A framework for understanding the psychological effects of working with victims. *Journal of Traumatic Stress, 3*(1), 131–149.

McCann, L., & Pearlman, L. A. (1992). Constructivist self-development theory: A theoretical model of psychological adaptation to severe trauma. In D. K. Sakheim & S. Devine (Eds.), *Out of darkness: Exploring satanism and ritual abuse* (pp. 185–206). New York: Lexington Books Macmillian.

McCaul, K., Solomon, S., & Holmes, D. (1979). The effects of paced respiration and expectations on physiological responses to threat. *Journal of Personality and Social Psychology, 37,* 564–571.

McConkey, K. M., & Sheehan, P. W. (1995). *Hypnosis, memory, and behavior in criminal investigation.* New York: Guilford Press.

McFarlane, A. C. (1988). The longitudinal course of posttraumatic morbidity. *Journal of Nervous and Mental Disease, 176,* 30–39.

McFarlane, A. C., Weber, D. L., & Clark, C. R. (1993). Abnormal stimulus processing in posttraumatic stress disorder. *Biological Psychiatry, 31,* 1050–1056.

McGeer, E., & McGeer, P. (1988). Excititoxins and animal models. In C. Calli, L. Manzo, & P. Spencer (Eds.), *Recent advances in nervous system toxicology* (pp. 107–131). New York: Plenum Press.

McGrath, P. J. (1999). Clinical psychology issues in migraine headaches. *Canadian Journal of the Neurological Sciences, 26*(Suppl. 3), S33–S36.

McGuigan, F. J. (1991). *Calm down: A guide for stress and tension control* (Rev. ed.). Dubuque, IA: Kendall/Hunt.

McNally, R. J., Kaspi, S. P., Riemann, B. C., & Zeitlin, S. B. (1990). Selective processing of threat cues in posttraumatic stress disorder. *Journal of Abnormal Psychology, 99,* 398–402.

McNally, R. J., Lasko, N. B., Macklin, M. L., & Pitman, R. K. (1995). Autobiographical memory disturbance in combat-related posttraumatic stress disorder. *Behaviour Research and Therapy, 33,* 619–630.

Meehl, P. 1973. *Psychodiagnostics.* New York: Norton.

Mefford, R. (1979). The developing biological concept of anxiety. In W. Fann, I. Karacan, A. D. Porkorny, & R. L. Williams (Eds.), *Phenomenology and treatment of anxiety* (pp. 111–124). New York: Spectrum.

Meissner, W. W. (1987). *Life and faith: Psychological perspectives on religious life.* Washington, DC: Georgetown University Press.

Miller, L. (1999). Critical incident stress debriefing: Clinical applications and new directions. *International Journal of Emergency Mental Health, 1,* 253–265.

Millon, T. (1969). *Modern psychopathology.* Philadelphia: Saunders.

Millon, T. (1983). *Millon Clinical Multiaxial Inventory manual.* Minneapolis, MN: Interpretive Scoring System.

Millon, T. (1987). *Manual for the MCMI–II* (2nd ed.). Minneapolis, MN: National Computer Systems.

Millon, T. (1990). *Toward a new personology.* New York: Wiley.

Millon, T. (1994). *Manual for the MCMI–III.* Minneapolis, MN: National Computer Systems.

Millon, T., & Davis, R. (1996). *Disorders of personality* (2nd ed.). New York: Wiley.

Millon, T., & Davis, R. (2000). *Personality in modern day life.* New York: Wiley.

Millon, T., & Everly, G. S., Jr., (1985). *Personality and its disorders.* New York: Wiley.

Millon, T., Grossman, S., Meagher, S., Millon, C., & Everly, G. (1999). *Personality Guided Therapy.* New York: Wiley.

Mitchell, J. T. (1983). When disaster strikes . . . The critical incident stress debriefing process. *Journal of Emergency Medical Services, 8,* (1), 36–39.

Mitchell, J. T., & Everly, G. (2001). *Critical Incident Stress Debriefing: An operations manual* (3rd ed.). Ellicott City, MD: Chevron.

Mitchell, J. T., Schiller, G., Eyler, V., & Everly, G. S., Jr. (1999). Community crisis intervention: The Coldenham tragedy revisited. *International Journal of Emergency Mental Health, 1,* 227–238.

Monahon, C. (1997). *Children and trauma: A guide for parents and professionals*. San Francisco: Jossey-Bass.

Monroe, R. (1970). *Episodic behavioral disorders*. Cambridge, MA: Harvard University Press.

Monroe, R. (1982). Limbic ictus and atypical psychosis. *Journal of Nervous and Mental Disease, 170,* 711–716.

Montada, L., & Lerner, M. J. (1998). *Responses to victimization and belief in a just world*. New York: Plenum Press.

Morey, L. C., Waugh, M. H., & Blashfield, R. K. (1985). MMPI scales for *DSM–III* personality disorders. *Journal of Personality Assessment, 49,* 1645–1653.

Morgan, C. A., Grillon, C., Southwick, S. M., Davis, M., & Charney, D. S. (1995). Fear-potentiated startle in posttraumatic stress disorder. *Biological Psychiatry, 38,* 378–385.

Morgan, S. (2001). Brief hypnosis for needle phobia. *Australian Journal of Clinical & Experimental Hypnosis, 29*(2), 107–115.

Moursand, J. (1993). *The process of counseling and therapy* (3rd ed.). Englewood Cliffs, NJ: Prentice-Hall.

Murray, H. A. (1943). *Thematic Apperception Test manual*. Cambridge, MA: Harvard University Press.

Mynard, H., Joseph, S., & Alexander, J. (2000). Peer-victimisation and posttraumatic stress in adolescents. *Personality & Individual Differences, 29*(5), 815–821.

Najavits, L. M., Weiss, R. D., Shaw, S. R., & Muenz, L. R. (1998). "Seeking safety": Outcome of a new cognitive–behavioral psychotherapy for women with posttraumatic stress disorder and substance dependence. *Journal of Traumatic Stress, 11*(3), 437–456.

National Institute of Mental Health (NIMH). (2002). Mental health and mass violence (NIH Publication No. 02-5138). Washington, DC: U.S. Government Printing Office.

Newman, E. C. (2000). Group crisis intervention in a school setting following an attempted suicide. *International Journal of Emergency Mental Health, 2,* 97–100.

Newman, E., Kaloupek, D. G., & Keane, T. M. (1996). Assessment of posttraumatic stress disorder in clinical and research settings. In B. A. van der Kolk, A. C. McFarlane, & L. Weisaeth (Eds.), *Traumatic stress: The effects of overwhelming experience on mind, body, and society* (pp. 242–273). New York: Guilford Press.

Norris, F. H. (1990). Screening for traumatic stress: A scale for use in the general population. *Journal of Applied Social Psychology, 20,* 1704–1718.

Norris, F. H., & Perilla, J. (1996). Reliability, validity, and cross-language stability of the Revised Civilian Mississippi Scale for PTSD. *Journal of Traumatic Stress, 9,* 285–298.

North, C. Nixon, S., Shariat, S., Mallonee, S.,McMillen, J., et al. (1999). Psychiatric disorders among survivors of the Oklahoma City bombing. *Journal of the American Medical Association, 282,* 755–762.

Nurmi, L. (1999). The sinking of the Estonia: The effects of Critical Incident Stress Debriefing on Rescuers. *International Journal of Emergency Mental Health, 1,* 23–32.

NVOAD Emotional and Spiritual Care Committee. (2003, January). *Meeting on early psychological intervention.* Washington, DC: Author.

Occupational Safety and Health Administration (OSHA). (1996). *Guidelines for preventing workplace violence for health care and social service workers.* OSHA 3148-1996. Washington, DC: Author.

OSHA. (1998). *Recommendations for workplace violence prevention programs in late night retail establishments.* OSHA 3153-1998. Washington, DC: Author.

Olafson, E., & Boat, B. W. (2000). Long-term management of the sexually abused child: Considerations and challenges. In R. M. Reece (Ed.), *Treatment of child abuse: Common ground for mental health, medical and legal practitioners* (pp. 14–35). Baltimore: Johns Hopkins University Press.

Olney, J. W. (1978). Neurotoxicity of excitatory amino acids. In E. McGeer, J. Olney, & P. McGeer (Eds.), *Kainic acid as a tool in neurobiology* (pp. 95–122). New York: Raven Press.

Orr, S. P., & Kaloupek, D. G. (1997). Psychophysiological assessment of posttraumatic stress disorder. In J. P. Wilson & T. M. Keane (Eds.), *Assessing psychological trauma and PTSD* (pp. 69–97). New York: Guilford Press.

Orr, S. P., Lasko, N. B., Metzger, L. J., & Pitman, R. K. (1997). Physiologic responses to non-startling tones in Vietnam veterans with post-traumatic stress disorder. *Psychiatric Research, 73*(1–2), 103–107.

Orr, S. P., Lasko, N. B., Shalev, A., & Pitman, R. K. (1995). Physiologic responses to loud tones in Vietnam veterans with posttraumatic stress disorder. *Journal of Abnormal Psychology, 104*(1), 75–82.

Othmer, E., & Othmer, S. (1994). *The clinical interview using DSM–IV.* Washington, DC: American Psychiatric Press.

Overmier, J. B., & Seligman, M. E. P. (1967). Effects of inescapable shock upon subsequent escape and avoidance learning. *Journal of Comparative and Physiological Psychology, 63,* 28–33.

Pagano, R. (1981). Recent research in the physiology of meditation. In G. Adam, I. Meszaros, & E. Banyai (Eds.), *Brain and behavior: Advances in physiological sciences* (Vol. 17, pp. 443–451). Budapest: Pergamon Press.

Paige, S. R., Reid, G. M., Allen, M. G., & Newton, J. E. O. (1990). Psychophysiological correlates of posttraumatic stress disorder in Vietnam veterans. *Biological Psychiatry, 27,* 419–430.

Pallmeyer, T. P., Blanchard, E. B., & Kolb, L. C. (1986). The psychophysiology of combat-induced post-traumatic disorder in Vietnam veterans. *Behavior Research Therapy, 24,* 645–652.

Papez, J. (1937). A proposed mechanism of emotion. *Archives of Neurology and Psychiatry, 38*, 725–743.

Parad, L., & Parad, H. (1968). A study of crisis oriented planned short-term treatment: Part II. *Social Casework, 49*, 418–426.

Paris, J. (1997). Childhood trauma as an etiological factor in the personality disorders. *Journal of Personality Disorders, 11*(1), 34–49.

Paris, J., & Zweig, F. H. (1997). Dissociation in patients with borderline personality disorder. *American Journal of Psychiatry, 154*(1), 137–138.

Parson, E. R. (1997). Traumatic Stress Personality Disorder (TrSPD): Intertheoretical therapy for the PTSD/PD dissociogenic organization. *Journal of Contemporary Psychotherapy, 27*(4), 323–367.

Parson, E. R. (1998). Traumatic Stress Personality Disorder (TrSPD), Part III: Mental/physical trauma representations—From focus on PTSD symptoms to inquiry into *who* the victim has become. *Journal of Contemporary Psychotherapy, 28*(2), 141–171.

Pearlman, L. A., & Saakvitne, K. W. (1995). *Trauma and the therapist: Countertransference and vicarious traumatization in psychotherapy with incest survivors.* New York: W. W. Norton.

Pennebaker, J. (1999). The effects of disclosure on physical and mental health. *International Journal of Emergency Mental Health, 1*, 9–18.

Pitman, R. K., Orr, S. P., Forgue, D. F., de Jong, J. B., & Claiborn, J. M. (1987). Psychophysiologic assessment of post-traumatic stress disorder imagery in Vietnam combat veterans. *Archives of General Psychiatry, 44*, 970–975.

Platman, S. R. (1999). Psychopharmacology and posttraumatic stress disorder. *International Journal of Emergency Mental Health, 1*, 195–199.

Pomeroy, W. (1995). A working model for trauma: The relationship between trauma and violence. *Pre- & Peri-Natal Psychology Journal, 10*(2), 89–101.

Posner, M. I., Walker, J. A., Freidrich, F. J., & Rafal, R. D. (1984). Effects of parietal injury on covert orienting of attention. *Journal of Neuroscience, 4*, 1863–1874.

Post, R. (1985). Stress sensitization, kindling, and conditioning. *Behavioral and Brain Sciences, 8*, 372–373.

Post, R. (1986). Does limbic system dysfunction play a role in affective illness? In B. Doane & K. Livingston (Eds.), *The limbic system* (pp. 229–249). New York: Raven Press.

Post, R. (1992). Transduction of psychosocial stress onto the neurobiology of recurrent affective disorder. *American Journal of Psychiatry, 149*, 990–1010.

Post, R., & Ballenger, J. (1981). Kindling models for the progressive development of psychopathology. In H. van Pragg (Ed.), *Handbook of Biological Psychiatry* (pp. 609–651). New York: Marcel Dekker.

Post, R., Rubinow, D., & Ballenger, J. (1986). Conditioning and sensitisation in the longitudinal course of affective illness. *British Journal of Psychiatry, 149*, 191–201.

Post, R., Uhde, T., Putnam, F., Ballenger, J., & Berrettini, W. (1982). Kindling and Carbamazepien in affective illness. *Journal of Nervous and Mental Disease, 170,* 717–731.

Post, R. M., Weiss, S., & Smith, M. (1995). Sensitization and kindling. In M. J. Friedman, D. Charney, & A. Deutch (Eds.), *Neurobiological and clinical consequences of stress* (pp. 203–224). Philadelphia: Lippincott-Raven.

Pynoos, R. S., Steinberg, A. M., Ornitz, E. M., & Goenjian, A. K. (1997). Issues in the developmental neurobiology of traumatic stress. In R. Yehuda & A. Saria (Eds.), *Psychobiology of posttraumatic stress disorder* (pp. 176–193). New York: New York Academy of Sciences.

Racine, R., Tuff, L., & Zaide, J. (1976). Kindling unit discharge patterns and neural plasticity. In J. Wada & R. Ross (Eds.), *Kindling* (pp. 19–39). New York: Raven Press.

Rahe, R. (1974). The pathway between subjects' recent life changes and their future illness reports. In B. S. Dohrenwend & B. P. Dohrenwend (Eds.), *Stressful life events: Their nature and effects* (pp. 73–86). New York: Wiley.

Rahe, R. (1976). Stress and strain in coronary heart disease. *Journal of the South Carolina Medical Association, 72*(suppl.), 7–14.

Rauch, S. L., van der Kolk, B. A., Fisler, R. E., Alpert, N. A., Orr, S. P., et al. (1996). A symptom provocation study of posttraumatic stress disorder using positron emission tomography and script-driven imagery. *Archives of General Psychiatry, 53,* 380–387.

Rauch, S. L., Whalen, P., Shin, L., McInerney, S., Macklin, M., et al. (2000). Exaggerated amygdala response to masked facial stimuli in posttraumatic stress disorder: A functional MRI study. *Biological Psychiatry, 47,* 769–776.

Redmond, D. E. (1979). New and old evidence for the involvement of a brain norepinephrine system in anxiety. In W. Fann, I. Karacan, A. Pikomey, & R. Williams (Eds.), *Phenomenology and treatment of anxiety* (pp. 153–204). New York: Spectrum.

Redmond, D. E., & Huang, Y. (1979). New evidence for a locus ceruleus-norepinephrine connection with anxiety. *Life Sciences, 25,* 2149–2162.

Reichle, B., Schneider, A., & Montada, L. (1998). How do observers of victimization preserve their belief in a just world cognitively or actionally? Findings from a longitudinal study. In L. Montada & M. J. Lerner (Eds.), *Responses to victimization and belief in a just world* (pp. 55–64). New York: Plenum Press.

Reiman, E., Raichle, M. E., Robins, E., Butler, F., Herscovitch, P., Fox, P., & Perlmutter, J. (1986). The application of positron emission tomography to the study of panic disorder. *American Journal of Psychiatry, 143,* 469–477.

Reitan, R. M. (1958). Validity of the Trail Making Test as an indicator of organic brain damage. *Perceptual and Motor Skills, 8,* 271–276.

Reitan, R. M. (1993). *The Halstead–Reitan Neuropsychological Test Battery: Theory and clinical interpretation.* Tucson, AZ: Neuropsychology Press.

Resnick, H. S., Kilpatrick, D. G., & Lipovsky, J. A. Assessment of rape-related posttraumatic stress disorder: Stressor and symptom dimensions. *Psychological Assessment, 3*(4), 561–572.

Richards, D. (2001). A field study of critical incident stress debriefing versus critical incident stress management. *Journal of Mental Health, 10,* 351–362.

Rinne, T., Westenberg, H. G., den Boer, J. A., van den Brink, W. (2000). Serotonergic blunting to meta-chlorophenylpiperazine (m-CPP) highly correlates to childhood abuse in impulsive and autoaggressive female borderline patients. *Biological Psychiatry, 47,* 548–556.

Ritchie, P. J. (2002). *Management of critical incident stress in a military environment. A review for the Canadian Armed Forces.* Toronto: Canadian Forces.

Robins, L. N., & Helzer, J. E. (1985). *Diagnostic Interview Schedule (DIS Version III-A).* St. Louis: Washington University, Department of Psychiatry.

Robinson, D. (1999). *Disordered personalities.* Port Huron, MI: Rapid Psychler Press.

Robinson, H., Sigman, M., & Wilson, J. (1997). Duty-related stressors and PTSD symptoms in suburban police officers. *Psychological Reports, 81,* 835–845.

Robinson, R. C., & Mitchell, J. T. (1993). Evaluation of psychological debriefings. *Journal of Traumatic Stress, 6*(3), 367–382.

Robinson, R. C., & Mitchell, J. T. (1995). Getting some balance back into the debriefing debate. *Bulletin of the Australian Psychological Society, 17*(10), 5 –10.

Rose, S., & Bisson, J. (1998). Brief early psychological interventions following trauma: A systematic review of literature. *Journal of Traumatic Stress,* 11, 697–710.

Rose, S., Bisson, J., & Wessely, S. (2002). Effectiveness of psychological debriefing. Oxford, UK: Cochrane Review.

Rosenbloom, D., Pratt, A., & Pearlman, L. A. (1995). Helpers' response to trauma work. In B. H. Stamm (Ed.), *Secondary traumatic stress.* Lutherville, MD: Sidran.

Rothbaum, B. O., Meadows, E. A., Resick, P., & Foy, D. W. (2000). Cognitive–behavior therapy. In E. B. Foa, T. M. Keane, & M. J. Friedman (Eds.), *Effective treatments for PTSD: Practice guidelines from the international society for traumatic stress studies* (pp. 60–83). New York: Guilford Press.

Rothschild, B. (2000). *The body remembers: The psychophysiology of trauma and trauma treatment.* New York: W. W. Norton.

Rubin, L. R. (1977). *Reanimation of the paralyzed face.* St. Louis: Mosby.

Rubin, Z., & Peplau, L. (1975). Who believes in a just world? *Journal of Social Issues, 31,* 65–90.

Ryan, C., & Butters, N. (1980). Learning and memory impairment in young and old alcoholics: Evidence for the premature aging hypothesis. *Alcoholism, 4,* 190–198.

Saigh, P., & Bremner, J. D. (1999). *Posttraumatic stress disorder.* Boston: Allyn & Bacon.

Sapolsky, R. M., Uno, H., Rebert, C. S., & Finch, C. E. (1990). Hippocampal damage associated with prolonged glococorticoid exposure in primates. *Journal of Neuroscience, 10,* 2897–2902.

Sarafino, E. P. (1998). *Health psychology* (3rd ed). New York: Wiley.

Saunders, B. E., Arata, C. M., & Kilpatrick, D. G. (1990). Development of a crime-related Post-Traumatic Stress Disorder scale for women within the Symptom Checklist–90–Revised. *Journal of Traumatic Stress, 3,* 267–277.

Schacter, D. L. (1992). Understanding implicit memory: A cognitive neuroscience approach. *American Psychologist, 47,* 559–569.

Scheel, K. R. (2000). The empirical basis of dialectical behavioral therapy: Summary, critique, and implications. *Clinical Psychology: Science & Practice, 7*(1), 68–86.

Scheibe, S., Bagby, R. M., Miller, L. S., & Dorian, B. J. (2001). Assessing posttraumatic stress disorder with the MMPI–2 in a sample of workplace accident victims. *Psychological Assessment, 13*(3), 369–374.

Schiraldi, G. R. (2000). *The Post-traumatic stress disorder sourcebook.* Los Angeles: Lowell House.

Schlenger, W., & Kulka, R. A. (1989). *PTSD scale development for the MMPI–2.* Research Triangle Park, NC: Research Triangle Park Institute.

Schmidt, M. (1996). *Rey Auditory–Verbal Learning Test.* Los Angeles: Western Psychological Services.

Seligman, M. E. P. (1995). The effectiveness of psychotherapy. *American Psychologist, 109,* 993–994.

Seligman, M. E. P., & Maier, S. R. (1967). Failure to escape traumatic shock. *Journal of Experimental Psychology, 74,* 1–9.

Selye, H. (1956). *The stress of life.* New York: McGraw-Hill.

Selye, H. (1976). *Stress in health and disease.* Boston: Butterworth's.

Sethi, A. S. (1989). *Meditation as an intervention in stress reactivity.* New York: AMS Press.

Shader, R. (1984). Epidemiologic and family studies. *Psychosomatics, 25* (Suppl.), 10–15.

Shakespeare, W. (1999). *Hamlet.* New York: Dover.

Shapiro, S. L., Schwartz, G. E., & Bonner, G. (1998). Effects of mindfulness-based stress reduction on medical and premedical students. *Journal of Behavioral Medicine, 21*(6), 581–599.

Shay, J. (1994). *Achilles in Vietnam: Combat trauma and the undoing of character.* New York: Macmillan.

Shea, M. T., Zlotnick, C., & Weisberg, R. B. (1999). Commonality and specificity of personality disorder profiles in subjects with trauma histories. *Journal of Personality Disorders, 13*(3), 199–210.

Shea, S. C. (1998). *Psychiatric interviewing* (2nd ed.). Philadelphia: Saunders.

Shipley, W. C. (1940). *Shipley Institute of Living Scale for Measuring Intellectual Impairment.* Los Angeles: Western Psychological Services.

Shweder, R. A., & Haidt, J. (1993). The future of moral psychology: Truth, intuition, and the pluralist way. *Psychological Science, 4,* 360–365.

Silver, S. M., Brooks, A., & Obenchain, J. (1995). Treatment of Vietnam war veterans with PTSD: A comparison of eye movement desensitization and reprocessing, biofeedback, and relaxation training. *Journal of Traumatic Stress, 8,* 337–342.

Sloan, P., Arsenault, L., Hilsenroth, M., Harvill, L., & Handler, L. (1995). Rorschach measures of posttraumatic stress in Persian Gulf war veterans. *Journal of Personality Assessment, 64*(3), 397–414.

Small, R., Lumley, J., Donohue, L., Potter, A., & Waldenstrom, U. (2000). Randomised controlled trial of midwife led debriefing to reduce maternal depression after operative childbirth. *British Medical Journal, 321,* 1043–1047.

Smith, K., Everly, G. S., Jr., & Johns, T. (1993). The role of stress arousal in the dynamics of stressor-to-illness processes in accountants. *Contemporary Accounting Research, 9,* 432–449.

Smith, K., & Green, D. (1984). Individual correlates of the belief in a just world. *Psychological Reports, 34,* 435–438.

Soloff, P., & Millward, J. (1983). Psychiatric disorders in the families of borderline patients. *Archives of General Psychiatry, 40,* 37–44.

Solomon, S. D., Keane, T. M., Newman, E., & Kaloupek, D. G. (1996). Choosing self-report measures and structured interviews. In E. B. Carlson (Ed.), *Trauma research methodology* (pp. 56–81). Lutherville, MD: Sidran Press.

Solomon, Z., & Benbenishty, R. (1986). The role of proximity, immediacy, and expectancy in frontline treatment of combat stress reaction among Israelis in the Lebanon War. *American Journal of Psychiatry, 143,* 613–617.

Somer, E. (1994). Hypnotherapy and regulated uncovering in the treatment of older survivors of Nazi persecution. *Clinical Gerontologist, 14,* 47–65.

Sorg, B. A., & Kalivas, P. (1995). Stress and neuronal sensitization. In M. J. Friedman, D. Charney, & A. Deutch (Eds.), *Neurobiological and clinical consequences of stress* (pp. 83–102). Philadelphia: Lippincott-Raven.

Southwick, S. M., Yehuda, R., & Giller, E. L. (1993). Personality disorders in treatment-seeking combat veterans with posttraumatic stress disorder. *American Journal of Psychiatry, 150,* 1020–1023.

Spiegel, D. (1994). Hypnosis. In R. E. Hales, S. C. Yudofsky, & J. A., Talbott (Eds.), *American Psychiatric Press textbook of psychiatry* (pp. 1115–1142). Washington, DC: American Psychiatric Press.

Spitzer, R. L., Williams, J. B. W., Gibbon, M., & First, M. B. (1990). *User's guide for the Structured Clinical Interview for DSM–III–R.* Washington, DC: American Psychiatric Association.

Stein, H. F. (1997). Trauma revisted: Culture, mourning, and the unconscious in the Oklahoma City bombing. *Journal for the Psychoanalysis of Culture & Society, 2*(1), 17–37.

Stern, A. (1938). Psychoanalytic investigation of and therapy in the border line group of neuroses. *Psychoanalytic Quarterly, 7,* 467–489.

Stoyva, J. M., & Carlson, J. G. (1993). A coping/rest model of relaxation and stress management. In L. Goldberger & S. Breznitz (Eds.), *Handbook of stress: Theoretical and clinical aspects* (2nd ed.; pp. 724–756). New York: Free Press.

Strupp, H. (1980). Success and failure in time-limited psychotherapy. *Archives of General Psychiatry, 37,* 947–954.

Sullivan, M. J., & Evans, K. (1996). Trauma and chemical dependence: A summary overview of the issues and an integrated treatment approach. *Sexual Addiction & Compulsivity, 3*(3), 228–249.

Summerfield, D. (2001). The invention of post-traumatic stress disorder and the social usefulness of a psychiatric category. *British Medical Journal, 322,* 95–98.

Swanson, L. W. (1983). Organization of the hippocampus. In W. Seifert (Ed.), *Neurobiology of the hippocampus* (pp. 3–20). New York: Academic Press.

Swanson, W. C., & Carbon, J. B. (1989). Crisis intervention: Theory and technique. In Task Force Report of the American Psychiatric Association, *Treatments of psychiatric disorders* (pp. 2520–2531). Washington, DC: American Psychiatric Association.

Taylor, R. E. (1985). Imagery for the treatment of obsessional behavior: A case study. *American Journal of Clinical Hypnosis, 27,* 175–179.

Taylor, S. (1983). Adjustment to threatening events. *American Psychologist, 38,* 1161–1173.

Taylor, S. E., Lichtman, R., & Wood, J. (1984). Attributions, beliefs about control, and adjustment to breast cancer. *Journal of Personality and Social Psychology, 46,* 489–502.

Thankachan, M. V., & Mishra, H. (1996). Behavioural management with peptic ulcer cases. *Indian Journal of Clinical Psychology, 23*(2), 135–141.

Thompson, B., Geller, N. L., Hunsberger, S., Frederick, M., Hill, R., et al. (1999). Behavioral and pharmacologic interventions: The Raynaud's treatment study. *Control Clinical Trials, 20*(1), 52–63.

Thompson, S. C. (1981). Will it hurt less if I can control it? *Psychological Bulletin, 90,* 89–101.

Thrasher, S. M., Dalgleish, T., & Yule, W. (1994). Information processing in post-traumatic stress disorder. *Behaviour Research & Therapy, 32*(2), 247–254.

Trimble, M. R. (1981). *Post-traumatic Neurosis.* New York: Wiley.

Turnbull, G., Busuttil, W., & Pittman, S. (1997). Psychological debriefing for victims of acute burn trauma. *British Journal of Psychiatry, 171,* 582.

Uddo, M., Vasterling, J. T., Brailey, K., & Sutker, P. B. (1993). Memory and attention in posttraumatic stress disorder. *Journal of Psychopathological and Behavioral Assessment, 15,* 43–52.

U.S. Department of Health and Human Services. (1999). *Mental health: A report of the Surgeon General.* Rockville, MD: Author.

van der Hart, O., Brown, P., & van der Kolk, B. A. (1989). Pierre Janet's treatment of post-traumatic stress. *Journal of Traumatic Stress, 2,* 379–396.

van der Kolk, B. A. (1987). *Psychological trauma*. Washington, DC: American Psychiatric Association.

van der Kolk, B. A. (1988). The trauma spectrum: The interaction of biological and social events in the genesis of the trauma response. *Journal of Traumatic Stress, 1*(3), 273–290.

van der Kolk, B. A. (1994, Jan./Feb.). The body keeps the score: Memory and the evolving psychobiology of posttraumatic stress. In M. Horowitz (Ed.), *Essential papers on posttraumatic stress disorder* (pp. 301–327). New York: New York University Press.

van der Kolk, B. A. (1996). The complexity of adaptation to trauma: Self-regulation, stimulus discrimination, and characterological development. In B. A. van der Kolk, A. C. McFarlane, & L. Weisaeth (Eds.), *Traumatic stress: The effects of overwhelming experience on mind, body, and society* (pp. 182–213). New York: Guilford Press.

van der Kolk, B., Brown, P., & van der Hart, O. (1991). Pierre Janet on posttraumatic stress. *Journal of Traumatic Stress, 2*, 365–378.

van der Kolk, B. A., & Ducey, C. (1989). The psychological processing of traumatic experience: Rorschach patterns in PTSD. *Journal of Traumatic Stress, 2*, 259–263.

van der Kolk, B., Greenberg, M., Boyd, H., & Krystal, J. (1985). Inescapable shock, neurotransmitters, and addition to trauma. *Biological Psychiatry, 20*, 314–325.

van der Kolk, B. A., Hostetler, A., Herron, N., & Fister, R. E. (1994). Trauma and the development of borderline personality disorder. *Psychiatric Clinics of North America, 17*(4), 715–730.

van Dixhoorn, J. (1998). Cardiorespiratory effects of breathing and relaxation instruction in myocardial infarction patients. *Biological Psychology, 49*(1–2), 123–135.

VanPeski-Oosterbaan, A. S., Spinhoven, P., van Rood, Y., Van der Does, W. A. J., & Bruschke, A. J. V. (1997). Cognitive behavioral therapy for unexplained noncardiac chest pain: A pilot study. *Behavioural & Cognitive Psychotherapy, 25*(4), 339–350.

Vaughan, K., Armstrong, M. S., Gold, R., O'Connor, N., Jenneke, W., et al. (1994). A trial of eye movement desensitization compared to image habituation training and applied muscle relaxation in post-traumatic stress disorder. *Journal of Behavior Therapy & Experimental Psychiatry, 25*(4), 283–291.

Vesterling, J. J., Brailey, K., Constans, J. I., & Sutker, P. B. (1998). Attention and memory dysfunction in posttraumatic stress disorder. *Neuropsychology, 12*(1), 125–133.

Vreven, D. L., Gudanowski, D. M., King, L. A., & King, D. W. (1995). The civilian version of the Mississippi PTSD Scale: A psychometric evaluation. *Journal of Traumatic Stress, 8*, 91–109.

Walsh, F. (1977). The family of the borderline patient. In R. Grinker & B. Werble (Eds.), *The borderline patient* (pp. 149–177). New York: Jason Aronson.

Watchorn, J. (2000, Aug.). *Role of debriefing in the prevention of PTSD*. Paper presented to the Inaugural Conference on Stress, Trauma, & Coping in the Emergency Services and Allied Professions. Melbourne, Australia.

Watson, C. G. (1990). Psychometric post-traumatic stress disorder measurement techniques: A review. *Psychological Assessment, 2*, 460–469.

Watson, C. G., Juba, M. P., Manifold, V., Kucala, T., & Anderson, P. E. D. (1991). The PTSD Interview: Rationale, description, reliability, and concurrent validity of a DSM–III–based technique. *Journal of Clinical Psychology, 47*, 179–188.

Weathers, F. W., Blake, D. D., Krinsley, K. E., Haddad, W., Huska, J. A., et al. (1992, November). *The Clinician-Administered PTSD Scale: Reliability and construct validity*. Paper presented at the Association for the Advancement of Behavior Therapy, Boston.

Weathers, F. W., & Keane, T. M. (1999). Psychological assessment of traumatized adults. In P. A. Saigh & J. D. Bremner (Eds.), *Posttraumatic stress disorder: A comprehensive text* (pp. 219–247). Needham Heights, MA: Allyn & Bacon.

Weathers, F. W., Litz, B. T., Herman, D. S., Keane, T. M., Steinberg, H. R., et al. (1996). The utility of the SCL–90–R for the diagnosis of war-zone related PTSD. *Journal of Traumatic Stress, 9*, 111–128.

Wechsler, D. (1945). A standardized memory scale for clinical use. *Journal of Psychology, 19*, 87–95.

Wechsler, D. (1981). *Wechsler Adult Intelligence Scale–Revised*. San Antonio, TX: Psychological Corporation.

Wechsler, D. (1987). *Wechsler Memory Scale–Revised*. San Antonio, TX: Psychological Corporation.

Wechsler, D. (1997). *Wechsler Memory Scale–Third Edition*. San Antonio, TX: Psychological Corporation.

Wee, D. F., Mills, D. M., & Koelher, G. (1999). The effects of Critical Incident Stress Debriefing on emergency medical services personnel following the Los Angeles civil disturbance. *International Journal of Emergency Mental Health, 1*, 33–38.

Weil, J. (1974). *A neurophysiological model of emotional and intentional behavior*. Springfield, IL: Charles C. Thomas.

Weiss, D. (1996). Psychometric review of the Impact of Event Scale–Revised. In B. H. Stamm (Ed.), *Measurement of stress, trauma, and adaptation* (pp. 186–187). Lutherville, MD: Sidran Press.

Weiss, D. S., & Marmar, C. R. (1997). The Impact of Event Scale–Revised. In J. P. Wilson & T. M. Keane (Eds.), *Assessing psychological trauma and PTSD* (pp. 399–411). New York: Guilford Press.

Weiss, D. S., Marmar, C., Metzler, T., & Ronfeldt, H. (1995). Predicting symptomatic distress in emergency services personnel. *Journal of Consulting and Clinical Psychology, 63*, 361–368.

Weissman, M., Prusoff, B., & Klerman, G. (1978). Personality and the prediction of long- term outcome in depression. *American Journal of Psychiatry, 135*, 797–800.

Wenger, M. A. (1948). Studies of autonomic balance in Army Air Forces personnel. *Comparative Psychology Monographs, 19* (Series No. 101), 1–111.

Wenninger, K., & Ehlers, A. (1998). Dysfunctional cognitions and adult psychological functioning in child sexual abuse survivors. *Journal of Traumatic Stress, 11*(2), 281–300.

Wessley, S., Rose, S., & Bisson, J. (1998). A systematic review of brief psychological interventions (debriefing) for the treatment of immediate trauma related symptoms and the prevention of post traumatic stress disorder (Cochrane Review). *Cochrane Library*, Issue 3, Oxford, UK: Update Software.

Western Management Consultants. (1996). *The medical services branch CISM evaluation report.* Vancouver, BC: Author.

Wetter, M. W., Baer, R. A., Berry, D. T. R, Robinson, L. H., & Sumpter, J. (1993). MMPI–2 profiles of motivated fakers given specific symptom information: A comparison to matched patients. *Psychological Assessment, 4,* 369–374.

Widiger, T., & Frances, A. (1985). Axis II personality disorders. *Hospital and Community Psychiatry, 36,* 619–627.

Wieraszko, A. (1983). Glutamic and aspartic acid as putative neurotransmitters. In W. Seifert (Ed.), *Neurobiology of the hippocampus* (pp. 175–196). New York: Academic Press.

Williams, D. E., & Page, M. M. (1989). A multi-dimensional measure of Maslow's hierarchy of needs. *Journal of Research in Personality, 23,* 192–213.

Wilson, J. (1989). *Trauma, transformation, and healing.* New York: Brunner/Mazel.

Wilson, J. P. (1995). The historical evolution of PTSD diagnostic criteria. In G. S. Everly, Jr., & J. M. Lating (Eds.), *Psychotraumatology* (pp. 9–26). New York: Plenum Press.

Wilson, J. P., & Moran, T. A. (1998). Psychological trauma: Posttraumatic stress disorder and spirituality. *Journal of Psychology and Theology, 26*(2), 168–178.

Wolberg, L. R. (1988). *The technique of psychotherapy* (4th ed.). Orlando, FL: Grune & Stratton.

Wolfe, J., & Charney, D. S. (1991). Use of neuropsychological assessment in posttraumatic stress disorder. *Psychological Assessment, 3,* 573–580.

Wolfe, J., Chrestman, K. R., Crosby, O. P., Kaloupek, K., Harley, R. M., et al. (2000). Trauma-related psychophysiological reactivity in women exposed to war zone stress. *Journal of Clinical Psychology, 56*(10), 1371–1379.

Woodward, S. H., Murburg, M. M., & Bliwise, D. L. (2000). PTSD-related hyperarousal assessed during sleep. *Physiology & Behavior, 70*(1–2), 197–203.

World Health Organization. (1990). *International classification of mental disorders,* (10th rev. ed.). Geneva: Author.

World Health Organization. (1992). *International classification of disease, mental and behavioural disorders* (10th ed.). Geneva: Author.

Yalom, I. (1970). *Group psychotherapy.* New York: Basic.

Yehuda, R. (1999). Biological factors associated with susceptibility to posttraumatic stress disorder. *Canadian Journal of Psychiatry, 44,* 34–39.

Yehuda, R., Keefe, R. S. E., Harvey, P. D., Levengood, R. A., Gerber, D. K., et al. (1995). Learning and memory in combat veterans with posttraumatic stress disorder. *American Journal of Psychiatry, 152,* 137–139.

Young, A. (1995). *The harmony of illusions: Inventing posttraumatic stress disorder.* Princeton, NJ: Princeton University Press.

Zanarini, M. C., Frankenburg, F. R., Chauncey, D. L., & Gunderson, J. G. (1987). The Diagnostic Interview for Personality Disorders: Interrater and test–retest reliability. *Comprehensive Psychiatry, 28,* 467–480.

Zanarini, M. C., Frankenburg, F. R., Dubo, E. D., Sickel, A. E., Trikha, A., et al. (1998). Axis I comorbidity of borderline personality disorder. *American Journal of Psychiatry, 155*(12), 1733–1739.

Zanarini, M. C., Gunderson, J. G., Frankenburg, F. R., & Chauncey, D. L. (1989). The revised Diagnostic Interview for Borderlines: Discriminating BPD from other Axis II disorders. *Journal of Personality Disorders, 3*(1), 10–18.

Zanarini, M. C., Williams, A. A., Lewis, R. E., Reich, R. B., Vera, S. C., et al. (1997). Reported pathological childhood experiences associated with the development of borderline personality disorder. *American Journal of Psychiatry, 154*(8), 1101–1106.

Zhang, J., Harper, R., & Ni, H. (1986). Cryogenic blockage of the central nucleus of the amygdala attenuates aversively conditioned blood pressure and respiratory responses. *Brain Research, 386,* 136–145.

AUTHOR INDEX

Graham, J. R., 76, 219
Gravitz, M. A., 171, 172, 227
Gray, J., 54, 58, 227, 228
Green, A., 169, 228
Green, D., 84, 243
Green, E., 169, 228
Greenberg, M., 62, 245
Gribkoff, V., 63, 221
Griffin, M. G., 87, 228
Grillon, C., 97, 169, 228, 237
Gronwall, D., 90, 92, 228
Grossman, R., 204, 228
Grossman, S., 2, 236
Gruzelier, J. H., 171, 228
Gudanowski, D. M., 82, 245
Gunderson, J. G., 201, 202, 203, 228, 248
Gurvits, T. V., 95, 228
Gusman, F. D., 217

Haddad, W., 246
Hafer, C. L., 182, 228
Haidt, J., 40, 243
Hale, R., 8, 226
Hall, C., 7, 228
Hallam, R. S., 166, 230
Hammarberg, M., 82, 228
Hammond, C., 172, 219
Hamsher, K. deS, 92, 217
Han, J. N., 164, 228
Handler, L., 90, 243
Hansenne, M., 220
Hanson, M., 157, 225
Harley, R. M., 247
Harper, R., 164, 226, 248
Harrison, B., 158, 229
Harvey, J., 164, 229
Harvey, P. D., 248
Harvill, L., 90, 243
Hathaway, S. R., 76, 229
Hays, J. R., 92, 229
Hazell, P. L., 231
Hedges, L. E., 42, 229
Heffernan, K., 203, 229
Helzer, J. E., 75, 241
Henry, J. P., 56, 57, 229
Heraclitus, 7, 14
Herbert, R., 170, 229
Herman, D. S., 246

Herman, J. L., 3, 41, 45, 48, 49, 178, 183, 200, 201, 208, 229
Herrmann, J., 222
Herron, N., 201, 245
Herscovitch, P., 240
Hertzberg, M. A., 216, 227
Hickling, E. J., 87, 217
Hiebert-Murphy, D., 45, 229
Hiley-Young, B., 166, 229
Hill, D., 154, 221
Hill, R., 244
Hills, A., 220
Hilsenroth, M., 90, 243
Hinchcliffe, R., 166, 230
Hobbs, M., 158, 229, 235
Holloway, E. A., 164, 229
Holmes, D., 164, 235
Holmes, R., 1, 229
Holstein, C., 40, 223
Homer, 18, 229
Horowitz, M. J., 67, 81, 178, 183, 184, 200, 229, 230
Horton, A. M., 90, 92, 230
Horton, A. M., Jr., 57, 224
Hostetler, A., 201, 245
Hotujac, L., 162, 216
Hough, R. L., 231
Howard, D., 9, 231
Huang, Y., 62, 240
Hub, E., 40, 223
Huber, M., 57, 230
Hughes, D. C., 27, 220, 221
Hunsberger, S., 244
Huska, J. A., 246
Hyer, L. A., 215, 232
Hyler, S. E., 203, 230

Innis, R. B., 219

Jacobson, E., 165, 166, 230
Jaffe, D., 48, 230
Jakes, S. C., 166, 230
James, W., 156
Janet, P., 19, 104, 107, 114, 115, 172, 178, 179, 230
Janoff-Bulman, R., 3, 40, 41, 48, 84, 178, 180, 181, 183, 230
Jaycox, L., 83, 226
Jenkins, 156, 159

Weisberg, R. B., 203, 242
Weiseth, L., 157, 222
Weiss, D. S., 28, 81, 246
Weiss, R. D., 45, 237
Weiss, S., 64, 66, 240
Weissman, M., 8, 28, 231, 246
Wenger, M. A., 85, 247
Wenninger, K., 42, 247
Wertheimer, M., 43
Wessley, S., 155, 247
Westenberg, H. G., 204, 241
Wetter, M. W., 77, 247
Whalen, P., 240
Wheeler, E., 231
Wheeler-Cox, T., 77, 234
Wiegartz, P. S., 91, 215
Wieraszko, A., 57, 247
Williams, A. A., 248
Williams, D. E., 44, 247
Williams, J. B. W., 203, 243
Wilner, N., 81, 200, 229, 230
Wilson, J. P., 19, 28, 48, 49, 241, 247
Wilson, W. P., 85, 222
Wolberg, L. R., 108, 140, 247
Wolf, S., 7, 34, 116

Wolfe, J., 86, 87, 90, 91, 234, 247, 247
Wood, J., 180, 244
Woodward, S. H., 162, 247
Worlock, P., 158, 229
Wortman, C. B., 181, 230
Woytkiw, L., 45, 229

Yalom, I., 247
Yehuda, R., 24, 27, 65, 93, 95, 201, 202, 204, 227, 228, 235, 243, 247, 248
Young, A., 28, 248
Young, G. P., 169, 219
Yule, W., 93, 244

Zaide, J., 240
Zanarini, M. C., 200, 203, 208, 248, 248
Zeitlin, S. B., 95, 236
Zhang, J., 248
Zlotnick, C., 203, 242
Zubizarreta, I., 166, 222
Zwaan, M., 222
Zweig, F. H., 200, 239

SUBJECT INDEX

ABOUT THE AUTHORS

George S. Everly, Jr., PhD, is chairperson of the Board Emeritus of the International Critical Incident Stress Foundation, a nonprofit organization affiliated with the United Nations that specializes in disaster and emergency mental health. He also serves on the faculties of Loyola College in Maryland and the Johns Hopkins School of Hygiene and Public Health. In addition, he is senior research advisor for the Office of His Highness the Amir of Kuwait and distinguished visiting professor at the Universidad de Flores, Buenos Aires. He has held appointments at Harvard College and Harvard Medical School. He was formerly chief psychologist and director of the Behavioral Medicine Department at the Johns Hopkins Homewood Hospital Center and the Union Memorial Hospital in Baltimore. A former president of the Maryland Psychological Association, he was the founding chair of Maryland's disaster mental health network for the Red Cross. In addition, he has published 12 textbooks and more than 100 professional papers. He has been awarded the Professor's Medal from the Universidad de Weiner, Lima, Peru; the Honor Award from the Baltimore City Police Department; and the Honor Award from the American Red Cross.

Jeffrey M. Lating, PhD, is an associate professor and director of clinical training at Loyola College in Maryland. He was formerly the chief psychologist and director of clinical training at the Union Memorial Hospital in Baltimore. A graduate of Swarthmore College and the University of Georgia, he also completed a postdoctoral fellowship in medical psychology at the Johns Hopkins Hospital. He is coeditor and coauthor of several textbooks and is the managing editor of the *International Journal of Emergency Mental Health*. He is also a faculty member of the International Critical Incident Stress Foundation.